George B. Smith

Canada: Its Rise and Progress

George B. Smith

Canada: Its Rise and Progress

ISBN/EAN: 9783337186418

Printed in Europe, USA, Canada, Australia, Japan

Cover: Foto ©ninafisch / pixelio.de

More available books at **www.hansebooks.com**

The Romance of Colonization.

CANADA:

ITS RISE AND PROGRESS.

BY

G. BARNETT SMITH,

AUTHOR OF "THE HISTORY OF THE ENGLISH PARLIAMENT,' "THE UNITED STATES" IN THE PRESENT SERIES, "THE LIFE OF GLADSTONE," ETC.

LONDON:

S. W. PARTRIDGE & CO.,

8 & 9, PATERNOSTER ROW.

1898.

THE ROMANCE OF COLONIZATION.

Special attention is requested to this well-written and up-to-date Series of books on the development of British Colonization from its commencement to the present day.

Crown 8vo. Frontispiece. 320 pages. Cloth extra, 2s. 6d. each.

   I.—THE UNITED STATES OF AMERICA TO THE TIME OF THE PILGRIM FATHERS. By G. BARNETT SMITH.

  II.—THE UNITED STATES OF AMERICA TO THE PRESENT DAY. By G. BARNETT SMITH.

 III.—INDIA: from the Aryan Invasion to the Great Sepoy Mutiny. By ALFRED E. KNIGHT.

  IV.—CANADA: its Rise and Progress. By G. BARNETT SMITH.

PREFACE.

THE story of Canada possesses many of the elements of romance, and is one of deep interest for the whole of the Anglo-Saxon race. It was on Canadian soil that the long and deadly struggle between the French and English took place. From the time of Champlain to that which is immortally associated with the names of Wolfe and Montcalm, the history of the Dominion presents one long series of stirring and memorable events. In the following pages an attempt has been made to trace that history, omitting nothing which is of real native or European importance; while due note has been taken of the growth of Provincial and Federal interests. The object has been to present a succinct narrative of the rise and growth of Canada from the earliest times to the present day.

With regard to the future of Canada, its prosperity seems to be well assured. The High Commissioner, Lord Strathcona and Mount Royal, in a recent speech recommended it as a land of promise for all who are willing to work. He pointed out that any Englishmen who were desirous of making a new home for themselves, would find in Canada land to be had for the asking, schools as good as any they had in the old country, and ministers of religion who were as earnest in looking after their people as they were in Great Britain. The Canadians also are loyal to the Empire which they have done so much towards building up.

The enterprise of the Dominion is one of its most characteristic features. Sir William Van Horne, Chairman of the Canadian Pacific Railway, has just stated that he shall only regard the railway service as complete when the Company can take a passenger at Euston Station, London, place him on one of its own cars, and land him in Yokohama without transfer to any other line. This is expected to be accomplished by the year 1900. In furtherance of this object, magnificent and powerful steamships will shortly be built for the Vancouver and Yokohama service.

Success to our brethren across the sea, who are thus resolved to place Canada in the forefront of the world's progress!

G. B. S.

CONTENTS.

CHAP.		PAGE
I.	THE EARLY FRENCH ADVENTURERS.	9
II.	THE COLONY FROM 1665 TO 1700.	27
III.	ITS HISTORY TO THE ARRIVAL OF MONTCALM.	49
IV.	CAPTURE OF QUEBEC—DEATH OF WOLFE.	65
V.	CANADA BECOMES A BRITISH POSSESSION.	115
VI.	THE COLONY FROM 1763 TO 1811.	132
VII.	THE SECOND AMERICAN INVASION.	152
VIII.	EVENTS FROM 1815 TO 1836.	182
IX.	THE REBELLION OF 1837-38.	198
X.	UNION OF UPPER AND LOWER CANADA.	223
XI.	GOVERNORS FROM SYDENHAM TO HEAD.	231
XII.	CONFEDERATION OF THE PROVINCES.	252
XIII.	THE RED RIVER REBELLION.	275
XIV.	THE DOMINION SINCE CONFEDERATION.	284
XV.	THE CANADA OF TO-DAY.	310

CANADA:
ITS RISE AND PROGRESS.

CHAPTER I.

THE EARLY FRENCH ADVENTURERS.

THE first settlements in the Canadian colonies were made by the French. Columbus having brought immortal honour to himself and the Spanish sovereigns Ferdinand and Isabella by his discovery of the American Continent in 1492, and this great event having been followed up by the explorations of the Cabots, which redounded to the credit of Henry VII. of England, Francis I. of France became moved to similar enterprises. "What!" he is reported to have exclaimed, "shall the Kings of Spain and Portugal divide all America between them, without suffering me to take a share as their brother? I would fain see the article in Adam's Will that bequeaths that vast inheritance to them."

Imbued with the combined ideas of glory and gain, Francis held out every inducement to his subjects to embark on American ventures; and he at length discovered in 1523 a Florentine named John Verrazani, then resident in France, who was a bold and resolute seaman, and eager to undertake a voyage to the newly discovered continent. The King ordered a vessel to be prepared for him, and in 1524 Verrazani put forth; but being overcome by stress of weather, he was obliged to return to port. Next year he sailed again, in another ship called the *Dauphine*, and proceeding by Madeira he eventually landed on the shores of Florida. Ranging along the coast from the twenty-eighth to the fiftieth degree of north latitude, he took nominal possession of the country, which he styled New France. But the reports he took back to France were considered very unsatisfactory by the King, who ordered him to explore the same route again in 1525. Verrazani departed on his second expedition, but he had no sooner landed on the continent than he was unfortunately murdered by the Indians.

It was reserved for Jacques Cartier, the celebrated French navigator, to become the real pioneer in Canadian discovery in the interests of France. Cartier's career was marked by a daring spirit of adventure. Born at St. Malo on the 31st of December, 1494, he became known as a bold and able seaman in his youth. It was not, however, until 1534 that he made the first of his great voyages to North America. Admiral Chabot having recommended him for this important service, the King appointed him to it, and had fitted out for him two vessels of sixty tons each, manned with 122 seamen. The little expedition sailed from St. Malo on the 10th of April, 1534, and on the 10th of

May it came in sight of Bonavista, in Newfoundland, and anchored in the harbour of St. Catherine. Cartier traversed the Labrador coast, crossed a gulf which he called St. Lawrence, and anchored in July in a bay which he called the Gulf of Chaleur, in consequence of the excessive heat prevailing. He next coasted the shores of Gaspé—now part of the province of Quebec—and took possession of the country in the name of his sovereign, Francis I. He remained for some time in the district, in order to conciliate and study the natives, and to acquire a knowledge of the country.

The quaint ceremony of taking possession of the land is described by one of the old historians. It appears that Cartier erected upon a height of land a Cross, thirty feet high, on which was suspended a shield, with three *fleurs-de-lis* carved on it, with the motto, " Long live the King of France." The natives followed the details of the ceremony with earnest attention. Cartier and his people knelt down before the Cross, and prayed devoutly, with their hands uplifted to heaven; and as soon as the ceremony was over he went on board his ship. "At the same moment, an Indian chief, clothed in a bear's skin, and attended by three of his sons and his brother, went in a canoe towards the vessels; when he had approached sufficiently near to be heard, he began a long oration, and pointed to the Cross just then set up; he then showed them the country round about, giving them to understand that it was his, and that they should not have it without his permission. While the Indians were alongside one of the ships, two sailors leaped into their canoe, and forced two of them on board. Cartier endeavoured to pacify the chief, and assured him that they should be treated kindly, that they should return again to their own country, and that the Cross was merely intended as a guide to them on entering the port when they should return. To these assurances he added a present of hatchets and knives, which so much pleased the chief that he returned perfectly satisfied. Leaving Gaspé on the 25th of July, he entered the St. Lawrence so far as to see the opposite shores, where, meeting with head-winds and boisterous weather, he sailed for France, and arrived on the 5th of September at St. Malo."

Cartier reported very favourably on the prospects of a plantation in this part of America, and the public mind was much stirred. On the advice of Vice-Admiral de Mailleraye, the King ordered an equipment of three vessels for the ensuing year; and, accordingly, Cartier again sailed from St. Malo on the 19th of May, 1535. The ships encountered such tempestuous weather, however, that they were dispersed, and did not meet again until the 26th of July, when they all reached the Bay of Castel, in Newfoundland. Cartier now navigated the Gulf of St. Lawrence, passing between the Island of Anticosti and the northern shore. After he had explored the coast, he proceeded up the River St. Lawrence, and on the 2nd of September arrived at an island which he named Bacchus, now Orleans. He moored his vessels, and went on shore with several of his men, accompanied by the Indians he had taken with him on his former voyage. The natives fled at their approach; but on hearing the good news that their countrymen had returned, their fears subsided, and they began to skip and dance.

The place Cartier was now at was Stadaconé, the site of the present city of Quebec. Donnaconna, the Indian chief, attended by his followers in twelve canoes, paid a visit to Cartier. The chief made a long oration, diversified with much grotesque posturing; and when the returned Indians informed him that they had been treated with great kindness in France, he expressed much joy, and laid Cartier's arm about his neck as a token of friendship. Not long after this interview, Cartier intimated to Donnaconna his desire to visit Hochelaga, the most considerable village in the country; but the chief was far from pleased at this, and sought to dissuade him from his intention. Cartier was resolute, however, and securing his vessels at Port de St. Croix, he sailed on the 19th of September with his pinnace and two other boats up the river, and arrived at Hochelaga on the 2nd of October. Next day Cartier, in sumptuous attire, with twenty-five of his men, went in procession to see the town. On the way they were met by various detachments of natives, who brought out their sick to be touched and healed by Cartier, whom they regarded as a superior being, sent from Heaven, with the power of healing diseases. Cartier did what could be done to gratify them; and to divert their attention from his supposed miraculous powers, he made presents of hatchets to the men, beads to the women, and trinkets to the children.

He then ordered the drums and trumpets to sound, which pleased the Indians mightily, so that they began to dance and skip about with great joy.

After the ceremony was over, Cartier ascended the mountain, at the foot of which the town of Hochelaga was built. From the summit of the mountain he beheld spread out before him a fine expanse of country, interspersed with rivers, woods, hills, and islands. To this mountain he gave the name of Mont Royal, which was afterwards corrupted into Montreal. As the course of the majestic river could be traced above several falls, the natives, on being appealed to, stated that they might sail up the river for three months, that it ran through two or three great lakes, beyond which there was a sea of fresh water to which they knew no bounds ; and that on the other side of the mountain there was another river, which ran in a contrary direction, to the south-west, through a country free from snow and ice.

Cartier subsequently returned to Stadaconé, where he and his companions remained through the winter with Donnaconna and his tribe. In April the ice broke up, and on the 3rd of May Cartier took possession of the country by erecting a Cross, thirty feet high, on which was suspended a shield, with the arms of France, and bearing this inscription, *Franciscus Primus, Dei Gratia, Francorum Rex, regnat.* " The same day, Donnaconna, accompanied by the two savages who had been in France, visited Cartier on board ; while they were regaling themselves, Donnaconna and two other Indians were seized, and confined on board Cartier's ship. The next night the natives came down to the shore, howling and beating their breasts, crying out for their friends. Cartier at first refused them admittance; but on his assuring them that he would bring them back again, they reluctantly consented to Donnaconna and the other Indians' departure. On the 6th of May, Cartier sailed from Port de St. Croix, touched at St. Peter's, in Newfoundland, and arrived at St. Malo on the 6th of July, 1536. The Indians that were taken to France had been so often told of the necessity of baptism in order to salvation, that on their arrival they were, at their own request, baptized; but neither of them lived to see their native land again."

As Cartier reported favourably on the nature and fertility of the new country, and his statements were confirmed by the Indians brought with him, the King resolved to send him on yet a third voyage. Francis de la Roche, Seigneur or Lord of Roberval, was appointed the King's Lieutenant and Governor of New France and Hochelaga. Cartier was appointed chief pilot, with five vessels under his charge. The inactivity of Roberval caused great delay, and at length Cartier was directed to sail without him. Leaving St. Malo on the 23rd of May, 1541, his ships being victualled for two years, Cartier experienced very severe weather, and did not arrive at Port de St. Croix until August. As soon as they anchored, the new chief and others came up, and made enquiries after the Indians in France. They were informed that Donnaconna was dead, and that the others had married and become great lords, and did not wish to return. Cartier remained in Canada for a year; but as Roberval did not appear, he resolved to return to France. Putting into St. John's, Newfoundland, on the way, he there met Roberval, the governor, with 200 settlers. Although Cartier reported that the Indians were strongly averse to the planting of a colony, the governor insisted upon his returning with him; but Cartier sailed away from St. John's in the night, unperceived.

Roberval prosecuted his voyage, and in July anchored at the place Cartier had left. Here he erected two forts, where he deposited his stores and ammunition. Iron ore was found, as well as crystals supposed to be diamonds, and a yellow substance believed to contain gold. Specimens were sent to France. The winter proved very severe for the settlers; and in addition to suffering great distress, they were severely oppressed by Roberval, who hanged, laid in irons, or whipped offenders according to his mood. Fifty persons died of scurvy, and all the survivors were bitterly discontented.

After this, the colonizing spirit in France languished for half a century. Then, in 1598, the Marquis de la Roche, a nobleman of Picardy, obtained letters patent conferring upon him powers similar to those granted to Roberval. The marquis sailed for Nova Scotia, his passengers consisting of a number of convicts who had been taken out of the French gaols. Falling in with the Island of Sable, the marquis landed forty of his wretched band, until he could survey the coast, and find a suitable place for a settlement. But he returned to France without doing this, and the miserable beings he had landed were left to their fate. For seven years they subsisted with the utmost difficulty; and when at last the French king (Henry IV.) sent a vessel to rescue them, only twelve survivors out of forty were found. They were taken to France, and the King pardoned their crimes, and rewarded them for the hardships they had undergone.

With regard to the origin of the name of Çanada, it is somewhat obscure. On Cartier's first arrival, the Indians were frequently heard to pronounce these two words, *Aca Nada,* nothing here, from which some supposed the name of the country was derived. But others believed the name to have originated in an Indian word, *Kannatha,* a village or collection of huts; and this is the derivation now most favoured.

The next effort at a French settlement after De la Roche's was made in 1600, when the King granted equal privileges to a M. de Chauvin, who had great interest at Court. Chauvin had been stimulated by the representations of one Pontgravé, who had made frequent voyages to Tadousac, and who reported strongly as to the value of the fur trade. Chauvin and Pontgravé sailed together for the St. Lawrence, where they obtained peltries and furs in great abundance. They were preparing for a second voyage in 1601 when Chauvin died. A number of merchants of Rouen now formed themselves into a company, with a view of carrying on the fur trade and effecting settlements in Canada. The patent was granted to Commander de Chatte. A squadron was fitted out, and the command given to Pontgravé who was accompanied by Samuel de Champlain, a brave and experienced seaman.

Champlain was destined to be the first real colonizer of the country. He was a Frenchman of gentle birth, maritime and military experience, and much religious enthusiasm. He was a native of Brouage, and for his share in the development of Canada he has been styled " The Father of New France."

Pontgravé and Champlain visited Tadousac, and then sailed up the St. Lawrence, and anchored at a place called by the Indians *Rebek*, or the rock. This place was deemed fitting for a fort or settlement, and it was here that Champlain ultimately founded the city of Quebec. On returning to France, Champlain found that the Commander de Chatte was dead, and that " a new patent had been given to M. de Monts, constituting him governor of the American territory lying between the fortieth and forty-sixth degree of north latitude, with an exclusive privilege of trade to Acadia and the Gulf of St. Lawrence, during the term of ten years. The patent was published in all the maritime towns of France. De Monts equipped two vessels, and sailed on the 7th of March for his new government. Champlain and Perrincourt accompanied him. They formed settlements at St. Croix and Port Royal, and retained quiet possession of Acadia, until they were attacked by Sir Samuel Argal in the year 1614, by the command of Governor Dale, of Virginia, when their settlements were broken up. While these attempts had been made in Acadia, De Monts and his company conceived that great advantages would result from the establishment of a colony in the River St. Lawrence by the extension of the fur trade, and they indulged the hope of penetrating westward through the lakes to the Pacific Ocean, and by that means of finding a nearer communication with China. With this view, one of their vessels had been sent, in the year 1608, to the River St. Lawrence, commanded by Champlain. In a former voyage, he had marked out a spot above the Island of Orleans, as a proper place for a fort. As soon as he arrived at Quebec, which was on the 3rd of July, he began to clear the woods, ordered houses to be built, and laid out gardens for the inhabitants. He passed the winter at this place, but some of his people suffered much from the scurvy. As soon as the navigation was open, he went up the River St. Lawrence, attended by several Indians, to explore the country; and on his way to the southward, he crossed a large lake, to which he gave his own name, which it retains to this day. On the shores of Lake St. Sacrement, now Lake George, he met a party of the Iroquois, of Five Nations, who were then at war with the Canada Indians; an action ensued, and the party of the Five Nations was defeated. Champlain killed two Indians with his own musket, and he brought fifty scalps in triumph to Quebec. In the autumn of the same year, he returned to France, leaving Captain Peter Chauvin in command, and in the following year returned to Quebec to establish a colony, of which he is justly considered the founder."

In 1610, as De Monts had lost his privilege of trade, Champlain revisited France, in order to find a powerful protector for the young colony. The Comte de

Soissons had obtained the viceroyalty, and he readily delegated his authority to Champlain, appointing him his lieutenant. The Prince de Condé succeeded, on the count's death, to the viceroyalty of New France, and he confirmed Champlain in his appointment, and obtained letters of incorporation for a new company, consisting of merchants of St. Malo, Rouen, and La Rochelle. Champlain pressed upon the Company the necessity for sending out settlers, as well as priests for Christianizing the natives. Four priests of the Recollets were accordingly sent out, and these were the first who settled in Canada.

The Prince de Condé disposed of the viceroyalty in 1620 to his relative the Marshal de Montmorenci, who retained Champlain in his position. The latter, who paid frequent visits to France, took his family out to Quebec. Troubles arose from the hostile attitude of the Five Nations, who dreaded an alliance between the Algonquins, Hurons, and the French. Representations as to the deplorable state of the colony were at length made to the French Government, which suppressed the old company, and granted an exclusive privilege to two brothers of the name of De Caen.

In 1623-24 Champlain built a fort to protect the little colony of Quebec, which at this time consisted of only fifty persons. Champlain then went to France again to represent the necessitous and comparatively insecure position of the colony, when he found that the Marshal de Montmorenci had disposed of his viceroyalty to his nephew the Duc de Ventadour. The duc had taken orders, and his chief object was the spiritual welfare of the colony. He consequently sent out in 1625 three Jesuits, Fathers L'Allemand, Masse, and De Brebœuf, and two lay brothers. They were well received by the Recollets at their small house, on the site of which now stands the present General Hospital, near the River St. Charles.

The Caens were Huguenots engaged in the fur trade. As religious dissensions broke out, Cardinal Richelieu revoked their privileges, and a charter was granted to an influential company called the Company of One Hundred Associates. Their powers were most extensive, including the right to declare war and to make peace, to enjoy the whole trade by sea and land for fifteen years, except the cod and whale fishery; and the beaver and fur trade in general were to belong to the Company for ever. The King gave them two ships of 300 tons each, and elevated twelve of the principal members of the Company into the Noblesse. The Company, on its part, agreed to bring into the colony, in the year 1628, 200 or 300 settlers, and 16,000 more before the year 1643.

But war having been declared between England and France, an expedition was sent against the colony under Admiral Sir David Kirk. In the meantime William de Caen sought to avenge himself for the loss of his exclusive privilege. Two brothers of Kirk, Lewis and Thomas, besieged Quebec, and in consequence of his distressful condition Champlain was compelled to surrender. Thus was the capital of New France first subdued by the power of England. Lewis Kirk became commander of Quebec, and Champlain proceeded to France.

Negotiations were afterwards set on foot for the restitution of the colony to France, and in 1632 this was accomplished. By the Treaty of St. Germain en Laye, all the old territory, as well as Acadia (Nova Scotia) and Cape Breton, became French possessions. The French Company having regained its rights, Champlain was reappointed governor in 1633; and he took out with him a number of respectable colonists, as well as two Jesuits, who were sent forth for the conversion of the Indians, and for the education of the youth of the settlement. The foundation of a Jesuit house had just been laid, when a severe loss overtook the colony by the death of its governor, who expired in December, 1635. Champlain seems to have been a zealous proselytizer, as well as an upright and valiant man, and it was a common saying of his that "the salvation of one soul was of more value than the conquest of an empire."

A terrible earthquake visited the colony in February, 1633. It was felt over 200 leagues of territory from east to west, and 100 from north to south. The shocks were no fewer than thirty in number; but fortunately, notwithstanding the general derangement of nature, no human lives appear to have been lost. Montmagny, Champlain's successor, founded various institutions for the benefit of the colonists, and peopled and fortified the Island of Montreal with a view of repressing the incursions of the Five Nations. The St. Sulpicians of Paris acquired this island for their operations. Succeeding governors were D'Aillebout and De Lauzon, and under the latter the religious orders made considerable progress. In 1653, Maisonville, Governor of the Island of Montreal, visited France, and returned with a hundred men, together with a pious lady, Marguerite Bourgeois, who in 1659 laid the foundation of the institution called the Sisters of the Congregation. The same year a new governor of the whole colony, the Marquis d'Argenson, went out; and in 1670, owing to the representations of the Jesuits, Quebec was created a bishopric, and François de Laval, titular Bishop of Petrea, was appointed to the see. Seminaries had already been erected for the education of a sufficient number of young men for the priesthood.

The Baron d'Avaugour succeeded D'Argenson; but the colony generally was in a deplorable state, and made no progress. The King sent out De Monts as his commissioner to visit Canada, and to report upon the state of the country. In the end, the Company resigned its charter to the King, who took the colony under the royal protection, and appointed M. de Mézy Governor-General.

The King created a Sovereign Council, " composed of De Mézy, as Governor-General, representing the Crown; De Laval, Bishop of Petrea; Robert, Intendant; and four other councillors to be elected by them, one to be Attorney-General, and a Clerk for the conservation of the minutes of arrêts, decrees, or orders of the Council. The Clerk to hold his appointment at the pleasure of the Governor and Bishop. The powers of the Sovereign Council were—' cognizance of all causes, civil as well as criminal; to judge sovereignly, and in the last resort, according to the laws and ordinances of the *Kingdom*; and

therein to proceed as near as possible in the form
and manner practised and observed in the jurisdiction
of our Court of our Parliament of Paris; reserving,
nevertheless, according to our sovereignty, the right to
change, reform, and amplify the said laws and ordinances, and to alter, repeal, or renew them, or such other
regulations, statutes, and constitutions, as we may
conceive to be useful to our service and the welfare
of our subjects in that country.' The Council was
directed to take order on the expenditure of public
money, the Indian trade, the colony's commerce with
France, the matters of public police, the appointment
of judges in the first instance for all private differences, without chicane or dilatory proceedings ; the
appointment of clerks, notaries, serjeants, and other
officers of courts ; the five councillors to hear and
determine petty causes, and see that the judgment
of the Council be executed ; to take more especial
cognizance in business touching syndics and trustees
of houses, their inhabitants, strangers, and others,
and render justice promptly ; to have such salary as
the State may order, and nothing else, nor to accept
of any presents without the royal leave, nor exercise
any other office. The Governor-General and Bishop
were directed to cause the Attorney-General and
Secretary to promulgate and enregister this Edict,
and see it executed, notwithstanding any impediments,
oppositions, and appeals. If any impediments should
intervene, the cognizance was to be referred to the
Sovereign Council, and all other courts were prohibited
from interfering. A copy of the Edict, under the
signature of the Clerk of the Sovereign Council, was

to have the same force and effect as the original. All acts of the Sovereign Council were directed to be under the Seal of the King's Arms, and universal obedience was commanded."

In 1679, the Custom of Paris and the Ordinances of the Kingdom of France were declared the law of Canada; and some years later Quebec, Three Rivers, and Montreal were constituted separate jurisdictions, and the Court of Justice Royale at Montreal was established.

Returning to the progress of the colony, in 1664 the King by an edict annexed it to the West India Company. The Company became possessed by this edict of the territory lying between the Rivers Amazon and Oronoko, as well as the Caribbee Islands, Canada, Acadia, Newfoundland, and Africa. This territory was conceded to the Company *en seigneurie*; and it was to be governed by the laws and ordinances of the empire and the custom of Paris, so as to avoid all difficulties and disputes. The Marquis de Tracy, who had been appointed Viceroy in North and South America, with authority over all governors, was ordered first to the West Indies, and then directed to visit Canada, there to adopt such measures as he deemed most expedient to ensure the tranquillity of the colony, and to put the country into a state of defence against the attacks of the Five Nations, who had now become more troublesome in consequence of the support and encouragement they received from the English.

The tribes confederated under the name of the Five Nations were the Mohawks, Oneidas, Onondagas, Cayugas, and Senecas—all Iroquois Indians. For generations they had been engaged in implacable warfare with the Algonquins and Hurons, the most powerful native races in Canada. During the progress of hostilities, the Iroquois Indians obtained guns and ammunition from the Dutch ; and as these gave them a great superiority over their rivals, the Algonquins were in course of time practically annihilated.

Such was the position of affairs when a new departure took place in the history of the colony.

CHAPTER II.

THE COLONY FROM 1665 TO 1700.

THE Viceroy, the Marquis de Tracy, took out with him the Seigneur de Courcelles as Governor of Canada, and M. Talon, Intendant. M. de Courcelles took the place of M. de Mézy, who had been recalled. The regiment of Carignan-Salières accompanied the Viceroy; and in 1665 a considerable number of new settlers arrived in Canada, bringing with them cattle, sheep, and horses, the first live stock as yet despatched to the colony.

The West India Company was to enjoy a monopoly of the territories and the trade of the colony for forty years; and it was not only granted further the exclusive navigation, but was to receive a bounty of thirty livres on every ton of goods exported to France. The Company was likewise to have a right to all mines and minerals, the power of levying and recruiting soldiers within the kingdom, manufacturing arms and ammunition for the defence of its possessions, building forts, and even declaring and carrying on war by sea and land against the native Indians, or neighbouring foreign colonies, in case of insult. A coat-of-arms was granted to the colony; but when used in war it was to be surmounted by the royal arms of France. To encourage emigration, all colonists and converts professing the Romish faith were invested with the rights of Frenchmen.

To check the irruptions of the tribes of the Five Nations, M. de Tracy erected three forts at the mouth of the River Richelieu, afterwards known as the Sorel. These forts proved unavailing, however, as the Indians discovered other means of harassing the settlements. De Tracy, therefore, determined to carry the war into the enemy's country. Although seventy years of age, he took the field in person, with a large force, with the object of exterminating the hostile Indians. On the 14th of September, 1666, his army, consisting of regular soldiers, militia, and friendly Indians, set forth; but great difficulties were encountered as they advanced, and the means of subsistence vanished. The Indians retired; and after a march of 700 miles, the governor had to return without effecting anything but the destruction of the villages, and the capture of a few old men, women, and children. Happily large stores of corn were found.

In the ensuing spring, De Tracy returned to France, leaving M. de Courcelles behind to administer the affairs of government. The latter succeeded in dealing with the Indians, and even in preventing his own allies from engaging in a war with the Iroquois. He further induced a large body of the Hurons to settle in a new district, and fixed upon Cataraqui on Lake Ontario—near the present site of Kingston—as an eligible situation for the erection of a fort, for the double purpose of protecting the fur trade and checking the incursions of the hostile tribes. De Courcelles suffered so much in health by his exertions that he was compelled to ask for his recall. He had only just left when small-pox broke out among the Indian tribes, causing the most fearful ravages. In the settlement at Sillery alone 1,500 perished, while one tribe was completely exterminated, and several others nearly so.

In 1672, De Courcelles was succeeded by the Count de Frontenac, who immediately erected the fort at Cataraqui, which was frequently called Fort Frontenac in consequence. The count was very able and ambitious, but also proud and overbearing, and he warmly resented any attempts to limit his jurisdiction. By the terms of the charter, all affairs of importance in the colony were to be decided in a Council of State, composed of the governor, the bishop, and the intendant, each with an equal vote. The bishop was supported by the clergy, whose influence was exerted in opposing the sale of spirits to the Indians, which the Viceroy, on the contrary, upheld as being profitable, and as a means he believed of attaching the Indians to the French interest. The count had also violent dissensions with M. Chesneau, the intendant; and as it was found impossible for them to act in concert, and there were other complaints against the governor, the French Government finally recalled them both. At the same time, it decided in favour of the clergy, and prohibited the sale of the fatal firewater.

Here we pause to relate the tragic story of the Sieur de la Salle, a young Frenchman of family and fortune, who was at this time residing in Quebec. He had emigrated to America in the hope of gaining both fame and wealth, being impressed with the idea of the practicability of effecting a passage to China and Japan through the unexplored regions to the west of Canada. He had heard of the success, in 1673, of a priest named Marquette, and a merchant of Quebec named Jolyet, who had penetrated as far as the mighty Mississippi ; and he became fired with the ambition of exploring the Missouri, which he believed must lead to the northern ocean. Having obtained the sanction of the Government to his enterprise, De la Salle went to France, where he was enabled, through the assistance of the Prince de Conti, to prepare an expedition. He was joined in his undertaking by the Chevalier Tuti, and on the 14th of July, 1678, they sailed from France with thirty men, and in two months reached Quebec. One Father Hennepin was of the party, which now made for the great lakes.

The following is Father Hennepin's deeply interesting description of the construction of the first vessel ever built on the Canadian lakes, and of the adventures it passed through : " It now became necessary for La Salle, in furtherance of his object, to construct a vessel above the Falls of Niagara sufficiently large to transport the men and goods necessary to carry on a profitable trade with the savages residing on the western lakes. On the 22nd of January, 1679, they went six miles above the falls to the mouth of a small creek, and there built a dock convenient for the construction of their vessel.

"On the 26th of January, the keel and other pieces being ready, La Salle requested Father Hennepin to drive the first bolt, but the modesty of the father's profession prevented. During the rigorous winter La Salle determined to return to Fort Frontenac; and leaving the dock in charge of the Italian named Chevalier Tuti, he started, accompanied by Father Hennepin, as far as Lake Ontario; from Ontario he traversed the dreary forests to Frontenac on foot, with only two companions and a dog, which drew his baggage on a sleigh, subsisting on nothing but parched corn, and even that failed him two days' journey from the fort. In the meantime, the building of the vessel went on under the suspicious eyes of the neighbouring savages, although the most part of them had gone to war beyond Lake Erie. One of them, feigning intoxication, attempted the life of the blacksmith, who defended himself successfully with a red-hot bar of iron. The timely warning of a friendly squaw averted the burning of their vessel on the stocks, which was designed by the savages. The workmen were almost disheartened by frequent alarms, and would have abandoned the work had they not been cheered by the good father, who represented the great advantage their perseverance would afford, and how much their success would redound to the glory of God. These and other inducements accelerated the work, and the vessel was soon ready to be launched, though not entirely finished. Chanting the Te Deum, and firing three guns, they committed her to the river amid cries of joy, and swung their hammocks in security from the wild beasts and still more dreaded Indians.

"When the Senecas returned from their expedition, they were greatly astonished at the floating fort, which struck terror among all the savages who lived on the great lakes and river within 1,500 miles. Hennepin ascended the river in a bark canoe with one of his companions as far as Lake Erie. They twice pulled the canoe up the rapids, and sounded the lake for the purpose of ascertaining the depth. He reported that, with a favourable north or north-west wind, the vessel could ascend to the lake, and then sail without difficulty over its whole extent. Soon after, the vessel was launched in the current of Niagara, about four and a half miles from the lake. Hennepin left it for Fort Frontenac, and, returning with La Salle and two other fathers, Gabriel and Zenobe Mambre, anchored in the Niagara on the 30th of July, 1679. On the 4th of August they reached the dock where the ship was built, distant eighteen miles from Lake Ontario, and proceeded thence in a bark canoe to their vessel, which they found at anchor three miles from the beautiful Lake Erie.

"The vessel was sixty tons' burden, completely rigged, and found with all the necessaries, arms, provisions, and merchandise; it had seven small pieces of cannon on board, two of which were of brass. There was a griffin flying at the jib-boom, and an eagle above. There were also all the ordinary ornaments and other fixtures which usually grace a ship of war.

"They endeavoured many times to ascend the current of the Niagara into Lake Erie without success, the wind not being strong enough.... While they were thus detained, La Salle employed a few of his men in clearing some land on the Canadian shore opposite the vessel, and in sowing some vegetable seeds for the benefit of those who might inhabit the place.

"At length, the wind being favourable, they lightened the vessel by sending most of the crew ashore, and, with the aid of their sails and ten or a dozen men at the tow lines, ascended the current into Lake Erie. Thus, on the 7th of August, 1679, the first vessel set sail on the untried waters of Lake Erie. They steered southward, after having chanted the Te Deum, and discharged their artillery in the presence of a vast number of Seneca warriors. It had been reported to our voyagers that Lake Erie was full of breakers and sandbanks, which rendered a safe navigation impossible ; they therefore kept the lead going, sounding from time to time.

"After sailing without difficulty through Lake Erie, they arrived on the 11th of August at the mouth of the Detroit River, sailing up which they arrived at Lake St. Clair, to which they gave the name it bears. After being detained several days by contrary winds at the bottom of the St. Clair River, they at length succeeded in entering Lake Huron on the 23rd of August, chanting the Te Deum through gratitude for a safe navigation thus far. Passing along the eastern shore of the lake, they sailed with a fresh and favourable wind until evening, when the wind suddenly veered, driving them across Saginaw Bay. The storm raged until the 24th, and was succeeded by a calm, which continued until next day noon, when they pursued their course until midnight. As they doubled a point which advanced into the lake, they were suddenly struck by a furious wind, which forced them to run behind the cape for safety. On the 26th, the violence of the storm compelled them to send down their topmasts and yard, and to stand in, for they could find neither anchorage nor shelter.

"It was then the stout heart of La Salle failed him. The whole crew fell upon their knees to say their prayers and prepare for death, except the pilot, whom they could not compel to follow their example, and who, on the contrary, did nothing all the time but curse and swear against La Salle, who had brought him thither to make him perish in a nasty lake, and lose the glory he had acquired by his long and happy navigation on the ocean. On the 27th, favoured with less adverse winds, they arrived during the night at Michillimakinac, and anchored in the bay, where they reported six fathoms of water and a clay bottom. The savages were struck dumb with astonishment at the size of their vessel, and the noise of their guns.

"Here they regaled themselves on the delicious trout, which they described as being from fifty pounds to sixty pounds in weight, and as affording the savages their principal subsistence. On the 2nd of September they left Mackinack, entered Lake Michigan, and sailed forty leagues to an island at the mouth of the Bay of Puara (Green Bay). From this place, La Salle determined to send back the ship laden with furs to Niagara. The pilot and five men embarked in her, and on the 10th she fired a gun, and set sail on her return with a favourable wind. Nothing more was heard from her, and she undoubtedly foundered in Lake Huron, with all on board. Her cargo was rich, and valued at 60,000 livres."

Dauntless in spirit, La Salle pursued his course with unabated energy; and after grappling with difficulties and dangers of all kinds—from both the Indians and his own party—he at length succeeded in reaching the mouth of the Mississippi. From here, the homeward journey to Quebec proved more difficult and dangerous than the outward one; but ultimately, after an absence of more than two years, the explorers arrived at Quebec. Shortly afterwards, La Salle left for France, where he was received with honour, and granted a commission as governor over the whole extent of country lying between the lakes and the Gulf of Mexico; and an expedition was equipped, consisting of four ships and a number of men, for the purpose of forming a settlement at the mouth of the Mississippi, and thus establishing a line of communication between that settlement and those already existing in Canada. Leaving Rochelle on the 24th of July, 1684, the vessels touched at St. Domingo and Cuba on their passage, and arrived in due time off the coast of Florida. Being unaware of the longitude of the mouth of the river of which he was in quest, La Salle proceeded about 200 miles beyond the mouth of the Mississippi before he became aware of his mistake. He then attempted to form a settlement on the coast, with the intention of afterwards making a search for the lost river. But this latter idea was at last abandoned; and without Indian guides to conduct him, he wandered into the interior parts of the country, after the fabulous mines of St. Barbe, and on the way he and his nephew were murdered by his mutinous followers.

This dramatic end to a strange career occurred in 1687. La Salle's death broke up the small colony on the coast, many of whose members died from hunger and fatigue. Those who were not murdered by the Indians were confined by the Spaniards in the mines, and only seven persons escaped to Canada to relate their dreadful misfortunes.

Returning to the history of the colony, the West India Company, being convinced of its inability any longer to carry out the complicated objects of its charter, resigned it into the hands of the Crown in December, 1674. At this period the whole population of the French settlements in Canada, including converted Indians, amounted to about 8,000 souls.

In 1682, Frontenac was succeeded as Viceroy by M. de la Barre, while M. de Meules was appointed intendant. The new governor was confronted by many difficulties. The English settlers on the Hudson regarded the Iroquois country as within their own territory, and used every means to court the alliance and good feeling of the Indians, and to draw their trade from the French settlements. To a large extent they succeeded, because they were able to offer the Indians more advantageous terms than the French traders. Remonstrances proved of no avail, and the French governor was further crippled by the reduction in the military strength of the colony.

M. de la Barre declared war against the two

Indian tribes which were most hostile to French interests, the Mohawks and the Senecas ; and having procured a reinforcement of 200 soldiers from France, he advanced up the river from Quebec. At Montreal he received deputies from the two tribes, but distrusted their assurances ; and he was proceeding against the Senecas, when other tribes informed him that they should make common cause with the attacked. Sickness broke out amongst the French troops ; and when De la Barre threatened the Indian deputies unless full reparation was made for injuries already sustained, they replied that he must be in a dream, and that if he would only open his eyes he must see that he was altogether unable to carry out his formidable threats. They guaranteed reparation for any actual plunder inflicted on French traders, but added that no more could be conceded, and that the army must be instantly withdrawn. De la Barre, convinced of the hopelessness of the struggle, acceded to these terms, and at once began his retreat. On reaching Quebec, he found that a fresh detachment of soldiers had just arrived from France, under the command of two captains of marines, who were commanded to proceed to the most important posts, and to capture as many of the Five Nations as possible, as his Majesty meant them to be employed on board the French galleys.

When the unsuccessful issue of the expedition against the Indians became known to the French Government, De la Barre was immediately recalled, and the Marquis de Dénonville was appointed his successor. This was in 1685. The new governor showed no disposition to conciliate the Indians. It is true he persuaded a number of chiefs to meet him on the banks of Lake Ontario; but he suddenly put them in irons, and sent them off to France to man the galleys, in accordance with the wish of the French king. It is said that in this act of treachery he even employed two missionaries to assist him. The marquis next urged upon the King the necessity of erecting a fort at Niagara to interrupt the communications between the British and the Iroquois, and the North-West Company at Quebec offered to pay an annual rent of 30,000 livres to the Crown for the privilege of a monopoly of the trade at the proposed station. This roused the English, and in the spring of 1686 Dénonville received a letter from Colonel Dongan, the Governor of New York, demanding explanations of the military preparations making against the Iroquois, whom he alleged to be subjects of England, and also remonstrating against the erection of a fort at Niagara by the French, all that country being considered by the British a dependency of New York. The French commander made a specious and temporizing reply, but continued his preparations for war, and at last started on an expedition into the country of the Senecas.

He inflicted a defeat upon the Iroquois; but they were, nevertheless, far from being subdued. Following their enemies on their homeward march, they "destroyed the newly erected fort of Niagara, and afterwards blockaded that at Cataraqui; and after making themselves masters of the whole upper country of the St. Lawrence, sent deputies to Montreal with proposals of peace, leaving, at two days' march behind, a band of 1,200 warriors. They insisted upon the restoration of the chiefs who had been sent to France, and all other captives, giving the commander only four days to agree to the terms. Dénonville had no choice but to submit. The treaty was interrupted by an act of treachery on the part of the Hurons. They had entered into the war on the misunderstanding that it was not to terminate till their enemies the Iroquois were completely subdued; and fearing lest their allies the French should leave them at the mercy of the Iroquois, they determined to interrupt the treaty. They therefore attacked a party of the deputies; and telling some who were taken prisoners that they had committed the act at the instigation of the governor, allowed them to depart. The consequences were such as the Hurons anticipated. A large party of Five Nations made a sudden descent on the Island of Montreal, and carried off 200 prisoners, without any resistance. The fort at Cataraqui was blown up and abandoned."

The affairs of the colony being now in a perilous state, the Marquis de Dénonville was recalled, and the province was for a second time committed to the governorship of the Comte de Frontenac. Taking out with him the captured chiefs, he landed at Montreal on the 27th of October, 1689. "On his arrival, he endeavoured to open a negotiation with the Iroquois; and by the advice of Oureouharé (one of the chiefs he brought with him from France), he sent a deputy, with four of the prisoners, to announce to the tribes his return to Canada, and his wish to conclude a treaty of peace. The Iroquois, after some deliberation, sent back the deputies with six belts, expressing their determination. Affecting to consider Onunthio (the governor) as always the same, they complained that his rods of correction had been too sharp and cutting. The roots of the tree of peace which he had planted at Fort Frontenac had been withered by blood; the ground had been polluted with treachery and falsehood. They demanded redress for these injuries, and that Oureouharé, with his captive companions, should be sent back, previous to the liberation of the French prisoners. Onunthio would then be at liberty to plant again the tree of peace, but not on the same spot.

"At this time, the Ottawas and other tribes, being desirous of having the English market to carry their furs to, were anxious to conclude a peace with the Iroquois, particularly as they felt that the alliance of the French was an injury rather than a benefit to them; they having to protect the French, instead of the French protecting them. It was not, however, the policy of the governor to allow of this union, as the Iroquois could depend upon the support of both the English and Dutch, and the whole or greater portion of the valuable trade in furs would be transferred from the Canadian to the New England settlements. The English and French nations were now at war, and the count determined to strike the first blow in order to endeavour to retrieve the reputation of his country in America. An expedition was sent out, therefore, in 1690, against Schenectady, the frontier town of New York. The party, composed of French and Indians, succeeded in surprising the place. The fort and every house was pillaged and burnt, and all the horrors of war were let loose on the inhabitants; sixty-three men, women, and children were massacred in cold blood, and two old Indians who were taken prisoners were cut into pieces to make soup for the Indians who accompanied the French. The Iroquois, after this affair, sent messengers to the survivors, promising to revenge the injury. Shortly afterwards, a second expedition was despatched to attack the English village of Sementels, which they succeeded in destroying, but were themselves waylaid on their retreat, and had considerable difficulty in escaping. The next measure adopted by the count was to send a detachment to strengthen the post at Michillimakinac, who were also bearers of presents to the chiefs in that neighbourhood. This party was attacked on their journey by a band of the Five Nations, whom they succeeded in defeating."

But the British now began to attack the French settlements as well as the Indians. Two expeditions were prepared, one by sea from Boston against Quebec, the other by land from New York directed against Montreal. Sir William Phipps commanded the sea expedition, having under him a fleet of thirty-four vessels, and a large body of troops. Sir William captured all the posts on the coasts of Acadia and Newfoundland, with several on the St. Lawrence, and was within a few days' sail of Quebec before news of his advance arrived there. The British fleet made its appearance before the city on the 5th of

October, 1690, and Sir William Phipps at once demanded its surrender. Frontenac replied that he should surrender to no one, and described King William as a usurper. A good deal of skirmishing ensued; but as Sir William found that neither the fire from his ships nor the efforts of his army made any impression, he resolved to return to New England. The expedition fared disastrously on its return journey, and several of the vessels foundered.

The British land force against Montreal was commanded by General Winthrop; but it effected nothing, and was obliged to retreat to Albany for supplies. The failure of both expeditions excited the liveliest dissatisfaction in England and the British American colonies.

In 1691, a large party of Iroquois made an irruption into the country about Montreal; but they were opposed by an officer named De Callières, at the head of the French troops and about 800 Indian allies. The invaders in the outset captured several posts; but in the end they were compelled to retreat. There was little to choose between the barbarity of the French and that of the Indians in the conduct of these campaigns.

Frontenac made several attempts to bring about a peace with the Five Nations, but in vain. He therefore collected an army of regulars, militia, and Indians, to the number of about 700 men, and in February, 1693, invaded the Mohawk country. Three Indian entrenchments were captured; and when the news reached Albany, Major Schuyler, with 500 men, including Indians, advanced to attack the French, with whom he had several successful skirmishes. The count returned to Montreal; and learning from the Indian prisoners that an important British expedition was being prepared against Canada, he put the capital into a state of defence, and augmented the fortifications of Chambly, Sorel, and Montreal.

As he also rebuilt the old fort of Cataraqui, the Five Nations appealed for succour to Colonel Fletcher, Governor of New York. This was not forthcoming; but the Indians proceeded to harass the French. The allied Indians complained greatly of the disadvantageous terms under which they were forced to trade with the French, compared with those obtained from the British by the Five Nations, and threatened to desert the French, and, joining the Iroquois, place themselves under the protection of the British. This danger demanded vigorous action on the part of Frontenac. He consequently determined upon such proceedings as should impress his enemies with a sufficient idea of his power, and at the same time rivet the chains of his allies. A strong force was collected, which in June, 1695, marched to Cataraqui, and thence into the country of the Onondagas. They discovered, on entering a lake, two bundles of rushes suspended to a tree, from which they learned that upwards of 1,400 warriors were waiting to receive them.

We learn from Charlevoix's narrative that "the French army then passed the Onondaga Lake; and having formed themselves in order of battle, the better to deceive the Indians, the two wings took a circuit round the borders of it : the engineer, Le Vasseur, that accompanied the count, then marked out a fort, where the provisions and batteaux were deposited, with a guard of a hundred men. A Seneca Indian, who had been out as a scout, apprised the Onondagas of the near approach of the French. It had been their determination to have defended their castles ; but when they were informed of the strength of the French army, and of the nature of the mortars they had brought with them, which, if they fell on their castles, would burst and bury them in the ruins, they instantly set fire to their village, and retired to the woods. The French by this time came up, and, finding no enemy, were idle spectators of the burning of a few miserable huts. The Oneidas, more to amuse than determined to make peace, on the 5th of August sent a messenger with a belt to assure the count that his nation was desirous of peace, and wished to live on the best terms with the French. The count answered that he sincerely wished peace with them, and that it should be concluded ; on condition, however, that those Oneidas who had left Canada should return and settle in the colony, as he was to be no longer amused with idle negotiations. The count, to add weight to his proposition, and to convince them of his ability to punish them in case of resistance, sent forward the Marquis de Vaudreuil with a detachment of 600 men to the Oneida village, with orders, in case of resistance, to put every Indian to the sword. The Oneidas did not wait the approach of the detachment, but fled with the utmost precipitation, leaving behind an old sachem of a hundred years of age. He was delivered over to the Indians belonging to the French party, who put him to the torture, which he bore with more than manly presence of mind. To one who stabbed him with a knife, 'You had better,' said he, 'make me die by fire, that these French dogs may learn to suffer like men. You Indians, you dogs of dogs, think of me, when you are in a like condition.' Never, perhaps, was a man treated with more cruelty, nor did any man bear it with more magnanimity and resolution. In a council of war, which was called on the 9th of August, it was resolved to destroy the Seneca tribe, and to leave a considerable French force in the country during the winter. On the evening of the same day, to the astonishment of the whole army, the count relinquished his former plan, and marched with the army for Montreal, where it arrived on the 20th of August, having only lost six men during the whole march. The count was in hopes that the late incursion would dispose the natives to peace; and to increase their distress, and to harass them the more, as soon as the troops had recovered from their fatigue, large parties were sent into their country to prevent supplies of provisions being sent to them, of which they were in the greatest want. The Five Nations, to convince the count that they were still unsubdued, sent several parties into Canada, one of which advanced near to Montreal, where, meeting a small French force, an action commenced, in which the French were routed, and the commanding officer and several were killed. As soon as M. de Callières was informed of their approach, Captain de Repentigni and several men went in pursuit of them; they were soon come up with, and the French losing their captain, they were routed by the Indians of the Five Nations."

Early in 1697, Frontenac was apprised by the French Government of another impending attack on Canada by the British, and he was ordered to have all his defences ready, together with an available army of some 2,000 men. The alarm proved to be a false one, however; for the British, instead of attacking, were fortifying their own places, under apprehension of incursions from Canada.

Meantime, causes of dissatisfaction multiplied, and the Indians were further incensed on discovering through their intercourse with the British that they were being cheated by the French regulations of the fur trade. On the 11th of September, the Peace of Ryswick was concluded by France and Great Britain; and as news of this reached New York before it was known in Canada, the Five Nations, under the protection of the treaty, went out to hunt near Cataraqui. Taking this opportunity for revenge, Frontenac sent out a French force, with a number of Algonquins, to attack them. Black Kettle, a famous Onondaga chief, and forty of his warriors, were disporting themselves in the hunting grounds, when they were attacked and defeated. Several were slain, and among them Black Kettle himself. After he was mortally wounded, he cried out: "Must I, who have made the whole earth tremble before me, now die by the hands of children!"

The Sieur de Révérin formed a company in 1697, and established a fishery at the harbour of Mount Louis, about half-way between Quebec and the extremity of the Gulf of St. Lawrence on the south side. The settlers were much disturbed by the English in the outset; but their exertions in both fishery and agriculture were fairly successful.

A warm and lengthy controversy took place in 1698 between the Earl of Bellamont, who had just been appointed Governor of New York, and the Comte de Frontenac. It arose out of an exchange of prisoners between Canada and the Five Nations, and Lord Bellamont demanded that the exchange should be made through him, the Five Nations being under the protection of England. Frontenac stoutly resisted this, and absolutely refused to acknowledge the Five Nations as subjects of Great Britain.

The dispute still remained undecided when, on the 28th of November, 1698, the Comte de Frontenac died in the seventy-eighth year of his age. His governorship had lasted for seventeen years, and by the French Canadians he was deeply regretted as the Father of the Country. The clergy honoured him for his virtues, the noblesse esteemed him for his valour, and the people generally held him in affectionate regard for his goodness. In his old age, his former infirmities of temper had somewhat softened.

The Chevalier de Callières was appointed governor on the 20th of April, 1699, the Marquis de Vaudreuil succeeding him as Governor of Montreal.

The policy of Callières was to bring together all the Indian tribes within reach of the Canadian settlements into one bond of union. In this he was partially successful for a time, and as the seventeenth century closed he effected a treaty of peace with the deputies of several Indian tribes.

CHAPTER III.

ITS HISTORY TO THE ARRIVAL OF MONTCALM.

THE interregnum of peace secured by the Treaty of Ryswick proved of short duration. It lasted barely five years, for in 1702 a rupture occurred between France and England, and war broke out afresh. Its disastrous effects were speedily felt in the respective colonies. Before the outbreak, however, the deputies of the Five Nations and those of the Indians of the north-west had met at Montreal, and concluded an amicable arrangement, with a mutual restoration of prisoners.

But as soon as the news reached Canada that war had been declared between England and France, Callières, apprehensive lest the British should incite the Five Nations to break the peace just concluded, perceived the necessity for undertaking the most vigorous measures to forestall the action of the English. He consequently represented to the Court of France the imperative importance of sending over troops for the preservation of the colony, and urging that the fortifications should be put into a complete state of repair.

While engaged in translating his views into action, the chevalier died suddenly on the 26th of May,

1703, his loss being deplored by the whole country. He was succeeded by the Marquis de Vaudreuil, who took out with him M. Beauharnois as intendant. The marquis followed in the footsteps of his predecessor, and seized the earliest opportunity of gaining over the Five Nations to the French interest.

The wisdom of this step was made apparent in the spring of 1708, when a council was held at Montreal to adopt measures to check the intrigues of the English among the Indian allies. A number of Indian chiefs were present, and it was resolved that a blow should be struck against the British colonies. The Five Nations were appealed to by the English to turn against their old enemies the French; but these tribes were unwilling to disturb the existing peaceful relations. "When they concluded a treaty," they replied, "they did so with the intention of keeping it; while the Europeans seemed to enter into such engagements solely with the view of immediately breaking them. One chief, with the rude freedom of his nation, intimated his suspicion that the nations were both drunk."

In 1709, however, a serious attempt against Canada was made by the British. Colonel Vetch, an Englishman who had resided for some years at Quebec, was the moving spirit in this enterprise. The Ministry in England approved of it, and Vetch went to Boston and New York to prevail upon the English colonies to join in the scheme. De Vaudreuil received intelligence that "a fleet of twenty ships was being prepared for the expedition, and that a large force of regular troops was to sail under its protection, while 2,000

English and as many Indians were to march upon Montreal by way of Lake Champlain. He was desirous of carrying the war into the enemy's country; but his allies objected, and he was obliged to content himself with acting on the defensive. The British, in the meantime, after forming a chain of posts from New York, had occupied with considerable detachments Lakes George and Champlain, and were erecting forts, with a view to cover their descent upon Canada. The Iroquois had joined them, according to promise; but in a grand council of the tribes which was held at Onondaga one of the chief orators remarked, that their independence was only maintained by the mutual jealousy of the two European nations, each of whom, if they could, would domineer over them, and that it would therefore be highly imprudent to permit the English to conquer Canada. These views of the subject were generally adopted by the rest of the council; and the English, losing their assistance, and being weakened by a pestilential disorder which broke out among their own people, burnt the forts they had just erected, and abandoned the enterprise."

Another British expedition was undertaken in 1710, but this likewise proved abortive; yet matters remained in such an unsettled state, that in 1712 the merchants of Quebec subscribed 50,000 crowns for the purpose of strengthening the fortifications of the town. The Fox Indians now began to cause much trouble; but they were severely repulsed in their attempt to burn the French fort at Detroit and destroy its inhabitants.

The Treaty of Utrecht was signed on the 30th of

March, 1713, and once more peace was restored between France and England. France retained Canada, but surrendered Acadia and Newfoundland; she also resigned all claims to the sovereignty of the Five Nations. At this time the population of Canada numbered about 25,000 souls.

A period of peace now set in, which proved beneficial to the development of the colony. Charlevoix, who visited it in 1720-21, gives a lively picture of the social life of the cities, as well as an attractive description of the beautiful scenery in the vicinity of the great lakes. He found, however, that little had been done as regards trade and the cultivation of land, no doubt owing to the disturbed state of the country; but now this state of things began to be remedied to some extent. A considerable trade was done in shipbuilding in 1723, and there was a sensible increase in the exports to and imports from France.

In 1725, M. de Vaudreuil died, after a lengthened governorship of more than twenty-two years.

Heriot, in a description of Canada at this time, states that, " when the French began their settlements in Canada, property was granted in extensive lots, called *seigneuries*, stretching along either coast of the St. Lawrence for a distance of ninety miles below Quebec, and thirty miles above Montreal, comprehending a space of 300 miles in length.

"The *seigneuries* each contain 100 to 500 square miles, and are parcelled out into small tracts on a freehold lease to the inhabitants, as the persons to whom they were granted had not the means of cultivating them. These consisted of officers of the army, of gentlemen, and of communities, who were not in a state to employ labourers and workmen. The portion to each inhabitant was of three acres in breadth, and from seventy to eighty in depth, commencing on the banks of the river, and running back into the woods, thus forming an entire and regular lot of land.

"To the proprietors of *seigneuries* some powers, as well as considerable profits, are attached. They are by their grants authorized to hold courts, and sit as judges in what is termed *haute* and *basse justice*, which includes all crimes committed within their jurisdiction, treasons and murders excepted. Few, however, exercised this privilege, except the ecclesiastical *seigneurs* of Montreal, whose right of jurisdiction the King of France purchased from them, giving them in return his *droit de change*. Some of the *seigneurs* have a right of villain service from their tenants.

"There are in Canada upwards of a hundred *seigneuries*, of which that of Montreal, belonging to the Seminary of St. Sulpice, is the richest and most productive. The next in value and profit is the territory of the Jesuits. The members of that society who resided at Quebec were, like the priests of Montreal, only agents for the head of their community. But since the expulsion of their order from France, and the seizure by the Catholic sovereigns of Europe of all the lands of that society within their dominions, the Jesuits in Canada held their seigniory in their own right.

"Some of the domiciliated savages held also in the province land in the right of *seigneurs*.

"Upon a representation of the narrow circumstances to which many of the noblesse and gentlemen of the colony were reduced, not only by the causes already assigned, but by others equally powerful, Louis XIV. was induced to permit persons of that description to carry on commerce by sea and land without being subjected to any enquiry on this account, or to an imputation of their having derogated from their rank in society.

"To no seigniory is the right of patronage to the Church attached; it was upon the advancement of the pretensions of some *seigneurs*, founded on their having built parochial churches, that the King, in 1685, pronounced in council that this right should belong to the bishop, he being the most capable of judging concerning the qualifications of persons who were to serve."

As regards the spread of Christianity, Recollet and Jesuit missionaries traversed the country in all directions, suffering great hardships in their endeavours to convert the Indians. Their work was watched with much interest and enthusiasm in France, and it has always been admitted that they were the first explorers of the country, and the pioneers of civilization in the Far West. There were not only Jesuits at the beginning of the eighteenth century in such centres as Tadousac, Lorette, Béçançour, St. François, and Sault St. Louis, but in every Indian village. The Jesuit priest suffered all imaginable inconveniences, such as walking all day in the snow, lying in the open air all winter, lying out in both good and bad weather, lying in the Indian huts, which swarmed with vermin, etc. They went through all these hardships with a double object—one being political, and the other the conversion of the Indians. They were clever and cunning, and of great service to the French king, for they were frequently able to persuade the Indians to break their treaties with the English. The ordinary priests were a far more numerous class. They were nearly all stationary, few acting as missionaries. The Recollets, the third order of clergymen in Canada, had taken vows of poverty, and lived chiefly on the alms which people gave them.

The Marquis de Vaudreuil having died on the 10th of October, 1725, he was succeeded by the Marquis de Beauharnois, a natural son of Louis XIV. of France. The deceased governor had ruled the country well for twenty-two years, and his death was sincerely mourned in consequence. Beauharnois continued a similar course in his rule, and by judicious management the affairs of the colony began to revive. Peace was restored with the Indians by the adoption of a just and conciliatory policy, and there were frequent intermarriages between the two races; cultivation was greatly extended, and little occurred to disturb the repose of the colonists or the governor, save the growing importance and the encroachments of the active inhabitants of the British colonies.

Governor Burnet of New York erected a fort and trading post at Oswego on Lake Ontario, in the hope of diverting the Indian trade on the lakes to New York; but the Marquis de Beauharnois immediately sent an envoy to obtain the consent of the Indians in the neighbourhood of Niagara to the erection of a fort and establishment on the banks of the river. He also erected a fort at Crown Point on Lake Champlain, and another at Ticonderoga. These retaliatory measures surprised and annoyed Burnet, and an epistolary warfare ensued between the two governors, but no serious action followed.

The religious communities continued to acquire property to such an extent, that in 1743 the King of France issued an edict prohibiting all mortmain acquisitions, and all changes and alienations. Various religious decrees were also promulgated, and an order made, with regard to the registration of the royal edicts and ordinances, that in future no edict, declaration, or letters patent should be registered in the Supreme Council of Quebec but by his special order, signified by the Secretary having the Department of the Marine.

War was again declared in 1745 between France and England. Louisburg and Cape Breton were taken by an expedition under the command of a New Englander named Pepperel, who was immediately created a baronet of the United Kingdom for his brilliant service. Pepperel was actively assisted by a squadron under Admiral Warren. As soon as the news of the capture of Cape Breton reached France, an expedition was prepared to endeavour to retake the island, and to retrieve the French honour. "A fleet of eleven ships of the line, thirty smaller vessels, and transports, containing 3,000 soldiers, set sail on the 22nd of June, with the intention in the first place of attacking and taking Nova Scotia. Four ships of the line from the West Indies were ordered to join the squadron, and Canada sent a party of 1,700 men to assist the enterprise. The French fleet, however, met with stormy weather, which separated the ships; the admiral died suddenly; and the shattered remnants of the squadron returned to France crestfallen and dispirited. A new expedition was soon equipped, consisting of six large men-of-war, the same number of frigates, and four armed East Indiamen; and a convoy of thirty merchant vessels sailed under their protection. They also took out with them Admiral de la Jonquière, who had just been appointed Governor of Canada. On the 3rd of May, 1746, they fell in with a British fleet, under Admiral Anson and Rear-Admiral Warren, which had been despatched to intercept them, and before night all the battle-ships had surrendered, while a large portion of the convoy escaped during the night. As soon as the capture of the governor was known in France, the Comte de la Galissonière was appointed to fill the vacancy. He endeavoured to prevail upon the French Government to send out a large number of settlers, to be located on the frontiers, to act as a check upon the British; his advice, however, was disregarded, and the admiral being shortly released from captivity and conveyed to Canada, the count returned to France."

The French governors of Canada were so inadequately paid, that Admiral de la Jonquière and his secretary confined to themselves the privilege of selling spirits to the natives. But the complaints against the governor became at length so numerous and so clamorous, that his friends at home were compelled to notice them, and he was consequently recalled. Before his successor was appointed, however, the admiral died at Quebec.

In 1752, the Marquis du Quesne de Menneville was appointed Governor of Canada, Louisiana, Cape Breton, St. John's, and their dependencies. He was a man of ability; but his demeanour was haughty in the extreme. Soon after reaching Quebec, Menneville perceived that peace could not be of long duration, so he directed his attention to the discipline of the troops and the militia. He formed the militia of Quebec and Montreal into several companies, and placed officers in command of each. A company of artillery was attached to the militia of both cities, who were on Sundays and holidays regularly exercised at the great guns. At stated intervals he reviewed the militia of the country parishes, and adopted other plans calculated to secure the safety and tranquillity of the colony.

Although there was no actual war during Menneville's governorship, France and England being then at peace, skirmishes frequently took place between the people of the two colonies, and the Governments in Europe did not hesitate to assist and encourage their respective colonies in hostile operations against each other. Detachments were sent from Canada to establish forts on the Ohio and Alleghany Rivers, and ultimately preparations were made for carrying on frontier operations both offensive and defensive. The British colonists were not slow in adopting similar measures, while the citizens of Virginia protested strongly against the French encroachments. It was while engaged upon a mission to the French that we first come upon the distinguished name of George Washington.

"To gain intelligence respecting the motions of the Virginians, frequent parties were sent out from Fort Du Quesne. One of these, under the command of Jumonville, a French officer, had proceeded but a short distance, when he was met by Lieutenant-Colonel Washington, who was then on his march to Fort Necessity. He had no sooner opened to Colonel Washington the object of his mission, to warn the English from taking possession of the country, than he and several of his party were killed. As soon as M. de Contrecœur was made acquainted with this circumstance, he assembled the Indians near the fort, and related to them the action that had just taken place. Availing himself of their indignation, and resolved on revenge, he assembled the officers of the garrison, who agreed on the immediate investiture of Fort Necessity. A small number of troops and Indians were put under the command of M. de Villier, a brother of Jumonville, who, proceeding with his people to the fort, compelled Colonel Washington to surrender."

When Great Britain was made aware of the French encroachments near the Ohio, she resolved on taking the most effectual measures to drive the French from the several posts they occupied. Orders were given to her governors in America to repel force by force, and several regiments were despatched from Ireland to assist in the work. Anticipating a rupture, France retaliated by making effective war preparations, and a large fleet was equipped at Brest, under the command of Admiral Bois de la Mothe, on board of which were several old regiments, a considerable supply of ammunition, and all other necessary war materials. Open war had not yet been declared ; but the English Ministry sent out Admiral Boscawen with eleven sail of the line to observe the movements of the French fleet.

The rival fleets reached Newfoundland in April, 1755. Thick fogs prevailed, and Admiral de la Mothe succeeded in getting his fleet away from the vicinity of the British, except two vessels, the *Alcide* and the *Lys*, which were captured respectively by Captain Andrews and Captain (afterwards Lord) Howe. On the news of these captures reaching France, the French Ambassador was recalled from London, and diplomatic relations were suspended between the two countries. In reply to French complaints, Great Britain retorted that the conduct of the French on the Ohio had rendered her own action both necessary and justifiable. The British colonies sent reinforcements to the English commander-in-chief in America, General Braddock, who began his march on the 10th of June, with 2,200 men, towards the place where Colonel Washington had been defeated during the preceding year.

The Marquis du Quesne de Menneville having requested his recall, he was succeeded this year by the Marquis de Vaudreuil de Cavagnac, son of the former governor of that name.

On the 9th of July, General Braddock pushed forward with a picked force to invest Fort Du Quesne, which occupied the present site of Pittsburg, Pennsylvania. Notwithstanding his proverbial obstinacy, he so far paid attention to the warnings of his American officers that he threw out flank and advance parties to guard against a surprise. He twice forded the Monongahela, in order to avoid a dangerous defile; and it was on the right bank of the river that his advance guard was attacked by a party of about 900 French and Indians from the fort. It was not a real ambuscade; but the dense cover of the forest, of which the Indians immediately took advantage to surround Braddock's force, and the latter's dogged insistence on his men fighting in line instead of imitating the tactics of the foe, exposed the British as a helpless living target to a withering fire, to which they could make but a very inadequate return. A fierce conflict of two hours ensued. Braddock, who exhibited remarkable bravery, had four horses shot under him, and was mortally wounded while vainly endeavouring to rally his men. The survivors made a hasty retreat under Washington, Braddock's aide-de-camp, who was the only one of the general's staff who escaped unhurt, although he had again and again been in imminent peril. No fewer than 63 out of 86 officers, and 914 out of 1,373 men engaged, were either killed or wounded. The loss of the French was trifling. Braddock was borne from the field, and died on the 13th at Great Meadows, about sixty miles from the scene of his fatal surprise.

" The English army, instead of fortifying themselves after the retreat, in case the late success of the French might have induced them to have penetrated into Virginia, left a few troops at Fort Cumberland, and marched with the rest, amounting to 1,600 men, on the 2nd of August, to Philadelphia, whence they were soon afterwards shipped to Albany, by order of General Shirley, on whom the chief command, on Braddock's death, devolved. Notwithstanding the late misfortune near Fort Du Quesne, the northern colonies, so far from being dispirited, set on foot two expeditions, one under the command of General Shirley, and the other under the command of General Johnson. Johnson, on the 8th of August, set out for Lake George, where General Lyman, with 6,000 provincials, had arrived. Here he took post on very strong ground, surrounded with thick woods, Lake George in his rear, and with a breastwork in front of felled trees. As soon as it was known that this army had marched from Albany, and that the object of General Johnson was to attack Crown Point, Baron Dieskau, a brave and experienced officer, was despatched with 3,000 men, composed of regulars, marine troops, and Canadians, to oppose him. On his arrival at Crown Point, he divided his army; and after leaving one half at this place, marched on by the way of South Bay, and at length arrived in sight of the English entrenchments at Lake George. At half-past eleven o'clock on the morning of the 8th of September, the Baron marched in regular order towards Johnson's centre, and when within 115 yards made his grand and centre attack with a heavy platoon firing, while the Canadians and Indians, dispersed on the flanks, kept up an irregular fire. The engagement soon became general on both sides. The French regulars kept their ground and order with great resolution, till overpowered by the warm and constant fire of the English; they then made a movement to the right of Johnson's encampment, and though a body of Canadians had advanced as a reinforcement, yet they could not again be brought into action. The French troops, no longer able to sustain the fire of the English, retreated at four in the afternoon in the most precipitate manner. Their loss is stated at 1,000 men, killed, wounded, and prisoners, among whom was the Baron, who was severely wounded. The remains of the French army made the best of their way to Crown Point. The English had 126 men killed, 94 wounded, and 60 missing. As soon as the news of this victory reached England, the King applauded General Johnson's bravery, created him a baronet, and gratified him with a donation of £5,000 sterling. The expedition under General Shirley went on so slowly, that he did not leave Albany before the end of July, and only arrived at Oswego in August. Here the general waited for the supplies of provisions, which by some mismanagement did not reach him until the end of September, when it was thought too late to undertake the expedition to Niagara. After leaving a garrison of about 700 men at Oswego, he returned on the 24th of October to Albany."

All through the year 1755 the civil affairs of the French colony were in a very unsatisfactory state. The cultivators of the soil being called away by the exigencies of the war, agriculture was neglected, and a scarcity of provisions ensued. To make matters worse, Bigot, the intendant, out of avaricious motives, shipped off large quantities of wheat to the West India Islands. The governor himself gave his sanction to the measures of a company which swallowed up everything. This company kept up the price of flour, in spite of the loud complaints of the people. Oppression, abuse, and peculation reigned everywhere, and petty officials all over the country followed the nefarious example set by their superiors. It is consequently not surprising that the Marquis de Vaudreuil soon lost the confidence of the colonists. They had looked to him for protection, and he had allowed the people to be harassed and plundered on all hands.

Both French and English were in a state of great expectancy as regards future war operations, when in the summer of 1756 the Marquis de Montcalm arrived in Canada with a large body of French troops. War had already been formally declared between France and England. The British colonies were by no means unprepared for the struggle, however. At this time, the State of Massachusetts alone could muster 40,000 men capable of bearing arms; Connecticut could furnish 27,000; and strong contingents might be expected from New Hampshire, Rhode Island, Pennsylvania, and Virginia. Adding the reinforcements from England, there could thus be put into the field a very formidable force.

CHAPTER IV.

CAPTURE OF QUEBEC—DEATH OF WOLFE.

WITH Montcalm there arrived from Europe two other brave and experienced officers, the Chevalier de Levi and Colonel de Bourlemaque. Montcalm remained a few days at Quebec, so that he could make himself acquainted with the position of affairs, and then he directed three regiments of regular troops to proceed to Montreal, whither he departed in advance to confer with the governor, the Marquis de Vaudreuil. He warmly approved the governor's conduct in pushing forward troops for the investiture of Oswego, where a number of French troops had already arrived from Fort Frontenac, under Captain de Villier. Bourlemaque was then directed to proceed to De Villier's camp with reinforcements, and to take the chief command.

Montcalm himself left for Ticonderoga on the 27th of June. There he made preparations for the defence of the frontier, and endeavoured to procure accurate intelligence of the movements of the British at Albany. On the 15th of July, he returned to Montreal, leaving De Levi and 3,000 men for the protection of Crown Point and Ticonderoga, and the maintenance of French supremacy on Lake Champlain and the

Richelieu. Still on the alert, the French commander next hastened from Montreal to Fort Frontenac, to make preparations for the assault on Oswego.

The British, meanwhile, were dilatory and comparatively inactive. Lord Loudoun, the commander-in-chief, was detained in England, and Major-General Abercromby was ordered to precede him, and to hold the chief command in America until his arrival. Abercromby took out with him the 35th and 42nd Regiments, and arrived at Albany towards the end of June. Deeming his force too weak to carry out the extensive plan of operations drawn up by General Shirley and the other colonial officers, and anxious to avoid responsibility, he determined to await the arrival of Loudoun before undertaking any important advance.

While the bulk of the British army thus remained stationary, Colonel Bradstreet, with a detachment of raw Irish recruits, conducted a large convoy of provisions in safety to Oswego. De Villier, with 700 French and Indians, had marched forward from Sackett's Harbour to intercept him, but got lost in the forest. On his return, Bradstreet, fearing an attack, divided his canoes and boats into three divisions, for better security in fighting. Gallantly proceeding himself in the first canoe, he left Oswego on the 3rd of July, and had only advanced nine miles up-stream, when a sharp volley from the French rang through the forest. The fire was deadly, and both Bradstreet and the enemy made for a little island. The former had not a dozen men with him, but he drove the French from the place. A few more of his band soon arrived, and twenty brave men beat back again double the number of Frenchmen. The enemy made yet a third onset with seventy men, but Bradstreet and his little band once more repelled them. The second and third British divisions now came up, and after a desperate struggle the French were completely routed, with the loss of 100 dead, 70 prisoners, and a large quantity of firearms. Bradstreet's Irish force had altogether 60 killed and wounded. Its leader hurried to Albany to warn Abercromby that Oswego was threatened by a large French force. Orders were given for the 44th Regiment to hasten to its relief, but its march was greatly delayed. Although Lord Loudoun joined the British army on the 29th of July, the force generally still remained inactive.

The historians, however, chronicle great activity on the part of Montcalm. "Having departed from Frontenac on the 4th of August, he arrived on the evening of the same day at Sackett's Harbour, the general rendezvous of his army, which amounted to more than 3,000 men. On the 9th, his vanguard arrived within a mile and a half of Oswego; on the night of the 10th, his first division also came up. The second division followed shortly after, and at midnight on the 12th he opened his trenches against Fort Ontario, which crowned a height on the opposite side of the river from Fort Oswego, and completely commanded the latter. From the following daybreak till evening the fire of the garrison was well kept up, when, their ammunition becoming exhausted, they had no alternative but to spike their guns, and retire across the river to Fort Oswego. The abandoned fort, which contained eight guns and four mortars, was immediately occupied by Montcalm, who now continued his parallel down the river-side, where a breaching battery was speedily erected, and next morning, at six o'clock, nine guns poured a destructive fire at point-blank range against Fort Oswego. At eight o'clock, Colonel Mercer, its commanding officer, was killed; and at ten, although its fire was still much superior to that of the French, the besieged hoisted a white flag and offered to surrender, much to the astonishment of Montcalm and his officers.

"The garrison, consisting of Shirley's and Pepperel's regiments, and a detachment of Schuyler's regiment of militia, was about 1,700 strong, and lost 150 in killed and wounded during the brief siege, and shortly afterwards, when 30 men, attempting to escape through the woods, were massacred by the Indians. The French had 80 killed and wounded. Over 1,600 prisoners of war, including 120 women, were sent down the St. Lawrence, and the colours of the captured regiments for a brief space decorated the walls of the churches of Montreal, Three Rivers, and Quebec. One hundred and twenty cannon and mortars, six sloops of war, 200 boats, and large stores of ammunition and provisions, with £18,000 in coin, fell to the conquerors."

This victory added to the rising fame of Montcalm, who, to curry favour with the Iroquois, razed Fort Oswego to the ground, and then returned to Fort Frontenac. The surrender of Oswego reflected discredit on the British troops, and it had the further effect of terminating the campaign of 1756 entirely in favour of the French. Their trade was reestablished, and their supremacy on Lake Ontario confirmed.

General Webb was advancing with the 44th Regiment to relieve the British garrison, when he heard of the capture of the fort, and turned back to Albany. Loudoun was pusillanimous, and did not venture to attack the victorious French army; and the unfortunate frontier settlers of Virginia, Pennsylvania, and New York were doomed to feel the full effects of the recent disasters. Their lands were overrun with marauding parties of French and Indians, whose course was marked by plunder and massacre. Reprisals followed, and the country was in a state of terror. The young Iroquois, disgusted with the supineness of the British, were with difficulty dissuaded from throwing in their lot with Montcalm.

All through the winter the French commander kept his scouts at work; and as he found that vast stores of provisions and warlike munitions had been collected at Fort William Henry, on Lake George, he resolved to capture it by a sudden assault, thus crippling the future operations of the British against Ticonderoga and Crown Point. Accordingly, at midnight on the 19th of March, 1757, a force of 1,100 French and 400 Indians, under Rigaud de Vaudreuil, attempted to carry the fort by escalade, but was repulsed. Vaudreuil then destroyed the adjacent storehouses and buildings, and returned to Montreal. Colonel de Bourlemaque was next despatched with two battalions to strengthen the works at Crown Point and Ticonderoga, while Captain Pouchot was sent to Niagara to fortify it in the best possible manner, and assume the command.

Lord Loudoun, having received large reinforcements from England, resolved on the reduction of Louisburg; but when he heard that a strong French fleet had arrived at Cape Breton, he abandoned the idea. To General Webb was entrusted the defence of New York and the New England States; while Colonel Munro, with a force of 2,000 men, was placed in charge at Fort William Henry.

Collecting an army of 6,000 regular troops and militia, and 1,700 Indians, Montcalm began the siege of Fort William Henry. On the way to the fort, he had several successful brushes with British parties. Many prisoners were taken; and when one of them tried to intimidate Montcalm by saying, " To-morrow or the next day General Webb will be at the fort with fresh troops," he replied, " No matter, in less than twelve days I will have a good story to tell about them." Webb certainly did go to Fort William Henry; but he took care to leave it again with a strong escort in sufficient time to avoid the siege. The cowardice of some of the British leaders at this time contrasts very unfavourably with the courage and resolution of the great French commander.

"Montcalm had not sufficient boats to carry his entire army by water, and the Iroquois agreed to guide De Levi with 2,500 men by land. Next day, which was the 1st of August, the main body of the army embarked in 250 boats, in front of which advanced the Indians in their decorated canoes. The rain fell in torrents, yet they rowed nearly all night, till at length the three triangular signal fires of De Levi broke upon their view, and the fleet pulled into North-West Bay. An hour after midnight, two English boats were descried upon the lake, which had been despatched to reconnoitre. Two canoes of the Algonquins boldly pushed out in pursuit, and with such celerity that one of the boats was captured. Of its crew, two prisoners alone were reserved; the rest were massacred. The Algonquins had one of their principal chiefs killed. Next morning no effort at concealment was attempted by the French; and the Indians, forming their canoes in a single line across the water, made the bay resound with their war-cry. The British were almost taken by surprise, and Montcalm disembarked without interruption a mile and a half below the fort, towards which his troops advanced in three columns. The Indians covered his flanks with vigilant skirmishes, or pushed on in advance to burn the barracks of the British, to capture their cattle and horses, and to cut off and scalp their stragglers. They speedily succeeded in surprising a foraging party, forty of whom they slew and scalped, and captured fifty head of cattle. During the day, they occupied, in connection with a force under La Corne, the road leading to Fort Edward, and interrupted all communication with the army of Webb. To the north, De Levi was posted with his regulars and Canadians; while Montcalm, with the main body of his army, established himself on the west side of the lake. Fort William Henry was defended by Lieutenant-Colonel Munro, of the 35th Regiment of the line, with less than 500 men; but 1,700 more lay entrenched at his side on the eminence to the south-east, where now may be seen the ruins of Fort George. Montcalm spent the 3rd of August in reconnoitring the fort and neighbourhood, and in erecting his batteries. Next day, he summoned Munro to surrender; but the gallant old soldier sent an answer of defiance. 'I will defend my trust,' said he, 'to the last extremity.' This bold reply hastened the preparations of the French, whose scanty supply of provisions must speedily run short. Montcalm felt, if he would conquer at all, it must be soon, and pressed forward his approaches night and day. The zeal of their general imparted itself to the men, who vigorously dragged the artillery over rocks and through forests, brought gabions and fascines, and laboured with untiring zeal in the trenches. The first battery of nine guns and two mortars was speedily constructed, and awoke a thousand echoes amid the surrounding hills as it opened on the fort amid the wild war-whoop of the savages. In two days more, Montcalm had constructed his second parallel; and another battery, at a shorter range, poured a destructive fire upon the fort, while the Canadians and savages, swarming into the zigzag of the trenches, swept its ramparts with murderous aim. The odds were great against him; still, Munro held out with stubborn valour, in the vain hope that Webb would advance to his aid. But the craven heart, who might speedily have collected a strong body of militia to assist his 4,000 men in raising the siege, sent nothing but a letter, with an exaggerated account of the French army, and advising him to surrender. Still the gallant old man held bravely out, and not till half his guns were burst, and his ammunition nigh exhausted, did he unfurl a flag of truce."

Knowing the terrible passion of the Indians for massacre and plunder, Montcalm insisted upon the stipulation that the British should be allowed to depart with all the honours of war, on condition of not serving against the French for eighteen months. They were also to surrender everything but their private effects, and to give up all captive Canadians and French Indians. The capitulation was signed on the 9th of August, and Munro delivered up the fort.

Unfortunately, Montcalm's Indian allies obtained spirituous liquors from the English, and they became so maddened under their influence, that when the British began to march out of their entrenchments they set upon them with great fury. De Levi rushed in among the infuriated savages, and endeavoured to check the spoliation and massacre, but without effect. So frightful was the scene, that many French officers were wounded in their endeavours to shield the British troops. " Kill me ! " exclaimed Montcalm, " but spare them ; they are under my protection." But all was of no avail. The British were compelled to defend themselves as best they could ; but the march to Fort Edward was a disordered flight, the surviving troops reaching it in detachments. A painful but eloquent description of this tragic occurrence is given in Fenimore Cooper's *Last of the Mohicans.*

Fort William Henry was demolished, and Montcalm left, bearing with him the vast stores found there. But instead of marching on Fort Edward, he dismissed the Canadian militia to gather in their harvest. Meanwhile, the capture of Fort William Henry excited great alarm in the New England colonies; but instead of adopting a bold policy, Lord Loudoun spent the remainder of the season in quarrelling with the colonies about the quarters for his troops and the royal prerogative, and the French were left undisturbed.

Loudoun's miserable inefficiency excited great indignation in England. The Ministry of the Duke of Newcastle was discredited by it, and Pitt came into office. He superseded the impotent commanders in America, and, disregarding military precedents, elevated Colonel Amherst to the rank of major-general, and placed him at the head of the force which was designed for the attack of Louisburg. Under Amherst, Whitmore, Lawrence, and James Wolfe were appointed brigadier-generals. The conquest of the Ohio Valley was assigned to Forbes; while Abercromby was to operate against Ticonderoga and Crown Point, with Lord Howe his second in command. The two men in whom both Ministers and the public placed the greatest confidence were Howe and Wolfe. The former was an able commander, with quick perceptions, and a manly and humane disposition. Wolfe was only thirty-one years of age, yet he had already been eighteen years in the army, and had served at Dettingen, Fontenoy, and Laffeldt. Merit made him a lieutenant-colonel at two-and-twenty. He was brave in spirit and firm in command, yet in private life he was gentle and humane; and though accustomed to command, he lovingly obeyed his widowed mother, whom he regarded with the greatest affection and veneration.

"On the 19th of February, 1758," says one narrative, "a magnificent fleet sailed from Portsmouth, which carried out General Amherst, and an army of 10,000 men. It was long detained by contrary winds, and after a stormy passage reached Halifax on the 28th of May, where Boscawen's fleet was met coming out of the harbour, the gallant admiral being weary of inaction. At dawn, on the 2nd of June, the entire armament, embracing 22 ships of the line, 15 frigates, 120 smaller vessels, and 11,600 troops, arrived off Louisburg. Amherst indulged in the hope that he would be able to surprise its garrison, and issued orders for the silent landing of the troops. But for six days a rough sea, and the heavy surf which broke upon the rugged beach, rendered a disembarkation impossible. During this interval, the French toiled night and day to strengthen their position, and fired upon the ships at every opportunity. On the evening of the 7th, the wind lulled, the fog cleared off, and the heavy sea gradually subsided, but a violent surf still continued to break on the beach. On the following morning, just before daylight, three divisions of boats received the troops; at dawn, Commodore Durell examined the shore, and reported a landing to be practicable. Seven frigates now opened fire to cover the advance to land. In a few minutes afterwards, the left division, led by Brigadier Wolfe, began to row in-shore, and was speedily followed by Whitmore and Lawrence, with their brigades ; while two small vessels were sent past the mouth of the harbour to distract the attention of the enemy, and induce them to divide their force. The left division was the first to reach the beach at a point about four miles from town. Wolfe would not allow a shot to be fired, stimulated the rowers to fresh exertions, and on coming to shoal water boldly jumped out into the sea to lead on his men. The French stood firm, and retained their fire till their assailants were close to land. Then, as the boats rose on the last swell, which brought them into the surf, they poured in a close and deadly volley from every gun and musket they could bring to bear. Wolfe's flagstaff was shivered by a barshot, many soldiers were killed, several boats were wrecked by the surf; but still he cheered on his men, who had not yet returned a shot, and in a few minutes, with fiery valour, they had burst through the breastworks of the French, who fled in disorder. The victors pressed rapidly on in pursuit, and, despite a rugged country, inflicted a severe loss on the fugitives, captured seventy prisoners, and invested Louisburg the same day.

" For the succeeding two days a rough sea rendered it impossible to land the siege artillery, and provisions were conveyed to the army with the greatest difficulty. On the 11th, the weather moderated, when tents were landed, and some progress made in the preparations for the siege. On the 12th, De Drucor, the French general, withdrew all his outposts, and even destroyed a battery which commanded the entrance to the harbour, being desirous to reserve all his force for the defence of the town. The garrison of Louisburg was composed of 3,000 regular troops and militia, with a few Indians. In addition to this force, six line-of-battle ships and two frigates guarded the harbour, at the entrance of which three other frigates had been sunk, to prevent the passage of the British fleet. Wolfe's light troops were speedily in possession of the different posts deserted by the French, and on the 20th a battery opened upon the ships and land defences. For many days the slow operations of the siege continued under great difficulties to the British, owing to the marshy nature of the ground, and heavy rains which flooded the trenches. But science, a sufficient force, union among the principal officers, and courage and endurance in sailors and soldiers, overcame every obstacle, and promised speedy success. A sortie on the 9th of July by the besieged was speedily repelled, and day and night the batteries thundered against the ramparts, the citadel, and the shipping. On the 21st, three of the French men-of-war were set on fire by a shell, the following day the citadel was in a blaze, the next the barracks were burned down, while Wolfe's trenches were pushed close to the town, and the French driven from their guns by the British sharp-shooters. On the night of the 25th, two captains of Boscawen's fleet swept into the harbour with a squadron of boats under a furious fire, and burned one of the remaining men-of-war and carried off another. Boscawen prepared to send in six ships of the line to attack the other French vessels ; but the town was already a heap of ruins, the greater part of its guns being dismounted, and its garrison without a safe place to rest in ; so De Drucor resolved to capitulate at discretion, such being the only terms he could get."

The capture of Louisburg was a triumph for the British Ministry as well as the British arms. No fewer than 5,600 soldiers and sailors were made prisoners, and eleven ships of war taken or destroyed. About 15,000 stand of arms, and large quantities of military stores and provisions, fell into the hands of the victors, as well as eleven stand of captured colours, which were conveyed to England. With Louisburg fell Cape Breton and Prince Edward's Island, and thus terminated the power of France for ever on the eastern seaboard of North America. Louisburg was deserted after this, and never recovered a position of importance.

While the siege of Louisburg was going forward, the largest army as yet seen on the American Continent assembled at Albany, under the command of Abercromby, now general-in-chief, for the attack on Ticonderoga and Crown Point. It was composed of a strong detachment of the royal artillery, 6,350 troops of the line, and 9,000 provincial militia. Towards the end of June this force marched to Lake George, and encamped by the ruins of Fort William Henry till the 5th of July, when it embarked in 1,035 boats, and, protected by artillery mounted on rafts, proceeded towards Ticonderoga, or Fort Carillon, as it was named by the French. Within half a mile of the fort, Montcalm had marked out his lines, which he fortified by felled trees and entrenchments of earth.

Early on the morning of the 6th, the British advance guard, consisting of 2,000 men under the command of the gallant Bradstreet, safely landed, and, meeting with no opposition, was speedily followed by the entire army. Montcalm did not expect Abercromby so early, and was rather taken by surprise. "These people," said he, "march cautiously; yet if they give me time to gain the position I have chosen on the heights of Carillon, I shall beat them." The British pushed forward in four columns, covered by skirmishers; but the guides knew little of the country. In the midst of the dense forest, the right centre of the British army, led by Lord Howe, came upon a belated detachment of French troops. A severe conflict ensued; but although the French were soon defeated, Lord Howe fell at the beginning of the skirmish, being fatally wounded by a bullet in the breast. His death caused great sorrow, for he was much beloved; but it had even a more disastrous effect than this, for the army lost all courage and order, and fell into a state of infatuation and dismay.

Abercromby retired with the main body of the army to the landing-place; but Bradstreet, with a large detachment, having found a strong position at some saw-mills, about two miles from Montcalm's lines, the whole army moved thither. On the morning of the 8th of July, the whole French garrison was ordered under arms. The La Reine, Bearn, and

Guienne Regiments were posted on the right, and the Regiments de la Sarre, Languedoc, and two strong pickets on the left. The centre was composed of the regiments of Berry, Roussillon, and the pickets of M. de Levi. The volunteers attached to the army took possession of the open wood between the river and the falls. The colonial and Canadian troops were posted in the entrenchments on the plains towards Fort St. Frederick, supported by a corps of reserve. The right was commanded by the Chevalier de Levi, the left by Colonel Bourlemaque, and the centre by the Marquis de Montcalm. A skilful general would have attacked the French flanks; but Abercromby rashly determined to throw his best troops against the enemy's centre, in order to cut their line in two, while his other troops assailed their right and left. The American rangers, Bradstreet's boatmen, and some companies of light infantry, formed Abercromby's first line; the Massachusetts militia formed the second line; and in the third line were the British regiments and Murray's Highlanders, the gallant 42nd. The reserve consisted of the Connecticut and New Jersey militia. While the army was forming, several French detachments came forward and skirmished, but were driven back.

"At one o'clock, having received orders not to fire till they had surmounted the breastwork, the British moved forward in three heavy columns, with skirmishers in the intervals, to force the French defences. Montcalm, who stood just within the entrenchments, while Abercromby occupied a secure post in the rear of his army, threw off his great-coat, the heat of the

July afternoon being excessive, and ordered his men not to fire a shot till he commanded. No sooner had the heads of the British columns become entangled among the trees and logs in front of the breastwork, than the word of fire was given, when a sudden and incessant discharge from swivels and small arms mowed down brave officers and men by hundreds. The light troops and militia were now moved aside; and the grenadier companies of the line, followed by Murray's Highlanders, pushed forward with quick but steady step, and despite the heavy fire of the French, without one hesitating pause or random shot, their column gallantly dashed against the abatis. Through this the grenadiers with desperate valour endeavoured to force their way; but the cool and well-aimed fire of the French smote them rapidly down. Maddened by the delay, the Highlanders, who should have remained in reserve, were not to be restrained, and rushed to the front. For a moment they appeared more successful; but they fiercely won their way through the abatis to die upon the summit of the breastwork, till ere long half of these gallant men and the greater part of their officers were slain or severely wounded. Then fresh troops pressed on, and for nearly four hours the attack was renewed again and again by the British; now fiercely rushing forward, then broken and shattered by the murderous fire of the foe, they sullenly retired to re-form their ranks for another desperate effort. But the valour of these brave men, thus sacrificed by an incompetent commander, was unavailing; and against that rude barrier so easily turned, and which one hour of well-plied artillery would have swept away, the flower of British chivalry was crushed and broken. At length, in the confusion, an English column lost their way, and fired in mistake on their comrades. This event produced hopeless dejection, the disorder in a few minutes became irretrievable, and Highlanders and provincials, rangers and grenadiers, joined in one disgraceful flight. During the confusion of battle, Abercromby cowered safely at the saw-mills in the rear. When his presence was necessary to rally the fugitives, he was nowhere to be found; and his second in command lost the opportunity of distinguishing himself, and gave no orders. But the disordered troops, finding the French did not pursue them, gradually recovered from their terror, and rallied of their own accord near a few unbroken battalions whom the general had retained in his vicinity, most probably with a view to his own safety. Yet scarcely had confidence been partially restored, than an unaccountable order from Abercromby to retreat to the landing-place renewed the panic. The soldiers, concluding they were to embark immediately to escape the pursuit of their victorious enemy, broke from all order and control, and crowded towards the boats. Fortunately, the gallant Bradstreet still held together a small force, which he now with prompt decision formed across the landing-place, and would not suffer a man to embark. Had the disordered masses been allowed to rush into the boats, numbers must have perished in the lake; and thus to the prudence of one man the salvation of many lives may be justly attributed. Owing to Bradstreet's spirited conduct, order was in a little time restored, and the army remained on the lake-shore for the night. It still exceeded the French force fourfold, yet next morning Abercromby re-embarked, did not rest till he was safe across the lake, and even then sent on his artillery and ammunition to Albany, to prevent the possibility of their falling into the hands of Montcalm."

The British loss in this sanguinary engagement was 1,950 in killed, wounded, and missing, nearly all of whom were regular troops, and amongst them were a great number of officers. The loss would have been heavier still if the French had pursued the enemy. The French loss was 450 killed and wounded, including thirty-eight officers. Montcalm employed the night in strengthening his lines, expecting a fresh assault when the British had brought up their guns. But he had nothing to fear from Abercromby, for that poltroon was far away. "Had I to besiege Fort Carillon," said Montcalm, "I would only ask for six mortars and two pieces of artillery." The English general, though still possessing a siege-train and an army of 14,000 men, spent the ensuing season in lining out a new fort near the site of Fort William Henry.

Bradstreet, with more of the true British spirit, insisted upon attacking Fort Frontenac, and was at length supported by the council of war. At the Oneida portage, he was joined by Brigadier Stanwyx with nearly 3,000 militia, and by forty-two Onondaga Indians led by their chief Red Head. Bradstreet quickly marched to Lake Ontario, and on the 25th of August he arrived within a mile of Fort Frontenac. He found the position defended by thirty guns and sixteen small mortars; but the works were weak, and the garrison small and dispirited. Bradstreet took possession of an old entrenchment near the defences, and at once opened the assault with his guns. As the garrison was quite incapable of sustaining a defence, it surrendered on the morning of the 27th. The victors made a splendid haul of provisions, ammunition, shipping, and sixty pieces of cannon and sixteen small mortars. But the commander had been strictly enjoined by Abercromby to destroy most of the stores and shipping captured. The fort was blown up and abandoned; but the French repaired it in the summer, and also strengthened and extended the works at Niagara.

While Bradstreet was operating against Fort Frontenac, Montcalm lost no opportunity of harassing Abercromby's outposts. The French light troops committed so much havoc and massacre, that Major Rogers was despatched with 700 men against them. This force was soon reduced by hardship and desertion to about 500. On the 8th of August, it encountered and defeated an equal number of French, whose loss amounted to 190 killed and wounded.

In the west, the French suffered a severe check by the capture of Fort Du Quesne. On the last day of June, Brigadier Forbes, with 1,500 regular troops and 5,000 militia, marched from Philadelphia *en route* for the Ohio Valley. Washington commanded two Virginian corps in the militia. The force had a long and laborious march over the Alleghanies, constructing a new road to the Ohio as it went. It was September before the army arrived at Raystown, ninety miles from Fort Du Quesne, and Forbes the commander was very ill. A force of 2,000 men, under Colonel Bouquet, was detached to take post at Loyal Hanna. A portion of this force, consisting of 800 Highlanders and a company of Virginian militia, was told off to make a reconnaissance of the works. Instead of this, the leader, Grant, directly challenged the garrison, and a conflict ensued, when the Highlanders were completely routed, with a loss of nearly 300 in killed, wounded, and prisoners. The whole army now moved forward as rapidly as possible. The French, however, abandoned the place on the 24th of November, first springing a mine under one of its faces. On the following day, the British took possession of the deserted stronghold, and at once proceeded to repair its works, changing the name of the fort to Pittsburg, in honour of the Minister who planned its capture.

The capture of Fort Du Quesne closed the campaign of 1758, which on the whole had gone distinctly in favour of the British. It was true that Abercromby had been defeated ; but the capture of Louisburg had left France without a safe port near the St. Lawrence, and effectually closed Canada in on the seaboard, while the reduction of Forts Frontenac and Du Quesne had given to Britain possession of all the territory out of which the war had arisen. Abercromby still had a large army, and Montcalm knew that it only required a skilful general to make it available. This it soon received, for in December Pitt superseded Abercromby, and appointed General Amherst commander-in-chief of the army in America.

The year 1759, which was destined to be a memorable one in the history of Canada, opened with vigorous measures on the part of the British. The House of Commons had voted £12,000,000 for carrying on the war, and Pitt drew up with great skill the arrangements for the ensuing American campaign. He selected the leading officers, not according to seniority of rank, but their ability. Stanwyx was entrusted with the capture of the French posts from Pittsburg to Lake Erie; Prideaux was to reduce Niagara; while Amherst was instructed to attack Canada by Lake Champlain and the Richelieu, to capture Montreal, effect a junction with the expedition against Quebec, and thus terminate French domination in North America by a single campaign. To Wolfe, who was Pitt's favourite general, was given the command of the important expedition against Quebec, which was regarded as the crucial undertaking of the whole campaign.

The French governor, De Vaudreuil, recognizing the critical position of Canada, sent De Bougainville to France for fresh troops and provisions, while Montcalm procceded diligently to put the colony into a state of defence. All male inhabitants in the province, from sixteen to sixty years of age, were ordered to be enrolled in the militia. What made the prospect of war worse was the comparative failure of the recent harvest.

In January, a census was taken of all the inhabitants in the three governments of the colony, and the number was found to be about 85,000. The number of men capable of bearing arms in the district of Quebec was 7,511, in that of Montreal 6,405, and in that of Three Rivers 1,313, making an aggregate of 15,229. Many of these were not available, however, from the necessities of agriculture; while the British had nearly 50,000 men under arms, or ready to take the field. Nevertheless, Montcalm gallantly went on with his duty, strengthening the fortifications, building vessels, and making strenuous efforts to collect provisions.

De Bougainville returned from France in May, bringing with him decorations and promotions for the officers who had already distinguished themselves, but little substantial assistance. The King and his Ministers urged the governor to take every possible step to defend the province, while Montcalm was told that his Majesty relied upon his zeal and courage. De Vaudreuil now addressed a circular to the militia officers, requiring them to be ready for marching in any direction at a moment's notice, and at the same time endeavoured to excite their patriotism by a stirring appeal. "This campaign," said he, "will afford the Canadians an opportunity of signalizing themselves. His Majesty well knows the confidence I have in them, and I have not failed to inform him of their services. His Majesty trusts they will make those efforts that are to be looked for from the most faithful subjects, more particularly as they have to defend their religion, their wives, and their property from the cruel treatment to be expected from the English.

"With respect to myself, I am resolved not to consent to any capitulation, in hopes that this resolution may have the most ruinous consequences to the English. It is most indubitable that it would be more merciful for the inhabitants, their wives and children, to be buried under the ruins of the colony, than to fall into the hands of the English.

"It being highly necessary that the most prudent precautions should be taken to prevent a surprise, I have established beacons from post to post, along the south shore, below Point Levi, to be set fire to as soon as the enemy are discovered.

"We promise every protection to the inhabitants, their wives, children, and property, to prevent their falling into the hands of the English, who would make them suffer the same hardships and miseries experienced by the Acadians. In addition to which, we have the testimony of their late ill-conduct, in their treatment of the inhabitants of Cape Breton, notwithstanding the capitulation, as well as those of the Island of St. John.

"Their hatred is so well known towards everything that is Canadian, that they even make them responsible for the cruelties of a few Indians, still forgetting the measures we have taken to prevent a repetition of these actions, and the good treatment which the nation has at all times shown to them when prisoners. We have a real satisfaction in declaring that we entertain no apprehensions for the safety of the colony, yet we shall adopt the most efficacious measures for securing to the inhabitants their rights and property."

But the most extraordinary document issued at this juncture was a pastoral letter from Dr. de Pont

Briant, the Bishop of Canada, to the clergy of his diocese. It drew a most deplorable picture of the civil and religious condition of the people, dwelling upon the impious hypocrisy which prevailed, and denouncing the widespread gambling, immorality, and crime, whose effects were to be perceived everywhere. His lordship ordered a series of special services of humiliation to be observed throughout the province.

A council of war held at Montreal decided that a strong body of troops should be posted at Quebec under Montcalm; and that Bourlemaque should take post at Ticonderoga, and blow up the works on the approach of the British, if he should be unable to resist them. Crown Point was to follow the same fate, if necessary; and then Bourlemaque was to retire to an island at the head of Lake Champlain, and there, aided by the shipping, make the most stubborn resistance, and if possible prevent the junction of the armies under Amherst and Wolfe. The Chevalier De la Corne, with 800 regulars and militia, was to entrench himself above Montreal, and withstand any force that might descend from Lake Ontario.

The campaign of 1759 opened with the advance of Brigadier Prideaux, at the head of nearly 4,000 regular troops and militia, and a large body of Iroquois led by Sir William Johnson, against the fort at Niagara. The army embarked on Lake Ontario on the 1st of July, and effected a landing on the 7th at one of the inlets six miles east of Niagara. The fort was invested on the land side, and the British boats effectually intercepted all communication by water. Pouchot, the French commander, sent to Frontenac, Detroit, and other western posts for aid, including as many Indians as could be collected. Relying upon such aid, he determined to defend the fort to the last extremity. To a demand from the British general to surrender, he replied : "My post is strong, my garrison faithful ; and the longer I hold out, the more I will win the esteem of the enemy."

Prideaux conducted his operations with skill, and the defences soon began to crumble under his vigorous fire. Having received slight reinforcements, the besieged made a sally on the 11th, but were driven back. For six more days Pouchot held bravely out, looking for the succours which Prideaux had taken measures to intercept. This brave English commander was killed in the trenches on the evening of the 19th, and the chief command now devolved on Sir William Johnson.

The incidents which followed are thus graphically described in Macmullen's history : "Meanwhile, De Aubrey rapidly descended from Detroit, at the head of 1,200 Frenchmen, collected from the different posts towards the Ohio, and nearly 1,400 Indians. On the 23rd, four savages made their way into the beleaguered fort with a letter to Pouchot informing him that succour was at hand, and that the British lines would speedily be attacked. But Johnson's scouts had given him ample intelligence of De Aubrey's approach, and he coolly prepared for the combat. Leaving sufficient troops to guard the trenches, he threw forward strong pickets, on the evening of the 23rd, to occupy the woods on either side of the rough forest road leading from Chippewa to Niagara, and connected these by a chain of Indian skirmishers. These arrangements completed, and no enemy appearing, the troops lay down to rest with their arms in their hands. It was a warm July night, and the stars glimmered brightly down upon the sombre forest, now unruffled by even the faintest breeze. To the contemplative mind, the scene must have been one of peculiar solemnity and grandeur. Close at hand, the stillness was unbroken, save by the monotonous breathings of the many sleepers, or the sentinel's tread. A little farther on, there was a brief pause around the beleaguered fort, and then its dark sides were suddenly illuminated by its own guns, or revealed by the red light of a salvo from the hostile trenches. From the distance, the dull boom of the cataract fell upon the ear like the noontide roar of life in London, or the rush of the approaching storm. The white tents of the besieging army, the watch-fires of the camp, the bright moon whose rays peered softly down amidst the sprays of the forest trees to glance from the polished muskets of the sleeping sentinel or the Indian's tomahawk, and the soft feathery cloud of spray that rose upwards from the Horse-Shoe Falls— all tended to complete a scene of surpassing interest. On the following morning, at daybreak, Johnson pushed forward his grenadier companies and part of the 46th Regiment to strengthen his fort, while the 44th Regiment was formed in reserve to preserve the communication with the troops in the trenches, and to act wherever its assistance might be needed. About eight o'clock, the head of the French column was perceived advancing through the woods, with large bodies of Indians covering either flank. As the enemy came on, the British outposts fell steadily back on the main body without firing, while the Iroquois pressed forward to parley with the French Indians, with a view of inclining them to peace. The latter refused to abandon their allies, and accordingly the warriors of the Six Nations again resumed their post on the flanks of the British. De Aubrey now speedily formed his force, and advanced to the attack. Shouting their appalling war-cry, the Indians burst through the woods, and fell furiously upon the British line, which coolly awaited their approach, and swept them away with a few rolling volleys. The close and steady fire with which they were received completely astonished the western warriors, and so thorough was their discomfiture that they disappeared altogether from the field of battle. Their flight left the flanks of the French completely exposed, and they were soon boldly turned by the Iroquois, who pressed rapidly forward through the woods, while the British held their ground in front with the utmost steadiness. Attacked on all sides by greatly superior numbers, the French hesitated, gave way, and after an action of little more than half an hour broke into utter rout. De Aubrey and his surviving officers, with a great part of his troops, were taken prisoners, while the fugitives were rapidly pursued and slain, or driven into the wilderness, where the numerous dead lay uncounted."

When the news of Johnson's victory had been confirmed, Pouchot, the French commander, surrendered up the fort and garrison, liberal terms being granted him. The French were to march out with the honours of war, and the women and children were to have safe conveyance to the nearest port of France. All stores, provisions, and arms were given up to the British general, and the garrison, 600 strong, were conveyed to New York under his protection. So important was the victory that the French forts as far as Erie fell without resistance. In announcing the British success to Amherst, Johnson said: "I have only to regret the loss of General Prideaux and Colonel Johnson. I endeavoured to pursue the late general's vigorous measures, the good effects of which he deserved to enjoy."

An attack made by a strong body of Canadians and Indians under La Corne upon the British detachment at Oswego completely failed. Meanwhile, the commander-in-chief had the greatest difficulty in keeping the main army together at Lake George, owing to the numerous desertions from the militia. General Amherst, having traced out the plan of Fort George, sailed down the lake on the 21st of July with his army of 11,000 men. He effected a landing near the place where Abercromby had disembarked the year before. Preparations were made for an assault on the French lines, which were guarded by a body of 3,400 men, composed of regulars, Canadians, and Indians. But on the morning of the 23rd the French withdrew from the lines which had enabled them to gain their victory of the preceding year, and fell back upon Fort Carillon. After a spell of sharp cross-firing, Bourlemaque recognized that even the defence of the fort was impracticable ; so he silently left it in the night, detaching 400 men to continue such resistance as might conceal his retreat. On the night of the 26th, intelligence was brought to Amherst that the fort had been abandoned, and a mine laid ; and immediately afterwards a tremendous explosion confirmed the news. Flames burst forth simultaneously from the wooden breastworks, barracks, and stores.

Amherst detached some light troops in pursuit of the French, and then began the work of repairing the fort. The fortress of Crown Point was next found by Major Rogers abandoned by the French ; and when Amherst came up, he encamped on the site, and traced out the lines of a new fort as a protection against the scouting parties of French and Indians. Bourlemaque had retreated to the Isle-aux-Noix, at the northern end of the lake ; and here, with a force of 3,500 men, 100 pieces of cannon, and four armed vessels, he strongly fortified himself. He resolved to defend the entrance of the Richelieu to the last extremity. In order to effect a junction with Wolfe at Quebec, two courses were open to Amherst. One was to open a road through the forest and push on to Montreal, leaving Bourlemaque in his rear ; the other, to obtain command of the lake, and drive him from his position. He adopted the latter plan ; but before it could be carried out, winter overtook him, and the main body of the British army was compelled to waste its strength in doing nothing. Brigadier Gage also, who was appointed to the command of Prideaux's force at Oswego, failed to advance upon and capture Ogdensburg, as he had been directed to do.

The indefatigable Major Rogers was the only British officer in this region who continued an active and successful course. He penetrated the forest to Lake St. Francis, and fell upon and completely crushed an Indian force which had detained an officer and a number of men sent with a flag of truce. The campaign in the west soon ended, and the British forces went into winter quarters.

The operations on the St. Lawrence now demand attention. Wolfe having assembled his army of about 8,000 men at Louisburg, he divided it into three brigades, led by Brigadiers Monckton, Townshend, and Murray, while the Adjutant-General was Isaac Barre, a fearless and ambitious Irishman, and one of the reputed authors of the *Letters of Junius*. The fleet, which consisted of twenty-two men-of-war, and as many frigates and armed vessels, was under the command of Admiral Saunders. On board one of the ships was Jervis, afterwards Earl St. Vincent; while James Cook, the celebrated navigator, was sailing-master of another.

The armament arrived safely off the Isle of Orleans on the 26th of June, and on the following day the troops effected a landing. Wolfe was astonished at the beauty of the scenery which spread out before him in all directions, and he was also struck with admiration at the ingenuity and skill displayed by Montcalm in devising his means of defence. Nothing was left undone, and for nine miles or more to Cape Rouge every landing-place was entrenched and guarded. The River St. Charles swept the rocky base of Quebec, affording additional security; and from the city to the Montmorency, a distance of eight miles, the position of the French army extended. It was protected by numerous redoubts and entrenchments, and the shoals and rocks of the St. Lawrence, and appeared well-nigh impregnable. For the defence of his formidable lines, Montcalm had 12,000 French and Canadian troops, and about 400 Indians. As he gazed upon the lines of defence, Wolfe fully appreciated the enormous difficulties which beset his enterprise.

As Admiral Saunders was not satisfied with the anchorage at the Isle of Orleans in tempestuous weather, he determined to pass up into the basin or harbour of Quebec. But before this could be done, it was necessary to drive the French from the headland of Point Levi, otherwise the enemy could fire into his vessels. This task was assigned to Brigadier Monckton, who fought his way to the point, and occupied the headland on the 30th, despite the resistance of a body of 1,200 Canadians and Indians. Montcalm had seen all through the importance of Point Levi, and had urged that 4,000 men should occupy it, and hold it to the last extremity; but he was overruled by the governor. However, he now made an unavailing attempt to dislodge the British. With a battery at Point Levi, and another at the western point of the Isle of Orleans, the British had sufficient security for their fleet.

Monckton marched his brigade along the opposite side of the St. Lawrence, in order to distract Montcalm's attention while Wolfe was taking post with the main body of his army on the eastern bank of the Montmorency. But the rapid current of the latter river, with its dangerous rocks and shoals, still kept the hostile armies apart. It was in vain that Wolfe endeavoured to discover some favourable point to turn Montcalm's flank, and thus compel a battle in rear of his lines. The French commander had apparently thought of everything; for not a spot along the Montmorency for miles into the interior, nor on the St. Lawrence to Quebec, had been left unprotected. British reconnaissances only led to the slaughter of the light infantry by the Indians and Canadians lurking in the forest.

After Wolfe had established himself on the Montmorency, Montcalm, moved by the representations of the inhabitants of the Lower Town, who feared the destruction of their houses by the British, made a night attack on Monckton's position at Point Levi; but it completely failed. On the 16th, a shell from the British fleet set a house on fire in the Upper Town, and the conflagration destroyed many buildings before it could be subdued, including the great cathedral, with all its pictures, images, and ornaments. The defences still remained uninjured, however, and the enemy was no nearer taking the place.

Towards midnight on the 18th, a small squadron under Captain Rous did manage to run the gauntlet of the French batteries without being even discovered by the sentinels, two of whom were hanged next day for their carelessness. The French opened fire on

Rous; but it only made him weigh anchor and proceed a little farther up the river. A boat which bore Wolfe and Admiral Saunders on their way to reconnoitre the city from the river's bank had its mast shot away; but Wolfe's keen eye had been able to trace before retreating the outline of the precipitous hill on which Quebec stood, and to note that this natural fastness was defended by cannon, boats, and floating batteries at every available point. So also above the town, as well as below it, every spot seemed impregnable, and Wolfe was almost in despair.

But the English commander determined to persevere, and his resolve was strengthened when a skirmishing party under Colonel Carleton brought in a number of prisoners and several packets of important letters. One of these said, "The governor and Montcalm have disagreed"; another, "But for our priests and the dread of the savages we would submit"; and a third, "We are without hope and food; since the English have passed the town, our communication with Montreal is cut off: God hath forsaken us." Their plight became still worse when the surrounding country was ravaged.

Skirmishes and reconnaissances took place every day almost, until the end of July, and still the British general had effected little towards the capture of Quebec. But although he might have awaited the arrival of Amherst, he still determined upon making every effort, though his own health was being seriously undermined. There was a point on the Montmorency where, after falling over a perpendicular rock, the river expanded into shallows for a distance of 300 yards, and then flowed into the St. Lawrence at an obtuse angle. Montcalm had placed a four-gun redoubt near the apex of this angle ; and Wolfe saw that if he could possess himself of this redoubt and turn the right of the French line, Montcalm must either fight or retreat. After a vigorous action on the 31st of July, Wolfe effected a landing on the opposite side, when the French abandoned the redoubt, and retreated to their entrenchments, which crowned the crest of the slope beyond. Instead of waiting for the support of other British troops, those which had landed rushed forward to storm the French entrenchments. They were repulsed with severe loss, and all that Wolfe could do was to effect an orderly retreat.

Brigadier Murray effected some successful operations about thirty or forty miles from Quebec, and upon some of his prisoners discovered papers which told of the occupation of Ticonderoga and Crown Point by Amherst, and the capture of Niagara by Johnson. But these victories brought little hope of aid to Wolfe before the close of the campaign, and his despondency and physical weakness were now aggravated by fever. Although the forces under Montcalm could scarcely be called an army, he knew that the French had probably the strongest country in the world to cover the approaches to the only vulnerable points of Quebec. The Indian scouts were keen to prevent surprises, and the French inhabitants were fighting for hearth and home.

Still, Wolfe laid a plan before his brigadiers, embracing three different and equally desperate methods of attacking Montcalm in his entrenchments below the town. These were all overruled, however, in favour of Brigadier Townshend's plan of landing an army above the town, in order to draw the French from their impregnable position to an open action. "I have acquiesced in their proposal," wrote Wolfe to Pitt, in a despatch dated the 2nd of September, "and we are preparing to put it into execution. There is such a choice of difficulties, that I am myself at a loss how to determine." One more examination of the citadel was made by Wolfe and Admiral Saunders, with a view to a general assault; but the general saw no prospect of success, especially as the fleet could render him no assistance.

"But if Wolfe's difficulties were great, so also were those which surrounded Montcalm. He knew not where to turn for a ray of hope, except to the now rapidly approaching winter. Danger menaced him on every side. Gage threatened him from Lake Ontario, Amherst from Lake Champlain, while the stately fleet riding securely at anchor below left no hope of succour from France. The peculation and misconduct of the civil officers wasted his resources, and he hesitated not to tell even the governor himself that he had sold his country. 'But while I live,' exclaimed the intrepid soldier, 'I will not deliver it up.' 'Of one thing I can assure you,' wrote he to a friend, 'I shall not survive the probable loss of the colony. There are times when a general's only resource is to die with honour; this is such a time: no stain shall rest on my memory.' But he found consolation in the fact that the conquest of Canada must speedily lead to the independence of the British colonies. Provisions and ammunition were becoming scarce in his camp, and the unhappy peasants stole to their homes by dozens to gather in their harvest. He scourged some offenders, hanged others, and threatened their villages with the vengeance of the savages, yet he could not keep them together, and was finally obliged to allow 2,000 of the militia to depart, to gather in their crops, at the most critical period of the campaign. The new plan of operations adopted by Wolfe rendered the concentration of his troops at Point Levi necessary, and preparations were at once made to evacuate the position at the Montmorency. These were all completed by the 3rd of September, when the troops safely crossed over the river. The vigilant eye of Montcalm had anticipated this movement from the unusual stir among the British, and he marched two strong columns to attack them while embarking. Monckton, from the heights of Point Levi, discovered the danger which menaced the retiring brigades, and, embarking a strong detachment in boats which were protected by some ships and frigates, rowed towards the Beauport shore as if about to assault the French lines. Montcalm was accordingly compelled to recall his battalions for their defence, and to permit the British troops at Montmorency to embark without molestation."

Wolfe having partially recovered, he and his brigadiers closely examined the bank of the river, in the hope of discovering some point by which his army could ascend to the Plains of Abraham. At last, about three miles above the city, he found a narrow path winding up the steep precipice from the water's edge, at a point where the bank curved slightly inward, and which has since been known as Wolfe's Cove. Although two men could scarcely ascend this path abreast, the general determined that his army should disembark here, and take the guard at the summit, amounting to about a hundred men, by surprise. This point taken, the French could no longer avoid giving battle.

Preparations began; and in order to deceive Montcalm as to the real point of attack, James Cook and others were sent to take observations up the river at Beauport, as though the attack were to be made from that quarter. On the 12th of September, a French deserter brought in most important intelligence to Wolfe. "The main force," he said, "is still below the city, and our general will not believe that you meditate an attack anywhere but from the Montmorency side. The Canadians are alarmed by the fall of Niagara, and in great distress for provisions. De Levi, with a large detachment, has left us for Montreal to meet Amherst; and De Bougainville, with 1,500 men, watches the motions of your fleet in the upper river." As evening came on, Wolfe made his dispositions. While he drew the enemy's attention in one direction, Monckton's and Murray's brigades moved up the river from Point Levi, and embarked on board the fleet without being observed. Then, at nine o'clock, the first division of the army, 1,600 strong, silently dropped into flat-bottomed boats, and waited the orders of their chief.

"It was a pleasant autumn night," observes Macmullen, "and the full lustrous stars of a northern firmament twinkled cheerfully down on the noble current of the St. Lawrence, as Wolfe quietly passed from ship to ship to make his final inspection, and utter his last words of encouragement. In a pure and gifted mind like his, the solemn hour could scarcely fail of awakening befitting associations. He spoke of the poet Gray, and the beautiful legacy he had given the world in his *Elegy in a Country Churchyard*. 'I would prefer,' said he, 'being the author of that poem to the glory of beating the French to-morrow'; and while the cautious dip of the oars into the rippling current alone broke the stillness of the night, he repeated:

> The boast of heraldry, the pomp of pow'r,
>   And all that beauty, all that wealth e'er gave,
> Await alike th' inexorable hour.
> The paths of glory lead but to the grave.

At one o'clock, on the morning of the 13th, the order to advance was given, and the flotilla dropped silently down with the receding tide, Wolfe commanding in person. He still continued his poetical musings; but his eye at the same time was keenly bent on the outline of the dark heights beneath which he floated past. He recognized at length the appointed spot, and leaped ashore.

"Meantime, the current had carried a few boats lower down, which had on board the light company of the 78th Highlanders. These were the first troops to land; without a moment's hesitation, they scrambled up the face of the wooded precipice, clinging to the roots and branches of trees. Half the ascent was already won, when for the first time the *qui-vive* of the French sentry above was given. 'La France,' promptly answered M'Donald, the Highland captain, with ready self-possession, and the sentinel shouldered his musket and pursued his rounds. In a few minutes, however, the unusual rustling among the trees near at hand alarmed the sentinels, their guard was turned out, and fired one hurried volley at the Highlanders, then, panic-stricken, turned and fled. By this time, another body of troops had pressed up the pathway, and possessed themselves of a four-gun redoubt which commanded it. As day dawned, Wolfe stood with his invincible battalions on the Plains of Abraham, the battle-field which gave a new empire to the Anglo-Saxon race. Only one gun, however, could be got up the hill, so difficult was the ascent."

Montcalm was completely deceived by the British manœuvres. Even when daylight approached, he was unable to realize the situation, it was so utterly unexpected. While the scattered roll of musketry was heard from above the beleaguered town, a horseman galloped up and told Montcalm that the British had ascended to the Plains of Abraham. "It can be but a small party come to burn a few houses and then retire," replied the general. But the man persisted that the British were there in force. "Then," said Montcalm, "they have at last got to the weak side of this miserable garrison; we must give them battle, and crush them before midday."

CAPTURE OF QUEBEC—DEATH OF WOLFE. 105

The story of the memorable engagement that ensued, which ended in the victory of the British and the death of both commanders, is thus dramatically told by the historian already quoted : " Leaving Governor De Vaudreuil behind with 1,500 militia, and despatching a courier to recall De Bougainville, Montcalm hurried his troops across the Valley of the St. Charles, over the bridge, and along the northern face of the ramparts to the battle-ground, where Wolfe, having already formed his line, calmly awaited his approach. The 35th Regiment were posted on the extreme right near the precipice ; on their left stood the Grenadiers of Louisburg ; the 28th, the 43rd, the 58th, the 78th Highlanders, and the 47th completed the front, led by Wolfe, and Monckton on the right, and Murray on the left. The second line, composed of the 15th Regiment and two battalions of the 60th or Royal Americans, was led by Townshend. The 48th Regiment, in four columns, formed the reserve under Colonel Burton. Colonel Howe, with the light infantry posted in houses, or scattered through the neighbouring coppices, covered the left flank and rear. The right flank was effectually protected by the precipice. The entire British army was somewhat under 5,000 men, but they were all well-trained veterans.

" About six o'clock, small bodies of the French troops deployed on the slopes near the ramparts of the city. By seven, they mustered more numerously, and brought up two field-guns, which caused some annoyance to the British. Towards eight o'clock, Montcalm had arrived with the bulk of his army, which he formed in three distinct masses on a slope to the north-west of the city, where they were sheltered from Wolfe's solitary but mischievous gun. At nine, he pushed to the front, and began to form his line of battle, being assured that De Bougainville was close at hand, and whose light cavalry, of which he had 350, already threatened the British left. His centre was formed of 720 regular troops and 1,200 militia. The right was composed of 1,600 veterans and 400 militia; on the left were 1,300 trained soldiers, supported by 2,300 of the Canadian levies. His total force thus amounted to 7,520 men, besides Indians, who were not less than 400. Of this force scarcely one half were regular troops; but the expected arrival of De Bougainville would add 1,500 veterans to his army, and, he trusted, enable him to win the battle, and save Quebec.

"Montcalm designed to avail himself of his superior force by outflanking the British left, and thus crowding them towards the landing-place, where he would assail them again with his own left and centre, while De Bougainville threatened the rear. Thus attacked on three sides of a square at the same time, he considered that the stubborn courage of the enemy must give way. The British position formed two sides of a square, one of which was occupied by their line of battle, the other by Colonel Howe's light infantry, who, as already stated, thus covered the left flank and rear.

"Agreeably to his plan of operations, Montcalm began the battle at ten o'clock by assailing Howe's position with a strong body of Canadian and Indian skirmishers, who speedily drove in the British pickets on their supports. Under cover of the cloud of smoke, which soon rose over this part of the battle-field, the veterans of the French right wing passed swiftly at an angle with the British left, and fiercely assaulted their light infantry. Howe felt the importance of his post, and made a stout resistance. His men fell fast; but in a few minutes Townshend, with the 15th Regiment and two battalions of the 60th, came to his aid, and the assailants were speedily beaten back with heavy loss.

"The attempt to outflank the British left being thus completely defeated, Montcalm's only resource was to attack their right and centre. Throwing forward a swarm of skirmishers, their fire speedily dislodged the few light infantry with which Wolfe had covered his front, and drove them back in disorder on the main body. This occurrence somewhat alarmed the British troops; but Wolfe, hurrying along the line, cheered them with his voice and presence, and directed them on no account to fire without orders. He speedily succeeded in restoring confidence. Recalling his troops, Montcalm now pushed forward his whole centre and left, which, with loud cheers and arms at the recover, moved boldly on to the attack. As the smoke of the skirmishers' fire cleared off from the battle-field, the long ranks of the French were seen rapidly approaching the British position. At the distance of 150 yards an oblique movement from the left gave their lines the appearance of columns, which chiefly threatened Wolfe's right wing. Another moment passed, the French paused, and from flank to flank poured a murderous and rapid fire upon the British line. The 35th and Grenadiers fell fast. Still not a shot was returned. Wolfe was struck in the wrist; but wrapping a handkerchief around the wound, he hurried from rank to rank, warning his men to reserve their fire for a shorter and deadlier range. Not a single trigger was pulled. With arms shouldered as if on parade, and motionless save when they closed upon the ghastly gaps made in their ranks by the French fire, these gallant men waited the word of command with that indomitable endurance which has ever characterized the British soldier when properly trained and led. The French were still unharmed, their confidence increased, and with a loud cheer they pressed forward against the British. A few moments more, and only forty paces separated the combatants. And now the clear voice of Wolfe giving the word to fire rises over the field. The order passes like an electric shot along the British line, its long row of muskets is swiftly levelled, and the next instant a well-aimed volley, almost as distinct as a single shot, rolls over the battle-field. It fell with terrible effect upon the advancing foe. Numbers of French soldiers reeled and fell at once; others staggered for a moment, then dropped aside to die; others, again, burst from the ranks shrieking in agony. Presently the breeze which blew gently across the battle-field carried away the smoke of one of the deadliest volleys that ever burst from British infantry, and the assailing battalions were soon reduced to mere groups among the slain. Scarcely fifteen minutes had elapsed since

Montcalm had made his principal attack, and already the battle was lost. The Brigadier de St. Ours was killed, and De Senezergues, the second in command, mortally wounded; while the Canadian militia had already broken and fled in confusion. Still the gallant Frenchman was not dismayed. Riding through the shattered ranks, he cheered the men with his voice, and induced them to re-form.

"Meantime, the British troops had reloaded, and Wolfe, resolving to take advantage of the disorder in the French ranks, ordered his whole line to advance, placing himself at the head of the 28th and the Grenadiers. For a few minutes they move forward steadily, then their pace increases to a run, and with bayonets at the charge they rush upon the French. Just then Wolfe was wounded a second time in the body; but still pressing forward, he received a ball in the breast. 'Support me,' he said to an officer near him; 'let not my brave fellows see me fall.' He was carried to the rear, and water was brought him to quench his thirst. Still the British pressed forward with fiery valour. On the right, the 35th swept all before them; in the centre, the 28th and Louisburg Grenadiers moved firmly on; on the left, the 58th and 78th overcame a stubborn and bloody resistance, and the last corps with its terrible claymore followed swiftly in pursuit, and supplied the want of cavalry. The fierce struggle fell heavily on the British, but was terribly destructive to the French. They wavered under the carnage; but Montcalm, galloping among his stubborn veterans, called on them to re-form, and again oppose the advancing foe. His efforts were

vain; the head of every formation was mowed down
by the terrible fire of the British, who, again rushing
forward at the charge, compelled his troops to give
way in every direction. At this critical period, he
fell mortally wounded, and from that moment all
was utter rout and confusion on the side of the
French. Wolfe's life ebbs fast away; yet from time
to time he essays to look upon the battle, and clear
away the death-mist that gathers on his sight.
Presently his spirit draws nearer 'to that bourne
whence no traveller returns'; he sinks backward,
and gives no signs of life beyond a heavy breathing
and the occasional groan of painful dissolution. The
French fly in all directions. 'They run! they run!'
exclaimed some of the officers who stood by their
dying general. 'Who runs?' eagerly asked Wolfe,
like one aroused from sleep. 'The enemy, sir,'
answered the officer who supported him; 'they give
way everywhere.' 'Go, one of you, to Colonel
Burton,' said Wolfe, 'and tell him to march Webb's
regiment (the 48th) with all speed down to the
St. Charles River to cut off their retreat.' His voice
grew fainter and fainter as he spoke, and he turned
as if to seek an easier position on his side. Four
days before, he had looked forward to an early death
with dismay; but he now felt he would breathe his
last breath on the field of victory, and that he had
well done his duty to his country. 'Now God be
praised! I die happy,' said the gallant soldier faintly,
yet distinctly; and Wolfe, who had won a new
empire for his race, passed from this material world
to immortality."

The body of Wolfe was taken home, and buried in Greenwich Church, and a monument was erected to him in Westminster Abbey. Although only thirty-two years of age at his death, he takes rank among the first six or eight of English generals. He had crowded into a brief span of life actions that would have reflected lustre on the oldest veteran. There are few instances where immortality has been conquered at so early an age.

The fires from the rampart of Quebec and the frigates stationed in the St. Charles checked the British pursuit of the flying enemy; and, moreover, Bougainville's formidable corps of veterans was hourly expected. Monckton had been severely wounded in the lungs; and Townshend, now the senior officer, recalled his disordered battalions to oppose the new enemy. He put himself into a strong position of defence; but no conflict occurred, for when Bougainville learned the news of Montcalm's total defeat, he declined meeting the victors, and hastily retreated to Cape Rouge. On the same day, De Vaudreuil, with 1,500 Canadians, deserted the lines below Quebec, and, leaving all his artillery, tents, ammunition, and stores behind, effected a hurried retreat to Jacques Cartier.

The loss of the British in this decisive and memorable battle on the Plains of Abraham amounted to 59 killed and 597 wounded of all ranks; that of the French was 600 killed, and upwards of 1,000 wounded and made prisoners. The Canadian militia ran away when they saw the victory inclining towards the British, and therefore suffered much less than the regular troops, who were almost destroyed.

The last scene in the life of Montcalm was very pathetic. "When his wound was dressed, he asked the surgeons if it was mortal; and being answered in the affirmative, calmly said, 'I am glad of it; how long can I survive?' 'Perhaps a dozen hours, and perhaps less,' was the reply. 'So much the better,' rejoined the general; 'I shall not live to see the surrender of Quebec.' To a council of war which hastily assembled, he showed that in twelve hours all the troops near at hand might be concentrated, and the British attacked before they had time to entrench themselves; but his proposition was overruled. With him, the hope of France in Canada was departing. De Ramsay, who commanded the garrison, asked his orders about defending the city. 'To your keeping,' he replied, 'I commend the honour of France. I wish you all comfort, and to be happily extricated from your perplexities. As for me, my time is short; I shall pass the night with God, and prepare myself for death.' To another he said, 'Since it was my misfortune to be discomfited and mortally wounded, it is a great consolation to be vanquished by so noble and generous an enemy.' He shortly afterwards called for his chaplain, who, with the bishop, administered the last offices of his religion, and remained with him till he died next day. Thus terminated the career of a great general and a brave man. Trained from his youth in the art of war, laborious, just, and self-denying, he offered a remarkable exception to the venality of the public men of Canada at this period, and in the midst of universal corruption made the general good his aim. Night, the rushing tide, veteran discipline, and more brilliant genius had given his rival the victory; yet he was not the less great. And while the name of Wolfe will never be forgotten, that of Montcalm is also engraved by its side on the enduring scroll of human fame. The latter has been censured for not abiding the chances of a siege rather than risking a battle. But with a town already in ruins, a garrison deficient in provisions and ammunition, and an enemy to contend with possessed of a formidable siege-train, the fire of which must speedily silence his guns, he acted wisely in staking the issue on the battle, in which, while he found defeat, he met also an honourable and glorious death."

Anticipating French reinforcements, Townshend set to work constructing redoubts, and placing his artillery in order. Admiral Saunders had already moved the whole of his fleet into the basin, preparatory to an attack on the Lower Town. Provisions in Quebec were very low, and the anxious citizens pressed the acting commander, De Ramsay, to capitulate before they were reduced to the last extremity. "We have cheerfully sacrificed our houses and our fortunes," they urged; "but we cannot expose our wives and children to massacre." De Levi, who was at Montreal, had been requested by De Vaudreuil to hasten to Quebec, and assume the chief command. He arrived at the French headquarters near Jacques Cartier on the 16th, and immediately convened a council of war, at which it was decided to raise the siege if possible.

A message was sent to De Ramsay to hold out to

the last extremity, as on the 18th the whole French army would be in motion, with a large supply of provisions, to relieve the city. But the information came too late. Capitulation had been agreed to on the 17th, and early on the ensuing day the terms were fully ratified, and Quebec surrendered. The keys of the city were delivered up in the evening, and the Louisburg Grenadiers marched in; while Captain Palliser of the navy took possession of the Lower Town.

The news of the fall of Quebec was received with joyful acclamations throughout the whole of the British provinces. Illuminations, bonfires, rejoicings were the order of the day. In Great Britain also there were triumphal celebrations, though the national joy was tempered by sadness over the death of the brilliant young general who had died in the moment of victory.

CHAPTER V.

CANADA BECOMES A BRITISH POSSESSION.

THE garrison of Quebec was permitted to march out with all the honours of war, and favourable terms were granted to the inhabitants. All the conditions were faithfully observed by the British. Many of the residents cheerfully and voluntarily took the oath of allegiance to King George II.

In October, the entire British fleet, with the exception of two small vessels, sailed from Quebec for Halifax, and then for England. Brigadier Townshend also proceeded home; while Monckton, who was recovering from his wounds, went to winter in the milder climate of New York. General Murray was entrusted with the government of Quebec, having Colonel Burton as lieutenant-governor, and a garrison of about 5,000 men. During a thick fog, a French vessel managed to elude the vigilance of the British fleet, and to escape away to France, bearing important despatches. Some of these despatches were full of recriminations, De Vaudreuil bitterly censuring De Ramsay for his precipitate surrender of Quebec, and De Ramsay condemning De Vaudreuil for his flight from the lines at the Montmorency.

As the result of one disastrous campaign, the

French position in Canada had passed into a practically hopeless phase. All the important posts now held by France were those of Three Rivers, Montreal, Frontenac, Detroit, and Mackinaw. She had been shut out from Lake Champlain by the loss of Crown Point and Ticonderoga, from the west by the fall of Niagara, and from the seaboard by the conquest of Quebec. The country was in a distressed condition everywhere, and sick and wounded men were found in every hamlet. Provisions were scarce even at Quebec, where scurvy carried off 800 men, and incapacitated nearly double that number.

Murray employed the winter in rebuilding a portion of Quebec and fortifying the city. He erected eight timber redoubts outside the defences towards the Plains of Abraham, and armed them with artillery, while he also laid in eleven months' provisions in the citadel. Outposts were established at all favourable points to conceal his movements from the enemy, and to confirm the country people in their allegiance. But the French likewise were not idle. The troops at Jacques Cartier harassed the British at every opportunity, and De Levi at Montreal pushed forward his preparations for the recapture of Quebec in the spring. He had all the French vessels remaining refitted, and built galleys to receive stores, provisions, and ammunition.

De Levi left Montreal on the 17th of April, 1760, with all his available force, and collected on his way downwards the detached corps at the various posts. On arriving at Cape Rouge, he had eight battalions of regular troops, 4,500 strong, 6,000 Canadians, and over 200 Indians. The artillery and stores were conveyed down the river in boats. It was not until the 27th that Murray received his first intelligence of the approach of this hostile force. He at once covered the retreat of his advanced posts at Cape Rouge and elsewhere, and, retiring, broke down all the bridges. But De Levi pressed on, and by the 28th was within three miles of Quebec. Murray had only an available force of 3,500 men, so greatly had his army been reduced by disease, desertion, and death.

Yet, with this small force at his command, Murray resolved upon giving battle. In a subsequent despatch to the Secretary of State, he said, " Having well weighed my peculiar position, and well knowing that in shutting myself within the walls of the city I should risk the whole stake on the chance of defending a wretched fortification, I resolved upon venturing an action in the field." The event, however, proved that he had come to a rash and disastrous resolution.

" Shortly after daybreak, Murray formed his skeleton battalions on the Plains of Abraham, supported by twenty pieces of artillery, planted at the most favourable points. Having completed his order of battle, he rode to the front to reconnoitre the enemy's position. The previous night had been wet, so he found the French occupied in putting their arms into order, and in other respects unprepared, as he supposed, for action. Thinking this a favourable opportunity to assail them, he gave orders for an immediate attack, which was gladly obeyed by his little army, who pushed forward in admirable order over the brow of the heights and into the plains beyond. De Levi at first could scarcely believe that the British seriously intended to attack his overwhelming force, and they had almost advanced within gun-shot range before he called his troops to arms. His line of battle, after a momentary confusion, was speedily formed, and some companies of grenadiers thrown into the woods on the right to cover his flank in that direction. These almost immediately encountered the skirmishers and light troops on the British left, who speedily drove them in on the main body, and, following too far in pursuit, got in front of their own artillery, and compelled its silence for a time. The advance of the British light troops was soon checked, however, by the steady front of the French supports, whose fire quickly compelled them to retire. De Levi's army was by this time formed in battle array, and the action speedily became general. For an hour and three-quarters did the battle rage with the utmost fury; but finally the numbers of the French prevailed. The British left was thrown into disorder, and gave way; the right was hardly pressed also; and Murray was compelled finally to retreat, leaving nearly the whole of his guns in the hands of the enemy, and 300 dead upon the field. The greater part of the wounded, amounting in all to 700, he succeeded, however, in carrying with him. Nearly a third of the British army were either killed or wounded; but still the French had dearly purchased their victory by a loss, according to their own admission, of fully 1,800 put *hors de combat*. So exasperated were they at the obstinacy of the contest by so small a force, that they stained their triumph by refusing quarter to several English officers, and by giving up the British wounded left on the field to the fury of the Indians. Out of nearly a hundred of these unfortunate men, unavoidably abandoned by Murray in his retreat, only twenty-eight were sent to hospital; the rest were massacred by the savages."

Murray retired within the walls of Quebec, and resumed the work of strengthening the fortifications. On the evening of the 28th, he issued a general order to his troops to the effect " that although the morning had been unfortunate to the British arms, yet affairs were not desperate, that a fleet might soon be expected, and it only remained for officers and men to bear patiently the unavoidable fatigues of a siege." The garrison now consisted of only 2,200 effective men; but they were all animated by a courageous spirit.

On the 10th of May, De Levi, who had taken up his position within 800 yards of the walls, opened his batteries, consisting of thirteen guns and two mortars. But Murray had stationed men on the walls, and his fire completely overpowered that of the French. Both besieged and besiegers were earnestly looking for the arrival of squadrons to aid them. On the 9th of May, a frigate was seen rounding the headland of Point Levi, and standing for the city. Great excitement prevailed as the Union-jack was run up the mast and a boat put off for the Lower Town. The garrison warmly welcomed this first instalment of British relief, and officers and men mounted the ramparts in the face of the enemy, and made the welkin ring with their hearty cheers. Two other vessels arrived on the 15th, under the command of Commodore Swanton; and next day the French vessels above the town were vigorously attacked, and forced on shore or destroyed.

De Levi was now compelled to retreat, and he fled precipitately, leaving his provisions, guns, tents, ammunition, and entrenching tools behind him. Murray went out rapidly in pursuit, but he was only able to capture a few stragglers; while De Levi made his way to Jacques Cartier, and afterwards to Montreal.

The French heads of departments in Canada had pursued such a shameful system of peculation and robbery, that the inhabitants of Quebec began to look forward to the English rule as a benefit instead of an injury. This feeling was strengthened by a judicious proclamation from Murray on the 22nd of May, to the effect that all peaceable residents would be fully protected, as well as those who at once laid down their arms and remained neutral. Defeated, France, with her exhausted treasury, could give them no assistance; and the bills of exchange of the preceding year, drawn upon the Government by the Canadian officials, still remained undischarged. There was a great depreciation of the colonial paper money, and the people could only obtain relief for their financial and other troubles by remaining true to their adhesion to Great Britain. The proclamation concluded with the assurance that "if they withdrew themselves from the army of M. de Levi, and gave it no assistance, further injury should not be done their homes or growing crops, and that thus the evils of another famine would be averted." The proclamation had a widespread beneficial influence, and the French general in Montreal endeavoured in vain to neutralize its effects.

On the 22nd of July, Amherst, who was at Oswego, found himself, owing to various reinforcements, at the head of an army of 10,000 men, with 700 Indians. He embarked with these forces, on the 10th of August, *en route* for Montreal, and invested the French fort at Ogdensburg on the way. After two or three days of heavy firing, the French surrendered at discretion on the 25th. Ascertaining that the Iroquois intended to massacre the French soldiers as soon as they gained entrance to the works, Amherst sternly forbade this, and stated that he should resist it by force. As they then sullenly threatened to return home, Amherst said they might do so, but he should exact vengeance for any atrocities they might commit on the way.

Amherst gave the name of Fort William Augustus to the conquered island. Writing to the Governor of New York, he said that, as he had destroyed French power at La Presentation (Ogdensburg), and also on the islands at the head of the rapids, the settlers on the Mohawk should be invited to return, for now they were assured of " a quiet and peaceable abode in their habitations."

The British army now passed down the St. Lawrence, and, after losing eighty-four men and several boats in the Cedar Rapids, landed on the Island of Montreal, about nine miles from the town, on the 6th of September. In the meantime, Murray, who had left Quebec on the 14th of June with 2,200 chosen men, was ascending the river, subduing various small posts on its banks, and compelling the inhabitants whenever practicable to submit to the authority of Great Britain. As he found Bourlemaque with 4,000 men posted at Sorel, Murray determined to await the arrival of an expected reinforcement from Louisburg. As soon as this came up, he pursued his way, and on the 7th of September his troops were disembarked, and posted to the northeast of the town. Next day, Colonel Haldimand, who had penetrated into Canada by Lake Champlain and the Richelieu, also arrived at Montreal, with a force of upwards of 3,000 men; so that there was now an army of nearly 16,000 men assembled beneath the walls of what was practically a defenceless town.

Negotiations for a capitulation had already been opened by De Vaudreuil on the 6th of September; but so many difficulties arose as to the articles of peace, that the capitulation was not signed until the 8th. The articles, like those of Quebec, were drawn up only in French. Dr. Kingsford, the Canadian historian, gives the following digest of the articles of capitulation: "No special privileges are granted in these conditions; they may be regarded as the acceptance of surrender by a conquered people. The troops were allowed the honours of war; but they had to lay down their arms, not to serve again during the war, and to be embarked as prisoners for France. A clause giving protection to deserters was refused. The demand that the Indians should be sent away after the articles were signed was refused, Amherst remarking, 'There has been no cruelty committed by our Indians, and good order shall be maintained.' M. de Vaudreuil and the officers were promised every consideration. All were allowed to carry away their private papers; but the archives and maps of the country were to be left behind. It was asked that, if peace was proclaimed, matters should return to the condition in which they had been. Amherst declared that everything must depend on the orders of the King. Those who had business in the country with the permission of De Vaudreuil could remain until they had arranged their affairs. No mention on either side was made of the use of the French language. The free exercise of religion was granted; the enforced payment of the dîme must depend on the King's will. The demand that the King of France should continue to name the Roman Catholic bishop was refused, as equally was the power to establish new parishes. The nuns were maintained in their constitutions and principles. The same consideration to the male communities of the Jesuits and St. Sulpicians was reserved for the King's pleasure. These communities were allowed to retain their property, with the right of disposing of their possessions, and withdrawing with the money to France. In answer to the condition asked for by De Vaudreuil, that those who remained in the colony should not be liable to bear arms against the King of France or his allies, he was told that the Canadians became subjects of the King of Great Britain. No special provision was entertained with regard to the Acadians; the demand that they should be sent back to their lands was specially refused. The remaining articles were the ordinary provisions made under circumstances of such surrender of a territory for the protection of the inhabitants, with the desire of granting them fair and equitable terms. It might be said that the whole spirit of the conditions was embraced in the remark of Amherst on Article 41, that the Canadians became the King's subjects. On the morning following the settlement of the articles of capitulation, the 9th of September, a detachment of troops with artillery proceeded to the *place d'armes*, and as a military force occupied the town ; the French regiments, one after the other, came upon the ground and laid down their arms, and returned to the camp on the ramparts, where they had been established. The ceremony over, a British force was sent to take possession of the gates, and guards were placed throughout the city. The British colours were now raised from the small fort which then stood at the east of Montreal, to show that the last stronghold of French Canada had surrendered."

By this capitulation, the whole of the vast territory extending from the fishing stations in the Gulf of St. Lawrence to Michigan and Illinois, passed into the hands of the British.

On the 11th of September, Amherst reviewed his whole force, in the presence of De Vaudreuil, with whom he became on friendly terms. The French troops next began to evacuate the town, and by the 22nd every French soldier had left Montreal, except those who had married in the country, and who had resolved to remain in it, and transfer their allegiance to the new Government. The provincial troops likewise returned to their respective homes in New Hampshire, Rhode Island, Connecticut, New York, and New Jersey. Major Rogers was despatched with 400 men, and letters from De Vaudreuil, to take possession of the French forts at Detroit, Miami, St. Joseph, and Michillimackinac. At the head of Lake Erie, Rogers encountered the great Ottawa chief, Pontiac, who was the head of a confederacy of Indian tribes, and who subsequently gave much trouble to the British.

General Amherst proceeded to establish a military government for Canada, with the double object of preserving the public tranquillity and administering justice. The colony was divided into three districts: the first was Quebec, over which Murray was placed; the second Three Rivers, at the head of which was Colonel Burton; and the third Montreal, which was entrusted to Brigadier Gage. Several courts of justice were established, composed of Canadian militia officers, who had summary jurisdiction, but with right of appeal to the commandant. This military authority was approved by the British Ministry, until France had relinquished Canada, and a proper form of government could be instituted.

Prosperity began once more to dawn upon Canada, now that the fears of British invasion and of Indian massacres were at an end. The bulk of the people soon blessed the events which had placed them under the rule of Great Britain. Even an able French author, the Abbé Raynal, wrote: " To the impenetrably mysterious transactions of a cruel inquisition, succeeded a cool, rational, and public trial ; and a tribunal dreadful, and accustomed to shed blood, was replaced by humane judges, more disposed to acknowledge innocence than to assume criminality. The conquered people have been still more delighted by finding the liberty of their persons secured for ever by the famous law of Habeas Corpus. As they had too long been victims of the arbitrary wills of those who governed them, they have blessed the beneficent hand that drew them from a state of slavery to put them under the protection of just laws."

At this period, General Amherst obtained a census of the population, which was reported at 76,172. It was thus distributed : Montreal, 37,200 ; Quebec, 32,584 ; Three Rivers, 6,388. Having traversed the new British possessions, Amherst made his way to New York, where he arrived on the 28th of October. He never subsequently visited Canada.

It remains to be stated that before the surrender of Montreal the French Court attempted to succour it in July. A number of store-ships had been sent out in the spring, under convoy of a frigate. Apprised of the sailing of an English squadron up the St. Lawrence before their arrival, the French vessels put into the Bay of Chaleurs. Here Commodore the Honourable John Byron (grandfather of the poet), with his squadron from Louisburg, attacked their whole fleet, consisting of one frigate, two store-ships, and nineteen sail of smaller vessels. These he destroyed, as well as two batteries which had been raised on shore for their protection. The town, consisting of 200 houses, met with the same fate.

When Great Britain had conquered Canada and Guadeloupe, she desired peace. Opinion in England and America was divided as to the desirability of these acquisitions. While there were a majority in favour of keeping Canada, the minority thought it might become burdensome and troublesome to us. One writer prophetically said that if England retained Canada, she would soon find North America itself too powerful and too populous to be governed at a distance. Yet Benjamin Franklin, the enlightened American statesman, strongly advocated its retention as a great safeguard for perpetual peace in North America. Pitt took the same view, and by his action unwittingly paved the way for the independence of the United States.

George II. died suddenly on the 25th of October, 1760. His successor, bent on governing in fact as well as in name, disliked Pitt, who had raised his country from an abyss of weakness and disgrace to be the first power in Europe. Relations became so strained, that the Minister resigned in October, 1761. George III. felt that he stood in the way of the peace he so much desired, and did not therefore ask him to remain; but Pitt still remained the Minister of the nation. While the King and Queen were received with coldness in the city of London, the appearance of Pitt drew forth the loudest acclamations. He had a further triumph when his successors were soon compelled to adopt his policy and to declare war against Spain. With the exception of Prussia and Portugal, Great Britain speedily found the whole of Europe arrayed against her.

Spain invaded Portugal; but with the aid of British auxiliaries, the latter drove her back. In her colonies, Spain suffered still more severely. Havannah was taken by the Earl of Albemarle and Admiral Pococke, with plunder to the amount of £3,000,000; Draper and Cornwallis captured the city of Manila; and as the cannon of the Horse Guards announced the birth of a Prince of Wales, waggons conveyed two millions of treasure to the Tower, a prize to the captors of two Spanish vessels. France, deprived of her colonies as well as Spain, found her commerce on the brink of ruin; and Austria and Prussia were weary of costly and useless campaigns. No wonder, under such circumstances, that Europe generally sighed for peace.

Lord Bute, George III.'s favourite Minister, had little to boast of personally in regard to these events. He had been compelled to adopt his rival's policy, but against his will. The French had almost succeeded in an attempt to seize Newfoundland, as Bute had left this important post badly protected. But British valour once more triumphed, and in September, 1762, the last French attempt on Newfoundland was decisively defeated.

On the 3rd of November, 1762, preliminaries of peace were signed at Paris by France and Spain on the one hand, and Great Britain and Portugal on the other. By this peace, Great Britain, in addition to its islands in the West Indies, gained the Floridas, Louisiana to the Mississippi, all Canada, Cape Breton, and the other islands on the Gulf of St. Lawrence, and Senegal; while the victories of Clive and Coote in Asia, and of

Watson and Pococke at sea, gave her the ascendency in the East Indies.

Although George III. declared that England had never signed such a favourable treaty before, Pitt opposed it on the ground that it did not give his country the advantages to which it was entitled by conquest. The nation at large took the same view; but Parliament sanctioned the treaty by a large majority, and it was finally ratified on the 10th of February, 1763. In Europe things remained substantially as they were; but in Asia and America everything was changed, and the Anglo-Saxon race became predominant in both continents.

By the thirteenth Article of this Treaty of Paris, the King of France "renounced all pretensions which he had formed or might form to Nova Scotia or Acadia in all its parts, and guaranteed the whole of it, with all its dependencies, to the King of Great Britain. He also added and guaranteed to his Britannic Majesty in full right, *Canada*, with all its dependencies, as well as the Island of Cape Breton, and all other islands and coasts in the Gulf and River St. Lawrence, and generally everything that depended on the said countries, lands, islands, and coasts, with the sovereignty, property, possession, and all rights, acquired by treaty or otherwise, which the most Christian King and the Crown of France have had till now over the said countries, islands, lands, places, coasts, and their inhabitants; so that the most Christian King ceded and made over the whole to the said King and to the Crown of Great Britain, and that in the most ample manner and form, without restriction, and without any liberty to depart from the said cession and guarantee, under any pretence, or to disturb Great Britain in the possessions above mentioned. His Britannic Majesty on his side agreed to grant the liberty of the Catholic religion to the inhabitants of Canada : that his new Catholic subjects might profess the worship of their religion, according to the rites of the Romish Church, as far as the laws of Great Britain might permit. His Britannic Majesty further agreed, that the French inhabitants or others, who had been subjects of the most Christian King in Canada, might retire with safety and freedom, whenever they might think proper, and might sell their estates, provided it be to the subjects of his Britannic Majesty, and might bring away their effects, as well as their persons, without being restrained in their emigration, under any pretence whatsoever, except that of debts or of criminal prosecutions. The term limited for their emigration was fixed to the space of eighteen months, to be computed from the day of the exchange of the Ratifications of Peace."

In September, 1763, General Murray suppressed by his vigorous action at Quebec a mutiny which broke out in consequence of an order from the commander-in-chief in America stopping, on the ground of necessity, fourpence for each ration of provisions to be issued to the forces under his command. Murray ordered the garrison to be under arms on the 21st on the Grand Parade. When they had assembled, he read the articles of war; and after demonstrating to the soldiers the enormity of their crime, he declared his fixed resolution to compel their submission, or to perish in the attempt. He then went to the head of Amherst's Grenadiers, determined to put to death the first man who refused to obey. He commanded them, in sign of compliance with orders, to march between two royal colours planted for that purpose. They did so, and returned cheerfully to their duty, expressing sorrow for their past behaviour; and all the rest followed their example. The general then declared they had recovered their character as good soldiers, and restored to the battalion its colours. The behaviour of the men ever afterwards deserved the warmest praise.

As for the colony generally, its condition under the new Government was all that could be hoped for. For years remonstrances had been transmitted to France against the oppressions of the former rulers, but all in vain; now every Canadian subject of Great Britain knew that he could no longer be harassed or misgoverned with impunity.

CHAPTER VI.

THE COLONY FROM 1763 TO 1811.

PEACE having been secured, Great Britain proceeded to give a settled form of government to its new possessions. In October, 1763, a proclamation was published under the Great Seal for erecting four civil governments in America ; namely, those of Quebec, East Florida, West Florida, and Granada. It was further announced that, as soon as circumstances permitted, general assemblies of the people would be convened as in the American provinces ; in the meantime, the laws of England were to be in force. All the laws, customs, and judicial forms which had long been in vogue were thus abolished at one stroke. It was not altogether a judicious proceeding, for the violent changes led to reactions which have been more or less felt ever since.

General Murray was appointed to the governorship of Canada, or the province of Quebec ; and he nominated a council of eight members to assist him in the government. Canada was at this time still without a printing press ; but on the 21st of June, 1764, the first number of the *Quebec Gazette* was published, and that journal has continued to appear ever since. Courts of King's Bench, Common Pleas, and Chancery were established in September; but the effort to settle all causes by the English laws failed, and the French laws and usages were allowed in certain causes. In 1765, complaints were sent to England relative to the establishment of the courts, the harsh conduct of law officers, and the enormous fees exacted. Redress was granted as far as possible, and Murray was held in high esteem by the French community for the consideration he invariably showed them, while the population was accustoming itself to the new order of things.

General Murray left for England in 1767; and as he did not return, Brigadier Sir Guy Carleton was appointed permanent Governor in his stead. The new administrator was a humane and just man, and proved himself a true friend to the colonists. When the criminal law of England became better understood, it worked more smoothly, and trial by jury and the Habeas Corpus Act gave general satisfaction to the people. Trade became prosperous, and emigrants returned from France, as well as large numbers of Acadians from the surrounding colonies. Between 1760 and 1773, it was estimated that the population increased by one-fourth. It was still, of course, overwhelmingly Roman Catholic.

Petitions began to be signed for the summoning of a House of Assembly, under the terms of the proclamation of 1763. Nothing was done, however; and Great Britain was so disturbed by the spirit of independence growing up in the colonies, that in 1774 it was determined to give Canada a new form of government. On the 2nd of May, a bill, usually known as the Quebec Act, " was brought into the House of Lords by the Earl of Dartmouth, which passed without opposition, and was sent down to the Commons for their concurrence. This bill repealed all the provisions of the royal proclamation of 1763, annulled all the acts of the Governor and Council relative to the civil government and administration of justice, revoked the commissions of judges and other existing officers, and established new boundaries for the province, which was now declared to embrace all ancient Canada, Labrador, and the counties west of the Ohio and Mississippi. The Quebec Act released the Roman Catholic religion in Canada from all penal restrictions; renewed their dues and tithes to its regular clergy, but as regarded members of their own Church only (Protestants being freed from their payment); and confirmed all classes, with the exception of the religious orders and communities, in the full possession of their properties. The French laws were declared to be the rules for decision relative to property and civil rights, while the English criminal law was established in perpetuity. Both the civil and criminal codes, however, were liable to be altered or modified by the ordinances of the Governor and a Legislative Council. This Council was to be appointed by the Crown, and to consist of not more than twenty-three, nor less than seventeen members. Its power was limited to levying local or municipal taxes, and to making arrangements for the administration of the internal affairs of the province; the British Parliament jealously reserving to itself the right of external taxation, or levying duties on articles imported or exported. Every ordinance passed by this Council was to be transmitted, within six months at furthest after enactment, for the approbation of the King, and if disallowed to be null and void on his pleasure becoming known in Quebec."

Canada was governed under the Quebec Act for seventeen years; but it was obnoxious to the English, who longed for the constitutional rights of the old country. The measure was opposed in the House of Commons; but its sponsors and supporters defended it, on the supposition that the French would remain the dominant race in Canada. The Earl of Chatham spoke strongly against it, as leading to a thousand difficulties, as well as the alienation of the British colonists; and the city of London agitated warmly against it. But the bill was carried, and, as we have seen, long remained the law of Canada. It was received in the most hostile spirit in the American colonies, and remonstrances poured in upon the Home Government for thus taking away all the ancient rights of English subjects. In the American Congress the Act was severely condemned. The Act annexed large territories to Quebec, including that part of the United States now forming Minnesota, Wisconsin, Michigan, Ohio, Indiana, and Illinois.

In 1775, the American War of Independence broke out. At an early stage, the colonists captured Ticonderoga and Crown Point, which commanded the Valley of the Hudson. The Americans believed that the Canadian people generally were favourable to their cause, and determined to anticipate the British by striking a decided blow in the north. They accordingly despatched a force of nearly 2,000 men.

under Schuyler and Montgomery, to penetrate into Canada by the Richelieu. Two expeditions were sent against Fort St. John; and the second, under General Montgomery, succeeded in reducing the fort in November, 1775. Fort Chamblée was likewise taken; and this important capture gave Montgomery a plentiful supply of provisions. Montreal being next attacked, Governor Carleton found himself not strong enough to defend it; so he abandoned the city, and the day following it was occupied by General Montgomery.. General Prescott, with a British force, shortly afterwards surrendered. Everything seemed to be in favour of the colonists; and although the season was now far advanced, Montgomery hastened towards Quebec. This indefatigable officer suffered nothing to deter him, notwithstanding that he had to weaken his small force of 2,000 men by discharging many soldiers whose term of service had expired. Being shortly reinforced by Colonel Arnold with about 1,000 men, he resolved on attacking Quebec. It was ably defended by Carleton; but on the night of the 31st of December a vigorous assault was made. It was repulsed with great loss, and the gallant Montgomery was killed. This brave officer, who was as formidable in war as he was gentle in peace, was much esteemed and beloved. He came of a good north of Ireland family, and had served with distinction under Wolfe; but after the Peace of 1763, he married an American lady, Miss Livingston, and when the rupture with England occurred, he joined the cause of the United States with genuine enthusiasm.

In May, 1776, the Americans retreated from Quebec,

under General Thomas, Montgomery's successor. The small-pox committed great havoc amongst the troops, and one of its victims was Thomas himself, who was succeeded in the command by General Sullivan. Various military movements subsequently took place ; but in the end the American forces withdrew altogether from Canada. The invasion resulted in no advantage to the American cause ; but, on the contrary, it roused the hostility of the inhabitants, and drew them into closer relations with Great Britain.

In the summer of 1777, Sir Guy Carleton was succeeded as Governor by Major-General Haldimand. He was a native of Switzerland, and knew little or nothing of the laws and customs of either the British or the Canadians. He was quite unfitted to administer the government, and his rule was distinguished by undue severity. For his violations of the liberty of the subject, several successful actions were brought against him, and the damages were paid by the British Government. After the Americans had achieved their independence, the Canadians more than ever desired a House of Assembly of their own. The British element in the colony was now strengthened by an emigration of loyalists from the State of New York. A census taken in 1784 showed that the population of Montreal, Three Rivers, and Quebec amounted to 113,012 ; and that 28,000 men were fit to bear arms, and had been enrolled in the militia. The other and more thinly populated portions of Canada probably contained 7,000 souls.

A new settlement was effected at this time upon the lands lying along the banks of the St. Lawrence, from the highest French settlement at Lake St. Francis upwards, and round the Bay of Quinte. The settlers consisted of Americans, loyalists, and disbanded officers and soldiers of the 84th Regiment, with a few other German and English soldiers. Settlements were also formed on the Niagara River and at Amherstburg, the latter being the first effective settlement of Upper Canada. Before the close of 1784, its population amounted to about 10,000 souls. Large allotments on moderate terms were made, on condition of actual occupation; and the benefits promised led to a considerable emigration from Great Britain.

As the English Ministers found that General Haldimand was not the proper person to rule the province, they sent out Mr. Henry Hamilton in 1785, to act as Lieutenant-Governor until a governor should be appointed. He summoned the Legislative Council, and with their sanction the law of Habeas Corpus was introduced into the province, to the great satisfaction of the colonists generally, including the Roman Catholics.

In 1786, the government was again entrusted to General Carleton, who had now been raised to the peerage under the title of Lord Dorchester. On his arrival at Quebec on the 23rd of October, his lordship was cordially welcomed by the inhabitants. The new Governor directed enquiries to be made into the state of the laws, the commerce, the police, and the education of the province. Commerce was declining; and education was at such a low ebb, that there was not a school in the province where the higher branches of learning were taught. The unsatisfactory condition of things, combined with the rapid increase of the English-speaking population, encouraged the efforts of reformers who advocated a division of the colony. A representative was sent to England, and the information he placed before Ministers led them to bring in a bill which gave a new Constitution to Canada.

The main provision of this bill, which came before the House of Commons in 1791, was the division of the province into Upper and Lower Canada. Mr. Pitt, in introducing the bill, briefly stated its provisions. The province of Quebec was to be divided into Upper and Lower Canada, in order to prevent any dissensions between the French Canadians and settlers of British origin. "Each province was to have its own Legislature, composed of a Legislative Council, the members of which were to be chosen for life, and a House of Assembly, to be elected in the usual manner by the people. The Habeas Corpus Act was to be a fundamental principle of the new Constitution. Provision was likewise to be made for the maintenance of the Protestant clergy in both provinces, by the allotment of lands (the Clergy Reserves); and while Parliament reserved to itself the right of regulating trade and commerce, the local legislatures were to have the sole power of internal taxation.

"Mr. Fox warmly opposed the bill on several grounds. He argued that it would be wiser rather to unite still more closely than to separate the British and French settlers; and that the Legislative Council should be also elective, with a higher qualification on the part of elected and electors than was necessary for the Lower House. 'By this means,' said he, 'Canadians will have a real aristocracy, chosen by persons of property, from among persons of the highest quality, who would thus have that weight and independence necessary to guard against the innovations of the people on the one part, or of the Crown on the other.'

"The Quebec reformers were also dissatisfied with the bill, and instructed Mr. Lymburner to oppose it, chiefly on the grounds that the division of the province would interfere with commerce, and would be really injurious to the inhabitants of Upper Canada. Mr. Lymburner was heard at the bar of the House of Commons against the bill on the 23rd of March, and opposed its principles in a long and lucid argument. But his efforts failed to prevent a separation of the province. The bill passed into law, and continued to be the Constitution of the Canadas until the Union."

Lord Dorchester having obtained leave of absence, Major-General Clarke was called upon to act as Lieutenant-Governor. The elections to the Houses of Assembly were held in June, 1792, and among the members returned were several of the principal merchants of Montreal and Quebec. General Clarke opened the first Parliament of Lower Canada on the 17th of December. A number of bills were passed, and an address was voted to the King, praying for the establishment of a Canadian College. Momentous events now transpired in Europe, the French Revolution being distinguished by the violence of its excesses. Eventually, war was declared between France and England. Meantime, the commerce and prosperity of Canada were steadily on the increase, and about a hundred vessels from British and foreign ports annually visited Quebec, while the net annual revenue of the Lower Province—from lands, customs, duties, and licences—was little less than £5,000 sterling.

In September, 1793, Lord Dorchester returned to Canada, and in November opened the second session of Parliament. Legislative zeal was not very strong, as only five or six bills were passed during the session. In consequence of the arrival of revolutionary emissaries from France, the Assembly aimed one of its measures against aliens who inculcated treason, and gave the Governor extensive powers to search out and punish such persons. Before the final session of the first Parliament of Lower Canada closed in 1796, the public revenue had largely increased since the division of the province.

Lord Dorchester finally left Canada in July, 1796, having accomplished much for the well-being and contentment of the province. He was succeeded as Governor-General by Major-General Prescott, who, in opening the new Parliament in January, 1797, alluded to the recent treaty of commerce and navigation between Great Britain and the United States as being highly favourable to the province. In the course of this year, the first execution for high treason took place in Canada. David M'Lean, a bankrupt American, endeavoured to persuade a number of the inhabitants of Quebec to assist him in seizing the city. His designs were discovered, and he was tried, condemned, and hanged as a traitor. This was the chief event in Prescott's administration, and he departed for England in 1799 much regretted by the colonists. He was followed by Sir Robert Shore Milnes as Lieutenant-Governor. All classes of the community in Lower Canada at this period were contented. "The inhabitants of British origin felt that they had all they could reasonably expect in a House of Assembly and a Legislative Council; while the population of French descent, in the full enjoyment of their language, their customs, and their religion, lived on in an easy and good-natured existence which nothing disturbed. Meantime, the province was steadily progressing in population and wealth. The inhabitants showed their devotion and loyalty to Great Britain by contributing liberal sums to carry on the war."

Father Casot, the last of the Jesuits in Canada, died in 1800, and the large possessions of the order now devolved to the Government. As the father had devoted his revenues to charitable purposes, his death was deeply regretted by the poor.

Slavery had always hitherto existed in Canada; but in 1803 Chief Justice Osgood at Montreal declared slavery inconsistent with the laws of the country, and gave freedom to all persons in that condition. From that time onwards Canada remained free soil, affording a safe refuge for slaves.

From 1803 to 1805—when the Lieutenant-Governor, who was personally unpopular, left the colony—trade and public affairs were in a satisfactory state. The revenue in 1805 amounted to over £33,000; and although the expenditure was about £40,000, the difference was far less in proportion than in previous years. One hundred and forty-six vessels, with an aggregate tonnage of 25,136, visited Quebec during the season.

Mr. Dunn, who assumed direction of the government as senior executive councillor, unpleasantly distinguished his rule by attempting to curb the liberty of the press. The *Montreal Gazette* having reported the proceedings at a dinner of the merchants of Montreal, which were regarded as reflecting on certain Parliamentary representatives, the House of Assembly voted the publication a breach of privilege, and ordered the publisher and editor of the *Gazette* to be taken into custody. As these gentlemen could not be found, however, the matter ended. But the manager of the *Quebec Mercury*, a journal which had criticized the illiberal proceedings of the Assembly, was summoned to the bar of the House, and compelled to apologize.

As members of the Assembly were not paid, and the novelty of being legislators had worn off, it was frequently difficult to obtain a quorum to transact the necessary business of the province. At the close of the session of 1805, many measures had failed to pass from this cause. At this period, a new journal, *Le Canadien*, appeared, exclusively devoted to French interests. It was an able and popular journal; but, unfortunately, it began a system of agitation and discord between the two races, which subsequently had lamentable results. The session of 1807 was marked by two incidents: a debate on a resolution for paying the expenses of members residing at a distance from Quebec, which was only lost by two votes; and the election of Mr. Ezekiel Hart, a Jew, by the people of Three Rivers.

On the 19th of October, 1807, Lieutenant-General Sir James H. Craig, who had been appointed to succeed General Prescott as Governor-General of

British North America, arrived at Quebec, and assumed charge of the government. During the first session under his rule, that of 1808, the Jewish member for Three Rivers was unseated, and the Militia, Alien, and Preservation Acts were continued. A new Assembly was now elected, which met in May, 1809. M. Panet, who had filled the office of Speaker during the four preceding Parliaments, was again elected. The Governor, displeased with the proceedings of the Assembly, dissolved it prematurely, and his otherwise arbitrary policy made him unpopular; and the feeling was not removed by a tour which he made through the principal towns of the province.

In 1809, John Molson, an enterprising and spirited merchant of Montreal, fitted out the first steamer that ever ploughed the waters of the St. Lawrence. On the 3rd of November, this memorable little craft, named the *Accommodation*, got up steam, shot out into the current, and, after a voyage of thirty-six hours, arrived safely at Quebec, where the whole city seemed to have turned out to welcome the nautical phenomenon. This venture gave a fresh impetus to the prosperity of Canada. The second steamer constructed in the province was launched at Montreal.

A new Assembly met in January, 1810, and Panet was once more elected Speaker. The Governor was more conciliatory in opening the first session; but he and the Assembly were soon at war again, the chief ground of difference arising out of the proposed disqualification of the judges from sitting in Parliament. The Governor accepted a measure of disqualification; but desired, with the Council, to have its operation postponed for a session. The Assembly retorted by declaring the seat of Mr. de Bonne, a judge, vacant by eighteen to six votes. The Governor, exasperated by this, again dissolved the Assembly. The press and the public now joined in the fray, the British colonists taking the side of the Governor, and the French espousing the cause of the more constitutional Assembly. The offices of *Le Canadien*, the French paper, were overrun by a party of soldiers, and its printer committed to prison. A number of influential French citizens were arrested for treasonable practices ; but as there was nothing against them, they were released, and the miniature Reign of Terror gradually subsided.

At the ensuing elections, the old members of the Assembly were for the most part re-elected, and Panet was again chosen Speaker. As a third dissolution would have been straining matters too far, the Governor exhibited a more peaceable spirit, and allowed the public business to proceed. Mr. Bedard, a member of the House who had been arrested, proved a bone of contention ; but eventually the Governor released him at his own pleasure. The session of 1811 passed over smoothly, and the bill to disqualify judges was passed and became law.

General Craig left Canada on the 19th of June, being then seriously out of health, and he died in England early in the following year. He had governed arbitrarily, imprisoning innocent men, and violating the rights of private property ; but he was probably not so much to blame as the system whose mouthpiece he was, an irresponsible Executive being at the root of most public disorders in Lower Canada.

Turning now to the affairs of Upper Canada, or Ontario, we find that when it was erected into a separate province in 1791, with a Constitution modelled on that of Lower Canada, it had a population of about 20,000 souls. These were scattered along the St. Lawrence from Lake St. Francis upwards to Kingston, thence around the Bay of Quinte, along the Niagara frontier at Amherstburg, in the old French settlement on the Thames, and in the Iroquois settlement at Grand River. Life was very lonely for the distant settlers in Western Canada. They had literally to cut their way, and clear the forests as best they could. Dangers and difficulties beset them on all hands; but they persevered, and in the course of half a century a great transformation was effected in the country and the people.

But when Governor John Graves Simcoe arrived in Upper Canada in 1792, there was nothing in the shape of a town beyond a small village at Kingston, and another at Newark, or Niagara, with an occasional cluster of log cabins elsewhere. As Newark was the most central spot, it was chosen for the capital, and here assembled the first Provincial Parliament of Upper Canada, on the 17th of September, 1792. The Lower House was composed of sixteen members, the Upper House of eight. Yet in its first session the Legislature displayed commendable wisdom and a just appreciation of the necessities of the province. Eight Acts were passed: one introduced the English civil law; another established trial by jury; and a third provided for the easier recovery of small debts. One Act regulated the toll to be taken on mills, and another made provision for building a gaol and courthouse in each of the four districts of Upper Canada. These districts comprised the Eastern, or Johnstown district ; the Middle, or Kingston district ; the Home, or Niagara district ; and the Western, or Detroit district. In closing the first Parliamentary session, the Governor complimented the honest farmers—for such were nearly the whole of the legislators—upon their satisfactory measures.

Simcoe still held the rank of brigadier in the English army ; and as he owned extensive estates in the mother country, people wondered why he should bury himself in the forests of Canada. His enlightened and liberal measures were probably due to patriotic motives ; but he might also have felt that, in the renewed struggle imminent, apparently, between America and Great Britain, the Governor of Upper Canada must play an important part.

When the Governor found that the strong fort on the American side of the Niagara River was to be surrendered by the British, he abandoned the design of making Newark his capital, as it would not do in case of war for the chief town of the province to be within reach of the enemy's guns on the frontier. Accordingly, after coasting along the upper shore of Lake Ontario, he fixed upon a place near the old French fort Toronto. Its geographical situation, viewed from every point, was excellent ; so in 1794 Toronto became the capital city. The result amply justified his choice, and on a site hitherto rarely visited by human footsteps one of the most beautiful cities upon the American Continent soon rose into view.

Land being granted to settlers on liberal terms, emigration from the United States to Upper Canada speedily became continuous, and its population rose to 30,000 souls. But now a new difficulty arose. Simcoe, who disliked the Americans, dreaded lest his capital should be chiefly settled by them ; so he began to cast about for a new metropolis on the banks of a river which he renamed the Thames. The Governor, however, was thwarted by Lord Dorchester, Governor-General and Commander-in-Chief of British North America, who held the Imperial purse-strings, and had the disposition of troops and vessels of war. He directed that Kingston should be the principal naval and military station of Lake Ontario ; and from that time forward it continued to remain so. But many years after Simcoe's death, Sir John Colborne partially carried out his plan of a metropolis by erecting barracks on the site he had chosen, and the London of Canada ultimately expanded into a flourishing city.

In 1793, a bill was carried providing for the payment of members at the modest rate of two dollars per day ; but by far the most important measure of the session was one against slavery. This Act declared that no more slaves were to be imported into the colony under certain pains and penalties, and that even voluntary contracts for personal services were to be limited to nine years. While the Act confirmed the existing property of masters in slaves imported under authorized licences, provision was made that their future children should be manumitted at the age of twenty-five years. The farmers of Upper Canada thus struck a fatal blow at slavery ten years before slavery was abolished in Lower Canada. As the Parliament of Upper Canada was to be elected every four years, the first Assembly accordingly terminated its existence in 1795, having enacted measures of a useful and eminently practical character.

The public press of the province at this time was limited to a demy sheet, issued as a Government *Gazette* at Niagara, and published weekly. The little press on which it was printed served also to print the Acts of the Legislature and the proclamations and circulars issued by the Governor.

In consequence of complaints made by the American Government, charging Governor Simcoe with exciting the hostilities of the Iroquois in both Canada and New York, he was recalled in 1796. During the interim, Mr. Russell, senior member of the Executive Council, assumed the direction of public affairs. As soon as Simcoe had departed, those portions of his policy which had been really praiseworthy were thrown over. Agreements with settlers were violated, and lands were seized upon by the favourites of men in power for the purposes of speculation.

In 1797, Niagara ceased to be the capital of Upper Canada, its place being taken by Toronto. There the second Parliament assembled in June, and conducted its business. Matters progressed without interruption until the autumn of 1799, when Major-General Peter Hunter arrived as Lieutenant-Governor of the province. As an international commerce had sprung up across Lake Ontario, St. Lawrence, and the Niagara River, an Act was passed in 1800 to regulate this commerce, and giving the Governor in

Council power to establish ports of entry, and to adopt such other measures as might appear desirable. There was still great jealousy in Canada against the Americans, who were credited with a desire for conquest; so in 1801 the Act for the better security of the province against the King's enemies was renewed. Another Act passed prohibited the sale of spirituous liquors and strong waters in the Indian settlement on the Thames.

There was now such a stream of Irish, Scotch, American, and English emigrants to Upper Canada, that when the Legislature met in 1802 the new district of Newcastle had been formed, and an Act was passed providing for the administration of justice therein. Other Acts increased the ports of entry, and granted £750 to encourage the growth of hemp. As the government of the province was practically in the hands of the Governor and his Council, and there was no check upon their action, the people at length began to chafe under this condition of things, and as early as 1805 there were two distinct parties in Canada West, closely assimilating to the Whig and Tory parties of Great Britain before the Revolution. The former desired more constitutional liberty, while the latter held by the irresponsible Executive.

For a long time the Tories held a decided superiority; and the system of favouritism by the Governor and Council led to the growth of abuses. Peculation prevailed, and even the administration of justice was not all that could be desired. As the judges were removable at the pleasure of the Crown, this weakened their personal influence, and in some cases affected their decisions. There were many irregularities in connection with the civil and criminal law, and a good deal of discontent prevailed, when a respectable English lawyer named Thorpe arrived, whose upright conduct tended to allay the public irritation.

On the recall of Hunter in 1806, Mr. Gore was sent out as Governor in his stead. He had every desire to govern justly, and personally he was an estimable man ; but he at once fell under the influence of the leaders of the Tory party. The oligarchy soon ruled as strongly as ever, and because Judge Thorpe was determined to pursue an upright course in redressing grievances, he was attacked by the official newspaper. Against the teeth of the Government opposition, Thorpe was elected to a seat in Parliament ; while an independent journal, the *Upper Canada Guardian*, was established. Gore procured Thorpe's recall ; and although the latter obtained a verdict against him for libel, he was left by the English Ministry to die in neglect.

The great majority of the people in Canada West continued loyal to Great Britain. They had grievances, of course ; but as they were lightly taxed, and prosperous, and certain concessions were made to them, they did not break out into open complaints. The want of a paper currency was a great drawback to the province, and the public morals—especially as regards intemperance—were not all that could be desired. In 1810, a good deal was done in laying out new roads and building bridges ; and when in the ensuing year Mr. Gore went to England on leave of absence, there seemed no indication of that international storm which was already brewing.

CHAPTER VII.

THE SECOND AMERICAN INVASION.

IT is necessary to glance at the predisposing causes which led to the second American invasion of Canada. First, there was the feeling of bitter animosity towards the British nation, which had prevailed in America since the revolutionary struggle. The election of Jefferson to the Presidency in 1801 completely established the ascendency of the Democratic party in the Union; and no longer checked by the counteracting influence of government, the jealousy and dislike of everything British made itself more than ever manifest. The nation even preferred the tyrannical Napoleon to constitutional England, the mother of its own race—a fact which sufficiently testifies to the temporary aberration of the national mind.

By Napoleon's celebrated Berlin and Milan Decrees, all the Continental ports were closed against British manufactures, the whole British Islands declared in a state of blockade, and the seizure ordered of all vessels bound from British harbours, as well also as that of British goods, wherever they could be found. Great Britain naturally retaliated by her famous Orders in Council, which declared all the ports of

France and her allies—from which the British flag was excluded—in a state of rigorous blockade. These decrees and orders pressed heavily upon neutrals, and especially upon Americans, who had now a large carrying trade to various parts of the globe. Instead of directing his attention against Bonaparte, however, President Jefferson encouraged the hostility against England by refusing to ratify a treaty of amity, commerce, and navigation concluded by the American Minister in London with the British Government. He followed this up in October, 1807, by an angry message to Congress, severely denouncing the British Orders in Council, but saying nothing of the French Decrees, to which they were the natural response.

A difficulty next arose in 1808 with regard to the right of searching for British deserters on board American ships; but the British offered to make reparation in a case where a captain had carried out this right by force instead of making a simple requisition. The election of Madison to the Presidency in 1809 led to the repeal of Jefferson's embargo law against American vessels leaving United States ports, and the substitution of an Act prohibiting all intercourse with France and England, but which provided at the same time that, if either of the belligerents should repeal its hostile edicts, this Act should cease to be in force with respect to that nation. Mr. Erskine was sent out to America to negotiate; but as he recommended that the Orders in Council should cease to be in force at a certain period, the English Government repudiated his action, which made the hostility between the two nations as bitter as ever, and strengthened the hands of the American war party.

By the early part of 1811 a rupture seemed inevitable. The American Minister left the British Court, and the United States openly renewed their intercourse with France. An accidentally hostile collision in May between the English war-sloop *Little Belt* and the American frigate *President* further precipitated matters. In January, 1812, Congress decided, by 109 to 22 votes, to increase the regular troops to 25,000 men, and to raise an immediate loan of £2,000,000 sterling. A general embargo was laid on all vessels in the harbours of the United States, hoping thereby to capture the British homeward-bound West India fleet. The President also tried to make capital against England by purchasing a correspondence supposed to be damaging from a Captain Henry, but he was outwitted.

On the 19th of June, 1812, Congress formally declared war against Great Britain, and directed that hostilities be immediately commenced. The Orders in Council were repealed about this time; but on learning the news America did not recede from her hostile position. There was a strong and honourable party in the United States, however, which denounced the war, though others supported it on the grounds of conquest. The majority were determined to ally themselves with the Emperor Napoleon, whose whole career was in flat contradiction to the principles of the American Republic. The men of New England lamented war; and when it was announced, the ships in Boston Harbour displayed flags half-mast high in token of mourning. The Democratic war party calculated upon an easy conquest of Canada, and upon being joined by many Canadians; yet in both points they were disappointed. But they managed to obtain an alliance with some of the Indian tribes, and especially with the Iroquois of New York State.

While the war fever was spreading in the States, in September, 1811, Lieutenant-General Sir George Prevost, recently the popular Governor of Nova Scotia, arrived at Quebec, and assumed charge of the government of Lower Canada, with the supreme military command of both provinces. In 1812, the Lower Canadian Parliament passed a very liberal militia act, and voted £12,000 for drilling the local militia, and £20,000 more for incidental measures of defence; while a further sum of £30,000 was placed at the Governor's disposal, should war be declared between Great Britain and the United States. Four new regiments of militia were embodied, as well as a regiment of Canadian Voltigeurs.

When it became known at Quebec that Congress had declared war, all American citizens were ordered to quit the province by the 3rd of July. Parliament passed a statute to legalize the issue of army bills to the extent of £250,000; and an annual grant of £15,000 was made for five years to pay whatever interest might accrue. General Brock in Upper Canada also made every preparation for the struggle. The Legislature passed an effective militia bill, and granted £5,000 to defray training expenses.

Hostilities speedily began, and the first success

of the campaign fell to General Brock, who, by the measures he ordered to be taken by Captain Roberts, acquired possession of the important fort at Mackinaw, which secured the entrance into Lake Michigan. Besides the value of the acquisition in itself, the capture of the fort had an excellent effect in retaining the north-west Indians in the British interest.

General Hull, the American commander in Upper Canada, crossed the Detroit River on the 12th of July, and planted his standard at Sandwich. Here he issued a bombastic proclamation, calling upon the inhabitants to surrender. "He did not ask for assistance," he said, "as he had a force that would break down all opposition, and that force was but the vanguard of a much greater. The United States offered peace, liberty, and security against war, slavery, and destruction." Few joined his ranks, however, and a counter-proclamation soon appeared from General Brock. The American and British forces came into battle array some miles from Amherstburg. Hull made several attempts to force a passage across the River Canard, a tributary of the Detroit, but in vain. He then fell back, and established himself at Detroit.

Brock proceeded to Amherstburg, where he met the Indians in council. Among the chiefs present was Tecumseh, who was destined to play a prominent part in Canadian history. He was prepossessing in appearance, of average stature, with a figure light, graceful, and finely proportioned, while his hazel eye, with its penetrating glance, showed him to be a man of energy and decision. Hull's despatches to his Government had been captured in one of the recent skirmishes, and they were of such a desponding tone, and painted his position in such gloomy colours, that Brock determined to attack him at once, before succour could arrive.

"By the 15th of August, a battery was constructed on the banks of the river opposite Detroit, and three guns and two howitzers placed in position, when Brock summoned Hull to surrender. He refused to comply, when the battery opened fire. Next morning, the British, numbering in all 700 regulars and militia and 600 Indians, crossed the river three miles below the town. Forming his men in column, and throwing out the Indians to cover his flanks, General Brock advanced steadily towards the fort. When at the distance of a mile, he halted to reconnoitre; and observing that little or no precautions for defence had been taken at the land side, resolved on an immediate assault. But Hull prevented this movement by capitulating; the garrison, with troops encamped in the vicinity, amounting altogether to 2,500 men, surrendering to little more than half their number. With Detroit a large quantity of military stores and provisions were given up, and the territory of Michigan also surrendered on the simple condition that life and property should be respected. The American militia were permitted to return to their homes, while the regular troops and officers, over 1,000 in number, were sent down to Quebec. Thus disgracefully, on the part of the Americans, ended the first attempt to conquer Upper Canada. Within the short space of five weeks, Mackinaw had fallen, Detroit had been captured, and the chief part of their army of invasion compelled to surrender; while their whole north-western frontier was left exposed to hostile incursions. The successes of British regular troops and militia, against a force so much their superior in numbers, had a most excellent effect in raising the spirits of the Canadian people, and securing the fidelity of the Indians. Had Hull been a man of energy and decision, matters must have been very different. Yet, in any event, with the force at his disposal, he could scarcely have established himself permanently in a hostile country difficult to traverse, and which, as at the River Canard, presented many favourable positions to check the progress of an invading force. But, aside from every consideration, his surrender was one of the most cowardly and humiliating occurrences which had ever taken place in North America. Hull's timid and vacillating conduct appears in strange contrast with the foresight, energy, and decision of the gallant Brock. The rapid movement on Mackinaw; the expeditious advance to Amherstburg, after he had dismissed the Legislature; and the passage of the Detroit River in the face of a superior force, when he had learned the timidity of its leader, unquestionably stamp the latter as a man of superior genius, and remind one of the most fortunate days of the gallant Montcalm."

England still believed that America would withdraw from her position, as the Orders in Council had been repealed; and in pursuance of this belief, Prevost, the governor-in-chief, had proposed an armistice to

Major-General Dearborn, the American commander-in-chief. Dearborn assented; but the American Secretary at War, General Armstrong, refused to ratify the armistice, which he believed to proceed from weakness and danger on the part of the British general.

The plan of the American campaign was as follows: Hull was to enter Canada at Detroit, and Van Ransallaer at the Niagara River, while Dearborn was to assail it by way of Lake Champlain and the Richelieu. Military posts were established at various favourable positions along the frontier, whence harassing excursions were to be made into Canadian territory. Slight successes were obtained in this way at Ogdensburg and Fort Erie. The British Government were still so sceptical as to the American designs on Canada, that only the 103rd Regiment and a battalion of Royal Scots had been sent out to the assistance of Prevost. Meanwhile, preparations were made by the Americans, both on land and water, for the conquest of Upper Canada before winter set in. General Harrison collected a large army at the west to avenge the fall of Detroit, while Dearborn instructed Van Ransallaer to penetrate Brock's line of defence on the Niagara at Queenston. Van Ransallaer had a large force, while Brock had scarcely 2,000 men for the defence, though these were in a high state of efficiency.

"During the 12th, Van Ransallaer completed his preparations for attacking Queenston. The following morning was cold and stormy; but, nevertheless, his troops embarked in boats at an early hour, and everything was made ready to push across the river with the first blush of dawn. These movements were soon discovered by the British sentries, who gave the alarm. Captain Dennis of the 49th, who commanded at Queenston, immediately collected two companies of his regiment and about a hundred of the militia at the landing-place to oppose the enemy, whom he held in check for a considerable time, aided by the power of an eighteen-pounder in position on the heights above, and a masked gun about a mile lower down. A portion of the Americans, however, landed higher up, and, ascending by an unguarded path, turned the British flank, captured the eighteen-pounder, and speedily compelled Dennis to retreat, after having sustained considerable loss, to the north end of the village. Here he was met by General Brock, who had heard the cannonade at Niagara, and pushed forward, in company with his aides-de-camp, Major Glegg and Colonel M'Donnell, to ascertain its cause. Having learned how matters stood, he dismounted from his horse, and, resolving to carry the heights, now fully in possession of the Americans, placed himself at the head of a company of the 49th, and, waving his sword, led to the charge in double-quick time, under a heavy fire from the enemy's riflemen. Ere long, one of these singled out the general, took deliberate aim, fired, and the gallant Brock, without a word, sank down to rise no more. The 49th now raised a shout to 'avenge the general!' when regulars and militia madly rushed forward, and drove the enemy, despite their superior numbers, from the summit of the hill. By this time, the Americans had been strongly reinforced, and the British, who had never exceeded 300 altogether, finding themselves nearly surrounded, were compelled to retire, having sustained a loss in killed, wounded, and prisoners of about a hundred men, including several officers. They re-formed in front of the one-gun battery, already stated as being a mile below Queenston, to await the arrival of assistance. Van Ransallaer had, therefore, made a solid lodgment on Canadian soil with nearly 1,000 men, and after giving orders to form an entrenched camp, recrossed the river to send over reinforcements. But the American militia, having now seen enough of hard fighting, were suddenly seized with conscientious scruples about going out of their own territory. Comparatively few crossed over to the assistance of their comrades beyond the river, who were thus left to shift for themselves. Early in the afternoon, a demonstration was made against the American position in the most gallant manner by young Brant, at the head of some fifty Mohawks. These, after a sharp skirmish, were compelled to retire, owing to the steady front presented by Colonel (afterwards General) Scott, who had meanwhile arrived, and assumed the chief command, Wadsworth, a militia general on the field, waiving his right thereto. But the British had no intention of surrendering Queenston so easily. Major-General Sheaffe, an American by birth, assumed the chief command on Brock's death, and, having collected all the troops at Niagara and the Chippewa, moved forward in admirable order to drive the enemy from their formidable position. His force, inclusive of 100

Indians, was under 1,000 men, of whom only 560 were regulars, with two small guns. After making a long détour to the right, to again open ground in rear of the heights, Sheaffe began the attack by an advance on his left, which, after delivering a volley, charged with the bayonet, and drove in Scott's right. He then advanced his main body, and, after a sharp conflict, a part of the enemy were driven back over the first ridge of heights to the road leading to the falls, while another portion let themselves down with the aid of the roots and bushes towards the river, hotly pursued by the Indians, who were with difficulty withdrawn. Resistance was now out of the question, and the Americans, to the amount of 950 regulars and militia, surrendered. So completely had they been scattered, that hardly 300 men remained with Scott when he gave himself up. Their loss in killed and wounded was also severe, but has never been correctly ascertained; it could scarcely, however, be under 300 men."

Thus was defeated the second attempt of the Americans to gain a permanent foothold in Canada. But to the Canadians the death of Brock was a terrible loss. Besides being a brave and sagacious soldier, he was a just and prudent civil governor, and he was esteemed by friends and foes alike as a man. By his death—he was only forty-two—a most promising career was suddenly cut short.

Van Ransallaer, disgusted with the conduct of the militia, resigned his command, and was succeeded by Brigadier-General Smyth, who procured an armistice of thirty days. The Americans were successful during October in several skirmishes. In November, Dearborn, at the head of 10,000 men, hung upon the confines of Lower Canada ; Smyth, with 5,000 men, occupied the Niagara frontier ; while Harrison, the bravest and most formidable of the American generals, with his Kentucky forest-rangers and Ohio sharp-shooters, threatened the weak British force under Proctor in the distant west. After a time, Dearborn saw the hopelessness of attempting a descent on Montreal, and withdrew his troops into winter quarters. In the meantime, General Smyth, who was in the vicinity of Fort Erie, issued an inflated proclamation, which read like a burlesque of the great Napoleon. His boast with regard to his "army of the centre" proved a very empty one, for his attempts against a much weaker force ended in failure and disgrace. His own soldiers despised him, and he was finally obliged to fly from the camp, being everywhere denounced as a traitor and a coward. He was cashiered by the American Government without trial.

The campaign of 1813 opened with bright prospects for the Canadians, whose Legislatures voted liberal supplies for carrying on the war. Before the close of January, Colonel Proctor achieved two striking successes against the Americans, and defeated and took prisoner Colonel Winchester, who commanded a brigade of Harrison's army. For this, Proctor was raised to the rank of brigadier-general. In Upper Canada, General Prevost directed successful operations against Ogdensburg and Fort La Presentation.

The American plan of campaign was for Harrison to recover Michigan, and threaten Canada at its western extremity; while Commodore Chauncey, aided by a strong land force under General Pike, was to capture Toronto, and invest Fort George at Niagara. Pike was next to assist in carrying the British posts at Erie and Chippewa. The combined American armies were then to descend to Kingston, in the reduction of which they would be aided by a third force under General Dearborn in person. Afterwards, Montreal and Quebec were to be assailed.

With fourteen armed vessels and 1,600 troops, Chauncey and Pike began the attack on Toronto on the 25th of April. The place was badly defended, and the first line was carried with little difficulty. The British commander, Sheaffe, however, or rather his artillery sergeant, Marshall, now blew up his magazine to prevent its falling into the hands of the enemy, and terrible havoc ensued. General Pike was killed, and 200 others of the British were killed and wounded. Still, General Sheaffe's force was so weak in numbers that he was compelled to retire towards Kingston. He was soon afterwards succeeded in the chief command in Upper Canada by Major-General de Rottenburg. Sheaffe returned to the Lower Province to command the troops in the Montreal district. Chauncey next proceeded with a powerful force to attack Fort George at Niagara. For its defence, against a large fleet and a strong army, General Vincent had scarcely 1,400 men. Still, he defended himself gallantly for a time; but finding at last the defence hopeless, he directed the guns to be spiked, the magazine to be blown up, and retreated in excellent order towards Queenston, leaving the Americans to take possession of the ruins of Fort George and a few dismantled houses.

Harrison, in spite of Winchester's defeat, still persevered in his determination to drive the British across the Detroit River and recover Michigan. On the 1st of May, Proctor invested Fort Meigs; the besieged made a sally, and carried the British batteries; but Proctor, having got his main body quickly under arms, cut off the retreat of his assailants by a rapid and judicious movement, and then achieved a brilliant and decisive victory. The enemy lost over 700 men in killed, wounded, and prisoners; while the casualties of the British were only fifteen killed and forty-five wounded. But as half of his militia left soon after the battle, Proctor was obliged to raise the siege of Fort Meigs and to retire. His victory had somewhat raised the spirits of the Canadians, which had been depressed by the American successes at Toronto, Fort George, and elsewhere.

In Central Canada, matters began to improve early in May, when Sir James Yeo, a naval officer of distinction, arrived at Quebec, with several officers of the royal navy and 450 seamen. The fleet at Kingston was already in a forward state of preparation to meet the enemy. The Governor-General and Yeo met at Kingston, and determined to make a dash at once at Sackett's Harbour, the great depot of the American naval and military stores. Unfortunately, when the British arrived and found the Americans to be not so formidable as they expected, Prevost postponed the attack for a day, and thus lost his opportunity of capturing Sackett's Harbour. The British fought one successful skirmish; but instead of following this up by a complete victory, as he might have done, Prevost retired, under the idea that a relief column was advancing to the aid of the enemy. By this weak action, Prevost's military reputation sustained a severe shock.

Meanwhile, in Western Canada, Dearborn sent a strong force—consisting of 3,000 infantry and 250 cavalry, with nine field-pieces—to dislodge Vincent and his British troops from the position they had taken on Burlington Heights. On the 5th of June, when the Americans arrived, Vincent directed a night attack to be made upon them by Colonel Harvey, which proved completely successful. Meantime, Commodore Yeo, on Lake Ontario, effected a communication with Vincent's little army. Dearborn was soon cooped up in Fort George, and the district in a critical position. His force had wasted away to less than 5,000 men. On the 28th of June, however, he sent out a detachment of 600 men under Colonel Boerstler to dislodge a British picket at Beaver Dam; but the whole detachment surrendered to a greatly inferior British force. This final failure completely ruined Dearborn's military reputation, and he was soon superseded in his command by Major-General Wilkinson.

On the shores of Lake Ontario, Vincent more than held his own, and inflicted several reverses on the Americans. The British fleet also captured several American vessels on the lake. Plattsburg was next captured by Colonel Murray. But on Lake Erie the British sustained a severe reverse, their fleet being captured by Commodore Perry.

The effects of this disaster were speedily felt by Proctor. With the enemy on both his flank and front, and lacking provisions and supplies of every kind, he was compelled to retreat. "Amherstburg, Detroit, and the minor fortified posts in the west were dismantled, stores of every kind destroyed, and the British, numbering 830, commenced to retreat along the Thames towards Lake Ontario, accompanied by 500 Indians under Tecumseh, who showed an honourable fidelity in misfortune. Harrison, following rapidly in pursuit with an army of 3,500 men, including several hundred cavalry, came up with Proctor's rear-guard on the 4th of October, and succeeded in capturing all his stores and ammunition and over 100 prisoners. The British general had now no recourse but to hazard a battle, and for this purpose he took up a position, on the following day, at the Moravian village on the Thames. Proctor's usual prudence appears to have forsaken him. The bridges in his rear had been left entire; he made no effort to strengthen his position by a breastwork; and it is even said that his field of battle was ill-chosen. But in any case his few worn-out and harassed soldiers, now reduced by casualties to nearly 600 men, were wholly unequal to a contest with Harrison's numerous and comparatively well-appointed army. The result was what might naturally be expected. The British were speedily beaten at all points, and Proctor fled from the field of battle, leaving the Indians to their fate.

Led by their gallant chieftain, they fought manfully against enormous odds, and only retired when Tecumseh no longer lived to rally them. The few British soldiers who escaped from captivity or death fled through the woods to reassemble, to the number of 240, at Burlington Heights. Nor did the reverses of the British terminate with this fresh disaster. On the same day that Proctor fled before Harrison, six schooners, having on board 250 soldiers, proceeding from Toronto to Kingston without convoy, were captured on Lake Ontario. These losses, in addition to the alarming intelligence that the enemy was making great preparations for the conquest of Lower Canada, and that Harrison was descending Lake Erie to reinforce the American army on the Niagara frontier, compelled Vincent, whose force was now reduced to 1,200 effective men, to raise the blockade of Fort George, and retreat to his old position on Burlington Heights. This movement was effected in most excellent order, although his rear was threatened by Brigadier M'Clure with a force fully as large as his own. At Stoney Creek, his rear-guard took up a strong position, and checked the further pursuit of the enemy. At Burlington Heights, Vincent was joined by the fugitives of Proctor's division, who made up his strength to nearly 1,500 bayonets."

Emboldened by their successes, the Americans now avowed their intention of invading Lower Canada, and taking up their winter quarters at Montreal. But the Canadians interfered with these projects. After sustaining defeats at Chrysler's Farm and Chateaugay, the Americans burnt the town of Niagara, and then retreated. This measure, which turned 400 helpless women and children into the streets of Niagara homeless in the depth of winter, excited great indignation among the Canadian people. Acts of retribution followed; for as the British now defeated the Americans all along the Niagara frontier, they burnt the towns of the enemy. The campaign of 1813 closed with no advantage whatever to the Americans, and the conquest of Canada seemed as remote as ever.

When the Legislature of Lower Canada met in January, 1814, an Act was passed increasing the issue of Army Bills to £1,500,000, and votes of thanks were accorded to Colonel de Salaberry and Colonel Morrison for their victories at Chateaugay and Chrysler's Farm. Difficulties arose with the judges of the province which had not been adjusted when this last session of the seventh Parliament closed on the 17th of March. The Legislature of Upper Canada met at Toronto in February, and passed several useful measures, besides making further provision for the war.

In view of the campaign of 1814, stores of all descriptions were forwarded by sleighs from Montreal and Quebec to Kingston at enormous expense. The first military movements began near the border of Lower Canada. Wilkinson marched to the western side of Lake Champlain on the 26th of March, with the view of attacking a small British force at La Colle Mill. His army consisted of 5,000 infantry and 100 cavalry, with eleven guns. The ordinary garrison of La Colle Mill, which was under the command of Major Handcock, was under 200 men; but he hastily drew together 300 more from the adjacent stations. With this small force of 500 men, he resolved to hold a post, which a few hours' fire of well-directed artillery would have levelled to the ground, against a well-appointed army.

"At one o'clock p.m. on the 30th of March, Wilkinson, after having made a demonstration against the outpost at Burtonville, occupied the woods close to La Colle Mill with his entire force, which he deployed into line, with the view of surrounding the British position and carrying it with the bayonet. His troops cheered loudly as they advanced; but the well-aimed and rapid fire with which they were received, soon compelled them to waver, and retreat into the wood for shelter. Three guns (an eighteen, twelve, and six-pounder) were now brought to bear upon the mill, within point-blank range. But these guns were badly served, and did little injury, while the artillerymen suffered severely from the British musketry and the fire of their two guns. The enemy was also held in check on the side of the Richelieu by the fire of two sloops and two gunboats, which had advanced towards the scene of action from Isle-aux-Noix; but these had to remain too far away to do much service. Desperate as were the odds, the flank companies of the 13th Regiment, and the Canadian Voltigeurs and Fencibles, made two gallant charges, in turn, to capture the enemy's guns, but were repulsed by the sheer force of numbers, the fire of his artillery, as well as two brigades of infantry, being directed against them. For full four hours did these few hundred gallant men withstand an army. As evening approached, their ammunition began to run short. Still they did not quail. Not a man spoke of surrender; and the daring front they had shown during the day deterred the enemy from assaulting their position with the bayonet. At six o'clock, Wilkinson retreated from the Canadian gristmill, completely foiled and beaten, and retraced his steps to Plattsburg. His repulse was infinitely more disgraceful than that sustained by Abercromby before the lines of Montcalm at Ticonderoga. There the British bravely endeavoured to storm; the American army made no attempt of the kind."

After this check, the American Government abandoned the idea of subduing Lower Canada for the present; and Wilkinson, after leaving garrisons in the principal posts on Lake Champlain, moved his army to the neighbourhood of Lake Ontario to operate against the Upper Province. The campaign was opened here, under favourable auspices for Canada, by Commodore Yeo and General Drummond. Oswego was captured by the British on the 6th of May, after a sharp action, and the fort was dismantled and the barracks and bridges were destroyed. The English proceeded to blockade the whole of the American seaboard. Overtures for peace were made, but they fell through, and America still determined to pursue its designs against Canada.

On the 3rd of July, two strong brigades, under Scott and Ripley, crossed the Niagara River from Buffalo to Fort Erie. Major Buck, the Canadian commandant at Fort Erie, surrendered the post, deeming it a useless loss of life to oppose a large army of upwards of 4,000 troops with a mere handful of men. Major-General Riall, who was commanding the British on the Niagara frontier, determined to check the enemy under General Brown at Chippewa early in July. But Brown made no attempt to carry the post, remaining content with establishing his position a short distance from it.

"On the morning of the 5th, Riall, having been reinforced by the 3rd Buffs, 600 strong, from Toronto, determined to become the assailant with 1,500 regulars, 300 Indians, and 600 militia. Brown had taken up a good position: his right rested on some buildings and orchards close on the river, and was strongly supported by artillery; his left extended to a wood, with a strong body of riflemen and Indians thrown out on his flank and in advance. Riall began the battle shortly after four o'clock in the afternoon, by pushing his main body in columns of echelon against the enemy's line, with the view of breaking through, and turning it at three different points. At the same time, a body of militia, with the entire Indian force, were thrown to the right to dislodge his light troops and savages from the wood. But the Kentucky riflemen fought stoutly, while the Iroquois effectually held the Canadian Indians in check, and neither were dislodged, until assailed by the light companies of the Royal Scots and 100th Regiment. Meanwhile, the heads of the attacking columns were crushed again and again by the discharges of the long and solid American line, which stood its ground bravely, and fired with rapidity and precision. Riall, at length finding himself unable to penetrate it, was reluctantly obliged to order a retreat, having sustained a loss of 157 killed and 320 wounded. The American loss was little more than half as severe. This battle was the most considerable fought as yet during the war, and the unusual steadiness and good conduct of the American troops showed the advantage of better discipline and superior general officers. Riall made a serious mistake in attacking an army strongly posted and twice his own strength, but he had doubtless been induced to take this step from the supposition that the enemy would be beaten as easily as usual. His defeat clearly proved that the British had now to contend against abler commanders and better troops, and that a nearer equality of numbers must be possessed to ensure success. Had Riall been content to act on the defensive, and cover himself by entrenchments at the favourable ground on the eastern side of the Chippewa Creek, his position would have been very difficult to force, and the attempt could scarcely fail to have resulted in the defeat of the enemy. His desperate bravery, however, had one good effect: it showed the Americans that, if they established themselves in Canada, it would only be by very hard fighting."

The Americans made no effort to improve their victory, and Riall retreated in order. The next engagement, which was at Lundy's Lane, or Bridgwater, was a triumph for the British arms. General Drummond, having heard of the advance of a large army on the Niagara frontier, left Kingston, and proceeded thither, where he arrived on the 25th of July. Here he learned of the advance of Brown and the retreat of Riall, and he determined at once to support the latter on the enemy's rear. On reaching Lundy's Lane, with 800 regulars, Drummond found that Riall had left; but he at once recalled him. Drummond then took possession of the little eminence at Lundy's Lane, on the summit of which he placed five field-guns and two brass twenty-four-pounders. His line of battle was formed of the 89th Regiment, a detachment of the Royal Scots, the light companies of the 41st, the Glengarry Light Infantry, bodies of militia, and of the 3rd Buffs, and a squadron of the 19th Light Dragoons. The entire force amounted to only 1,600 men. The enemy's brigades, under Scott and Ripley, with the militia and cavalry under General Porter, made up General Brown's army to fully 5,000 men.

"When Drummond arrived on the ground, the enemy was already within 600 yards of the advantageous position of which he at once so promptly and skilfully took possession. He had barely time to complete his formation, when the whole front was warmly engaged. But the decision and skill of the British general had already half won the battle. The battery, so judiciously placed, was admirably served, and swept the field with terrible rapidity, while the sharp rolling volleys of the infantry held Scott's superior numbers effectually in check. For three-quarters of an hour did the battle rage on something like equal terms in point of strength; then Ripley's brigade came on the ground, with another battery of artillery, and Drummond's little army had now to contend against three times its number.

Brown at once availed himself of his superior force to outflank his opponent's line. The 25th American Regiment swept round the British left, forced it back at an angle with the centre, gained temporary possession of the road, and the enemy's cavalry, following behind, made several prisoners,—General Riall, who had been severely wounded and was passing to the rear, among the rest. But the Canadian militiamen of the left gave way no farther than the brow of the road; and there, although pressed hard by immensely superior numbers, did they gallantly hold their ground, and effectually covered the rear of the centre and right. Meanwhile, the battle raged furiously at the centre of the British line, on which the Americans made fierce and repeated attacks, but were repulsed again and again with steady valour, to be afterwards smote down with terrible carnage by the fire of the artillery as they fell back to reform. Presently, night drew its sable pall over the battle-field; still the combat raged with desperate obstinacy. The assailants, maddened by their losses, pressed forward repeatedly to capture the British guns, and even bayoneted the gunners in the act of loading, but were as often repulsed. They next pushed up their own guns within a few yards of Drummond's battery, and thus maintained a combat of artillery. At one time, led by Colonel Miller, they forced the 89th back, and captured several of the British cannon; but a vigorous bayonet charge recovered them again, and took a gun in addition from the enemy, together with several tumbrils. About nine o'clock, there was a brief lull in the battle, while Scott's brigade, which had suffered severely, was being withdrawn by Brown and placed in reserve, and Ripley's fresher troops pushed to the front. Luckily, at this time the remainder of Riall's division, whose retreat on Fort George, as already stated, had been countermanded by Drummond, came up with two guns; and having been joined on its way by 400 militia, the hard-pressed British combatants were now reinforced by 1,200 fresh troops, with some of whom their line was prolonged at the right, which it was apprehended the enemy might outflank; the rest were placed in reserve. The moon now rose dimly over the battle-field, and flung its uncertain light from behind a mass of thin feathery cloud on the hostile ranks, enabling the eye to scan the slope in front of the British position, strewed thickly with the dying and the dead, the plaintive groans of the wounded mingling strangely and chillingly the while with the dull yet terribly voluminous roar of the mighty cataract close by. The contest was again resumed. Long thin lines of fire marked the discharges of the hostile infantry, while ever and anon the artillery shot out a red volume of flame, and then its thunders reverberated across the bloody field, to waste themselves in fitful echoes amid the continuous roll of the Niagara. A momentary pause now and then succeeded, and the cries of the wounded for water fell ominously on the ears of the still uninjured. Till midnight did this terrible combat continue, when Brown, finding all his efforts fruitless to force the British position, retreated to Chippewa, leaving Drummond in full possession of the battle-field."

The battle of Lundy's Lane was the most sanguinary, and the most fiercely contested, of any fought in Canada during the war. Had the whole American army been thrown at once against the British line, Drummond must have been hemmed in, and compelled to either retreat or surrender. But Brown and Scott were not skilful military tacticians, and Drummond won the victory by sheer bravery, with the aid of a strong position.

Drummond next made a daring attempt to capture Fort Erie. He would probably have succeeded, but his third column under Colonel Fischer was unable to co-operate with him. Drummond's troops fought bravely; but a great number of them were killed by the accidental explosion of a magazine, and the remainder retreated in dismay. The British loss was very severe, 157 men being killed, 308 wounded, and 186 made prisoners. The American loss was trifling. The British also sustained another reverse at Black Rock, where Colonel Tucker was defeated, though the Americans under Gaines did not follow up their advantage. When Drummond, therefore, received reinforcements from Lower Canada, he was enabled to retain his position.

An abortive attempt was made by the Americans to recapture the Fort of Mackinaw; but the British were more fortunate in their attempts upon Maine, a large part of which they captured. In fact, the whole country from Penobscot to New Brunswick was formally taken possession of, and remained under British rule till the end of the war.

The arrival at Quebec of 16,000 men of the Duke

of Wellington's army enabled Governor-General Prevost to assume the offensive. He consequently despatched General Kempt with a portion of this force to Upper Canada, with a view to a descent on Sackett's Harbour; while a body of 11,000 troops were concentrated on the Richelieu frontier, to operate against the enemy's posts on Lake Champlain. But the naval portion of this expedition—which was composed of one frigate, the *Confiance*, one brig, two sloops, and twelve gunboats—was in a lamentable state of inefficiency.

Early in August, the American general, Izzard, moved up Lake Ontario, with 4,000 men, to reinforce the besieged troops at Fort Erie, and to enable them to assume the offensive. Lake Champlain was, therefore, left very slenderly defended, and on the 6th of September, Prevost's army appeared before Plattsburg, having met with no opposition. Plattsburg was protected by two block-houses, and a chain of strongly fortified field-works, garrisoned by 1,500 troops and militia under Brigadier Macomb. The British artillery was brought up; but Prevost delayed his attack upon the enemy's works, until he could be supported by the British squadron. It was not until the 11th that the fleet appeared, and even then the shipwrights were busy on the hull of the *Confiance*, which bore Commodore Downie's flag.

"The squadron which the British vessels were now bearing down to attack was much their superior in men, tonnage, and weight of metal, besides being supported by powerful land batteries. Still, Downie relied upon Prevost's assurance that the enemy's position would be assailed by land while he attacked his fleet, and bore gallantly down to action. But instead of supporting this movement, Prevost directed his men to cook their breakfasts. The result was what might naturally be expected. After a desperate battle, the *Confiance*, *Linnet* brig, and *Chub* sloop were compelled to strike their colours; the *Finch* struck on a reef, and was of no use during the action; and nine of the gunboats fled. Prevost at length put his attacking columns in motion; but on finding that he could not expect succour from the fleet, he immediately withdrew them, and resolved to retreat. The works could have been easily carried; a success in this way would have been a set-off to the disaster of the fleet; and nothing could have equalled the indignation of the troops when they were ordered to retreat. Many of the officers indignantly broke their swords, declaring that they would never serve again; and the army sullenly retraced its way to the Canadian frontier, undisturbed by the enemy. The disgraceful course pursued on this occasion effectually destroyed the military reputation of the governor-in-chief; and as he died before he could be tried by court-martial, the stain still rests on his memory. On board the fleet, the loss in killed and wounded was 129, while the land force lost about 200. The loss of the American fleet was nearly as severe as that of the British. Among the killed of the latter was the gallant Downie. No sooner did the American force invested at Fort Erie learn the disaster of the British at Lake Champlain, than they made a vigorous sortie on the afternoon of the 17th of September. Owing to the rain falling in torrents, they succeeded in turning the right of the besiegers' pickets, and after a sharp contest obtained possession of two batteries. But a reinforcement speedily coming up, they were at once driven back, and pursued to the very glacis of the fort, whither they retired with precipitation, having sustained a loss in killed, wounded, and missing of 509 men. The British loss amounted to 600, of whom one-half, however, had been made prisoners in the trenches at the commencement of the sortie. Finding his men becoming very sickly, and learning also the advance of General Izzard's division, Drummond raised the siege on the 21st, and retired totally unmolested on Chippewa. During the autumn months, Chauncey had the advantage, in both the number and size of his vessels, of the British squadron on Lake Ontario. At length, on the 10th of October, the *St. Lawrence*, a vessel of 100 guns, was launched at Kingston, when the American commodore immediately withdrew, and was blockaded in turn at Sackett's Harbour. The lake freed from the enemy's ships, troops and stores were conveyed to the army on the Niagara frontier; and although Izzard had now a fine force of 8,000 men at Fort Erie, he blew up its works, recrossed the river, and left the harassed people of Upper Canada to repose. Beyond a foray of mounted Kentucky brigands, who marked their course with plunder and destruction at the extreme west, the retreat of Izzard was the last event of a war which completely burst the bubble of American invasion of Canada."

THE SECOND AMERICAN INVASION. 181

On the 24th of December, 1814, a treaty was signed at Ghent, which put an end to hostilities on the American Continent, and restored peace between Great Britain and Canada and the United States. The conquests on both sides were restored, and provision was made for settling the boundaries between the United States and Canada; though these have ever since been a subject of negotiation. The second invasion of Canada was very disastrous for the United States. She acquired not a single dollar of compensation, nor a single inch of territory. On the contrary, her commerce suffered terribly by her unjustifiable action. Her export trade had fallen from £22,000,000 sterling to £1,500,000 ; nearly 3,000 of her merchant vessels had been captured ; two-thirds of the mercantile and trading classes of the nation had become practically insolvent ; and the Union was threatened with the secession of the New England States.

If every war undertaken for spoliation and conquest could be punished in the same manner, we should soon witness fewer of those aggressive wars which are a scandal to civilized and Christian nations.

CHAPTER VIII.

EVENTS FROM 1815 to 1836.

WHEN the Legislature of Lower Canada met on the 21st of January, 1815, Mr. Louis J. Papineau was elected Speaker of the Assembly. A grant of £25,000 was passed for making the Lachine Canal, and another of £1,000 per annum as salary for the Speaker. A message from the Governor officially announced the conclusion of peace, whereupon the embodied militia were immediately disbanded. Returns showed that the public revenues had now more than overtaken the expenditure, the former being £204,550, and the latter £197,250.

Sir George Prevost left the colony in April, and died in England in the ensuing January. General Drummond assumed charge of the government, and his first public act was the redemption of the Army Bills issued during the war. Early in the session of 1816, it was announced that the Prince Regent had dismissed the charges against Chief Justices Sewell and Monk; and as the Assembly insisted on further prosecuting this matter, it was dissolved, and new elections were held.

Sir John C. Sherbrooke was appointed Governor-in-Chief of Canada, and he arrived at Quebec on the

21st of July, 1816. The new Assembly was as strong as ever against the recalcitrant judges. It again elected as its Speaker L. J. Papineau, who was destined to figure prominently in Canadian affairs. Votes of relief were passed for the distressed districts, and a grant of £20,000 was made for distribution in small loans to industrious farmers. As Governor Sherbrooke disliked remaining in Canada, foreseeing that the undecided policy of the British Government must lead to difficulties, he requested his 'recall, and was succeeded by the Duke of Richmond, who arrived in Canada in July, 1818. The duke speedily came into conflict with the Legislature on the question of the expenditure and official salaries and pensions. The Legislative Council practically made the unheard-of claim that it should appoint what officers it pleased at such salaries as it pleased, and that it was the duty of the Assembly to pay the estimates without enquiry. The House naturally resented this. In addition to Sewell and Monk, two other judges, named Bedard and Foucher, were impeached for malpractices ; but owing to the difficulties of a prosecution, nothing further was effected in either case. The Governor angrily prorogued Parliament on the 24th of April, 1819, and on the 27th of August following the Duke of Richmond died suddenly, while on a tour of inspection through Upper Canada, from the bite of a tame fox, which was not known to be in a rabid state.

Monk, upon whom the government devolved, dissolved the Assembly in February, 1820, because it refused to vote the amount necessary for the civil list. The elections again resulted unfavourably for the Executive; but owing to the death of George III. another dissolution became necessary. In the meantime, the Earl of Dalhousie was sent out as Governor, and he arrived on the 18th of June. When the new Assembly met, a quarrel arose between the two Houses on the question of supply, the Upper House being in favour of centralizing all real power in the Executive, while the Lower claimed the right to dispense the public revenue. A project for a union between the Upper and Lower Provinces was now brought forward; but it caused much dissatisfaction, and the scheme was abandoned.

Lord Dalhousie governed with a high hand, and his difficulties increased yearly, the French Canadians being bitterly opposed to his policy. At length, finding that there was little prospect of the Governor making any concessions to their demands, the anti-Executive party determined, in 1828, to lay their grievances by petition before the Imperial Parliament and the Crown. These grievances were chiefly based on the unconstitutional course of the Legislative Council, in throwing out useful bills passed by the Lower House, on the arbitrary acts of the Governor, and his expenditure of the public moneys without authority from the Assembly. The names of no fewer than 87,000 persons were affixed to the petition.

"The increasing embarrassment of the administration of Lower Canada determined the British Ministry to release itself from all responsibility in the premises by submitting the matter to Parliament. On the 2nd of May, Mr. Huskisson, now Colonial Secretary, moved in the House of Commons that a select committee of twenty-one members be appointed to enquire into the civil condition of Canada. 'The Assembly,' said he, in introducing his motion, 'in order to enforce their unreasonable pretensions, have refused to appropriate any part of the large revenue of which they have the command, unless the appropriation of the Crown revenue be also given up to them.' But despite the smooth glazing over of the members of the Ministry or their supporters, the committee, on the 22nd of July, reported in favour of the Canadian petition. They recommended the abolition of the seignorial rights of the Crown, the establishment of new electoral districts more in accordance with the progress of population, and the surrender of the whole of the public revenue to the Assembly; measures to be taken, at the same time, to render the Governor, Executive Council, and the Judges independent of an annual vote of supply. They also reported in favour of allowing the Canadians to have an agent in England, and generally indorsed the prayer of the petitioners. The report of this committee of the Imperial Parliament gave great satisfaction in Lower Canada, and the Assembly ordered four hundred copies to be printed and distributed among their constituents. The success which thus met the anti-Executive party was not known in Canada till the 15th of September, a week after the departure of Lord Dalhousie, who was, therefore, spared the mortification of seeing his policy so unequivocally condemned in presence of the people of his government. In England, he subsequently endeavoured to defend the course he had pursued, but was not very successful in the attempt. A coercive policy having so far completely failed, a conciliatory one was now determined on, and Lieutenant-General Sir James Kempt, promoted from the Government of Nova Scotia, deputed to carry it out."

With regard to the position of affairs in Upper Canada, which now demands some attention, great dissatisfaction prevailed when the Legislature met in February, 1817. The Assembly voiced this feeling by going into full committee on the 3rd of April, on the state of the province, as embraced under four heads. These were the impolicy of checking emigration from the United States, the insufficiency of postal facilities, the injuries sustained by the Crown and Clergy Reserves interfering with a more complete settlement of the province, and the propriety of the King granting lands to the embodied militia who had served during the war. The Executive being diametrically opposed to such an investigation, the Governor suddenly prorogued Parliament without previous notice—a contemptuous step which aggravated the discontent.

One Robert Gourlay, an English emigrant who had recently arrived in Upper Canada, now set on foot an agitation on the question of land settlements, and the causes which were retarding the improvement of the townships. He proposed that the people should petition the Imperial Parliament to investigate the affairs of the province, and that they should employ an agent in England to support their views. He further suggested that deputies from all the townships should meet in conference at Toronto ; and he had gone so far as to draw up the draft of a petition to the Crown, when the Executive, thoroughly alarmed at the posture of affairs, seized upon a passage in the petition, charging wholesale corruption against the officials, as a pretext for prosecuting him for libel.

While the storm raged, Mr. Gore was recalled, and was succeeded as Lieutenant-Governor of Upper Canada by Sir Peregrine Maitland. Gourlay was brought to trial at Kingston, and acquitted ; and a second trial took place at Brockville on another count, but with the same result. Gourlay was now very popular ; but the Assembly, disliking the idea of conventions, pronounced them illegal, and left him to his fate. He was ordered to quit the country ; and as he refused, was again thrown into prison. Subsequently, he was compelled to leave the province.

The Family Compact, as the party of the Executive came to be known, still continued to wield its influence, and it received a great accession of strength by the appointment of Bishop Strachan, an able and resourceful man, who continued to be one of the most active members of the body until its final overthrow.

In 1821, one Barnabas Bidwell was returned as member for Lennox and Addington. It being discovered, however, that he was a person of immoral character, a fugitive from justice, and a citizen of the United States, having taken the oath of allegiance there, he was expelled the House, though only by a majority of one. After this, a residence of seven years was made necessary for eligibility on the part of foreigners to membership in the Assembly. The project of the Welland Canal was now mooted, and it was eventually carried through, chiefly owing to the exertions of William Hamilton Merritt, of the Niagara district. The canal proved of inestimable benefit in ensuring the future prosperity of Canada.

In 1824, was formed the Canada Land Company, a corporation at first productive of benefit, but subsequently of injury to the province. Under its Imperial Charter, it began to buy up vast tracts of the Clergy Reserve and Crown lands at low prices, which it sold again in small lots at a large advance. In effect, it was a huge land monopoly, and, like all monopolies, brought evils in its train. Without the wishes of the Canadian Parliament being consulted, a vast quantity of the soil was withdrawn from public purposes, and passed into the hands of private speculators on the London Stock Exchange.

When Parliament opened in January, 1825, the Reform party carried their candidate for Speaker by a majority of two, the Family Compact being at length in a minority. William Lyon Mackenzie, a Scotch emigrant, now began to acquire great influence in the affairs of Canada. He attacked Government abuses and packed juries in the columns of the *Colonial Advocate*, and indirectly he assisted in securing for Canada a large measure of liberty and self-government. Moving to Toronto, where he issued the *Advocate* as a broadsheet, Mackenzie boldly attacked the abuses of the post office and other departments, until his printing office was broken into and completely wrecked, two magistrates coolly looking on. The Governor severely condemned this conduct, and the parties were sued for damages. Mackenzie was awarded £625, which was subscribed by friends of the aggressors, who thus escaped scot-free.

Great excitement occurred at Niagara Falls in May, 1827, when one Forsyth, who owned the principal inn at the falls and considerable landed property in the district, enclosed the Crown reservation. The Governor's officials removed the fence, and Forsyth was beaten in two suits for damages; but the Governor was blamed by the Home Government for his action. A good deal of feeling arose over the Orange processions and the Clergy Reserves; and the Governor further increased his unpopularity by suspending from office Mr. Willis, a judge who would not identify himself with the Family Compact, and who dared to pursue an independent course. The elections of 1828 went in favour of the Reformers, Mackenzie being amongst the members elected; and there was much satisfaction when Sir Peregrine Maitland left to assume the government of Nova Scotia, and Sir John Colborne was appointed in his place.

When the new Parliament met in January, 1829, Marshall Spring Bidwell—a son of the Bidwell previously mentioned—was elected Speaker. The first agitation now began for responsible government; but in the following year the death of George IV. necessitated a new election. Both the Reform party and the Family Compact were now to a large extent reconstructed, the former shedding most of its republican element, and the latter assuming a wider form as the Conservative party. In the Assembly, Mackenzie gave no repose to those who held by the Family Compact, and he showed that there were very few members in the Lower House who were not either paid officials of the Government or completely under their influence. He became so dangerous, that Attorney-General Boulton and others determined he must be got rid of. Nobody was safe, if light was going to be thrown fearlessly upon every abuse, as Mackenzie threatened to do. The fact of his having circulated some copies of the journals of the House was accordingly seized upon as constituting a breach of privilege. But the discreditable plot failed by a majority of twenty to fifteen against it.

Mackenzie was now more active than ever in his agitation for reform. He got up a petition, signed by 25,000 persons, asking the King for a rectification of abuses. In addition, the King was implored to give the Legislative Assembly the full control of all the revenues of the province, and the disposal of the public lands; to permit the secularization of the Clergy Reserves; the establishment of municipal councils, law reform, the power to impeach public servants, the exclusion of judges and clergymen from Parliament, and the abolition of the right of primogeniture. All these privileges were at a later date conceded; but the mover in them now was pursued with relentless hostility within the House, though outside he was extremely popular. Soon after Parliament assembled in November, 1831, an article by Mackenzie in the *Colonial Advocate* was voted by twenty-seven to fifteen to be a gross libel and a breach of privilege. Owing to the malevolent exertions of Boulton, Attorney, and Hagerman, Solicitor-General, he was expelled the House by twenty-four to fifteen. Public indignation now rose to fever heat; and when the new elections took place in January, 1832, Mackenzie became the object of great public demonstrations, and he was triumphantly re-elected for York. Again was he expelled, only to be once more returned by an immense majority. He was now the most popular man in the province, and was chosen by a mass meeting at Toronto to act as agent in laying the petition for the redress of grievances before the King. The summer of 1832 was marked by the ravages of Asiatic cholera throughout the province, it having been conveyed over from England in emigrant vessels.

"The Legislature assembled on the 31st of October. In his opening address, the Governor alluded to the rapid increase of population by immigration, the completion of the Rideau Canal, and the almost complete disappearance of cholera. Mr. Mackenzie still continued absent in England, and was busily engaged in attracting the attention of the Colonial Office, now controlled by Lord Goderich, to the affairs of the province. One of the first measures of the session was his third expulsion from the Assembly. But he was again re-elected by acclamation, no other candidate presenting himself, and the same day the first political Reform union of Upper Canada was organized, on a basis proposed by Dr. Morrison. Five times, altogether, was Mackenzie expelled by the Family Compact majority of the Assembly, to be as often re-elected. The Home Government disapproved of their conduct in this respect. It was decidedly opposed to its Whig policy, and to the principles of Reform professed by the Imperial Parliament, and although averse to complying with all the prayers of the petitions, for which Mackenzie acted as agent, the latter had the satisfaction of seeing Attorney-General Boulton and Solicitor-General Hagerman deprived of their situations for aiding prominently in his frequent expulsion. Hagerman, however, proceeding promptly to England, soon procured his own restoration to office; while Boulton got a judgeship in Newfoundland, where he soon embroiled himself with a large section of the population, and was finally dismissed from all employment by the Imperial Government. These occurrences added largely to the intensity of party spirit, and the agitation which they aroused reacted to some extent on the Legislature, which this year passed the long and much-desired Act making the judges independent of the Crown, and enabling them to hold their office for life, provided they behaved themselves properly. This Act also declared both branches of the Legislature a competent court to try impeachments against judges, giving, however, a right of appeal to the King in Council. Thus one serious and long-standing abuse was removed, and the flagrant case of a Thorp or a Willis could never again occur in Upper Canada. In November of this year, Mackenzie discontinued the publication of his *Colonial Advocate.*"

For two or three years the Family Compact party had been powerful again; but its arbitrary action lost it many friends, and at the elections in December, 1834, the Reform party secured a majority of ten in a House of fifty-eight members. This proved the death-knell of the Family Compact, and a new and better party sprang from its ashes, which began to call itself Conservative, and which certainly pursued a more constitutional course than the old. But a great deal of discontent arose when fifty-seven rectories were set apart from the Clergy Reserves for clergymen of the Church of England. The Reform party were likewise very hostile towards the Executive, on account of its reactionary measures.

As the English Colonial Office, however, now pledged itself to a policy of conciliation, and Sir John Colborne would not carry out the new views, he was recalled, and Sir Francis Bond Head was appointed his successor in 1837.

Returning to the affairs of Lower Canada, Sir James Kempt, who became Governor-in-Chief in 1828, pursued a conciliatory policy; but the financial disputes still continued between the Assembly and the Executive. These yet remained unsettled in 1830, when Kempt was succeeded as Governor by Lord Aylmer. The Imperial duties were at length surrendered to the Executive; but when the Assembly proceeded to memorialize the Crown to make the Legislative Council elective, this was refused by Lord Stanley, the Secretary of State for the Colonies.

The demands of the Papineau or Reform party in the Assembly were now embodied in a series of Ninety-two Resolutions, on which petitions to the King, Lords, and Commons of the United Kingdom were founded. Eventually, in April, 1828, a select committee of the House of Commons was appointed, on the motion of Lord Stanley, to enquire into the alleged grievances of the inhabitants of Lower Canada. The committee was made of the widest and most liberal character, and among its members were Bulwer Lytton and Daniel O'Connell.

"The committee sat until the 3rd of the following July, examined the various petitions and documents connected with Canadian grievances, as well as several witnesses, and spared no pains to acquire a just knowledge of the questions at issue. The result of the investigation was a report, which declared in the most unequivocal language 'that the Governors of Lower Canada had been unremitting in their endeavours to carry out the suggestions of the select committee of 1828, and that any want of success on their part was entirely owing to the quarrels between the two branches of the Canadian Legislature and other local causes.' The report further stated 'that it would be inexpedient to make the documents public, which had been submitted to the committee, and that the interests of the empire would be best subserved by leaving practical measures for the future administration of Lower Canada entirely in the hands of the Imperial Government.' In other words, the committee had come to the conclusion that every reasonable concession had been made to the French majority of Lower Canada, and that no further measures of conciliation could be adopted with regard to them, without serious injury to the British portion of the inhabitants, now more than a fourth of the entire population, and representing all its great commercial and monetary interests. They could not fail to see, from their minute enquiry, and the tenor of the

Ninety-two Resolutions, the extreme views of the Assembly, and the latent desire for a total independence which pervaded all their movements, as well as their thinly concealed hostility to Great Britain."

The differences between the British and the French inhabitants of Lower Canada now became every day more marked, and rival societies were formed in support of the two factions. The disturbed feeling of the population was intensified by a second severe visitation of the cholera.

When a new Assembly met in February, 1835, Papineau was again elected Speaker, and the hostility to the Executive was as strong as ever. Preparations began to be made on both sides for a deadly struggle, and a condition of general alarm prevailed, when Sir Robert Peel succeeded to the office of Premier. He determined to send out a special commission for the examination of existing grievances; but although his administration was succeeded by that of Lord Melbourne before he could effect his purpose, his successors carried out his intention. The commissioners were the Earl of Gosford, Sir Charles Grey, and Sir George Gipps, and Lord Gosford was likewise appointed to succeed Lord Aylmer as Governor-in-Chief.

The result of the Gosford Commission was such that all real grievances were offered to be redressed in the most liberal manner, and every point in dispute consistent with the retention of Lower Canada as a British province was conceded. But Papineau and his friends refused to be conciliated. Their hatred of British ascendency had reached its culminating point, and they now aimed at total independence.

The Lower House passed a bill appointing Mr. Roebuck their agent in England, with instructions to press their grievances ; but the Legislative Council threw it out. Papineau, in violent language, then announced himself a Republican in principle, and other members followed his example. The loyal population became alarmed. The Home Government remained firm on the question of not making the Legislative Council elective, which would have given the control of both Houses to Papineau and his friends. Papineau, therefore, determined upon revolution, counting on the support of the United States. Perceiving the serious aspect of things, the British population began to form themselves into defensive associations.

Session after session still saw the same deadlock in public affairs, with Papineau the idol of the country people. Indignation meetings were held by the French element, and violent resolutions passed. Though the Governor denounced these gatherings as seditious, they still continued. William IV. died in the midst of this excitement ; but the accession of Victoria led to no improvement in Canada. Indeed, so strong was the language of Papineau and his friends, that they were dismissed from the service as officers of militia.

One more attempt was made to smooth matters by summoning the Assembly ; but as it proved as recalcitrant as ever, it was prorogued. The " Patriots," as they now called themselves, organized military associations, with the avowed object of establishing a " North-West Republic of Lower Canada." Legal prosecutions would have been of no avail. The bench, the bar, and the people were alike animated by a spirit of hostility to Great Britain, and no jury would have convicted a political criminal. As for the intervention of the military power, that could only be called upon to quell actual rebellion. Meanwhile, the Roman Catholic clergy, perceiving the dangers likely to follow the spread of the revolutionary feeling, now sought to check the progress of the storm. But there was a critical period to pass through before the clerical influence could begin to make itself felt.

CHAPTER IX.

THE REBELLION OF 1837-38.

THE desire of the British Government to preserve the French element in Canada distinct from the English, as a safeguard against revolution, had unfortunately the very opposite effect from that intended, and it precipitated the conflict Ministers were anxious to avoid.

The French, being the dominant power in Canada, became also the aggressive power, though until the time of Papineau no systematic attempt was made to excite the prejudices of the masses against the natives of British origin. Governor Prevost pursued a French policy; and while he saved the country from the Americans, he excited hopes of a future nationality. The experiment of giving an English constitution to a French population failed completely in all its leading objects, though the Colonial Office vainly strove to preserve British ascendency by making the Executive and Legislative Councils almost exclusively English, and by excluding the French majority from all posts of real influence.

Yet the British were the real reformers, although the French Canadians claimed to be the Liberal party of Lower Canada. The British procured the Constitution, and they were foremost in agriculture, trade, and commerce, in all great public measures of utility, and in seeking the social elevation of the industrial classes. The French, on the contrary, clung to ancient customs, laws, and ordinances, and remained a stationary and non-progressive population. In brief, the Lower Canadians desired to acquire the legislative and administrative power to enable them to preserve their French nationality, and to shut out British immigration, enterprise, and competition. In Upper Canada, on the other hand, five-sixths of the Reform party desired to acquire administrative influence, with the view of placing the Constitution on a more secure and permanent basis, and not with a wish to overturn it altogether. They did not object to immigration, and sought to keep up with the advancing spirit of the age. They detested the Americans even more than they did the British, and only contemplated accepting aid from the former until they could achieve their independence.

Such was the condition of affairs when Louis Joseph Papineau precipitated the Revolution of 1837. He wielded an immense influence, yet he had neither a good cause, good counsel, nor money to reward his friends. If he had succeeded, his policy was only a disintegrating one; but he was destined to be worsted in his contest with Great Britain and the hardy Anglo-Canadian population. Though distinguished as an orator and a partizan leader, he had no solid qualities, and was a miserable failure in the field. He was the very opposite to Washington, whose country was ever his first thought, as it is with all true patriots.

The eloquent agitator Papineau was forty-eight years old in 1837. He knew how to excite the passions and prejudices of his race, but he was unable to guide them in a wise course. While he carried the Lower French Canadians with him, he had no understanding of the people of Upper Canada, who were necessary to the success of his scheme. One of his principal supporters was a Frenchified Englishman named Wolfred Nelson. The peasantry elected them their leaders, the tricoloured flag was displayed, and mobs paraded the streets of St. Hyacinthe, St. Denis, St. Charles, and Montreal. But the Roman Catholic clergy now used all their influence in favour of the Government, so that the insurgents could make little headway.

In consequence of a riot in Montreal, led by a French Canadian association called the Sons of Liberty, on the 12th of November, 1837, the Governor issued a proclamation directing the suppression of all unlawful meetings, and sixty disaffected magistrates in the district of Montreal were replaced by more loyal citizens in the commission of the peace. Perceiving the crisis which was at hand, Sir John Colborne moved to Montreal, where he concentrated the troops from Upper Canada and from Quebec. Warrants were issued for the arrest of Papineau, Storrow Brown (who had led the Montreal riot), and O'Callaghan, editor of the revolutionary *Vindicator*, on charges of high treason; but they escaped.

The insurgents who assembled at St. Charles were commanded by Brown; and those who collected at St. Denis on the Richelieu were directed by Dr.

Wolfred Nelson. Nelson came from loyal and respectable parents; but being elected to Parliament for the St. Denis district, he fell under the influence of Papineau, and enthusiastically imbibed his Republican principles.

Colonel Gore was despatched from Montreal, with 200 infantry, a party of volunteer cavalry, and three guns, to attack St. Denis; and Colonel Wetherall was directed to move down the Richelieu against St. Charles. Gore reached William Henry on the 22nd, where he was reinforced by a company of infantry. All through the wintry night they marched amidst showers of sleet and rain, which froze as they fell, to St. Denis, a distance of sixteen miles. The incidents which ensued are thus described by a Canadian historian :

"Meanwhile, Wolfred Nelson had been apprised of the simultaneous movement against his post and St. Charles, and threw out scouting parties before day, on the morning of the 23rd, to watch the approach of the troops, and break down the wooden bridges to retard their advance. About two o'clock on the preceding night, Lieutenant Weir, charged with despatches for Wetherall, had been captured by the insurgent guards, and taken to Nelson's house. He was dressed in coloured clothes, stated his name and rank with considerable reluctance, and after declining to partake either of refreshment or retire to rest, was given in charge by the doctor to '*three trustworthy habitants*' to be retained as a prisoner. Shortly before day, the alarm spread far and near, and bodies of insurgent peasantry pushed rapidly in from the surrounding country to support their comrades already in the villages, where a force of 300 or 400 men was soon collected, and posted with great judgment in buildings flanking and covering one another. In reconnoitring the advancing troops, breaking down bridges, and taking up defensive positions, Nelson showed considerable military skill, and was evidently better adapted by nature for a partizan leader than for a physician or a distiller. The courage of the doctor appeared in strange contrast with the cowardice of Papineau, who since his flight from Montreal had lurked at St. Denis. Here he remained as Nelson's guest till the appearance of the troops, when, instead of heading his misguided followers like a brave man, and showing them that he could fight as well as talk, he abandoned them in the moment of danger, and fled to Yamaska on the St. Hyacinthe River, whence he subsequently made his way into the United States. No excuses, no sophistry can palliate this act. No consideration should have made him desert his friends at such a time. Had he gallantly stood his ground, and borne himself like a man, the circumstance would have atoned, in the opinion of posterity, for much of his folly; whereas, the fact of his cowardly flight must stamp him with enduring ignominy. A strong loopholed or many-windowed dwelling-house, or building of any kind surrounded by others affording positions for a flanking or cross-fire, is always an admirable defensive position, when an assailing force lacks heavy artillery. Colonel Gore found this to be the case to his cost in the attack on St. Denis. The single field-gun he had been able to bring on made little impression on the buildings of the village; and although he attempted again and again, from ten o'clock in the forenoon till four in the afternoon, to turn the insurgents' position, he was completely foiled, and thought it prudent to retreat, as the peasantry were now rapidly collecting, and he had already sustained a loss of six killed, and one officer (Captain Markham) and sixteen men wounded. Five of the latter were left behind, and treated with the utmost humanity by Nelson. After endeavouring for several hours to drag it through the horrible roads, the gun—a brass one—was spiked and abandoned. The loss of the insurgents was much greater than that of the troops, being thirteen killed and several wounded. Still, the victory was decidedly on their side, and they had effectually prevented the sheriff from executing the warrants for the apprehension of Nelson and others. But they stained their triumph by the cowardly and cruel murder of the unfortunate Weir. When the firing commenced, his guard pinioned his arms with a rope, and put him into a cart, with the view of taking him to the rebel head-quarters at St. Charles. Possibly disliking his uncomfortable position, or fancying he might be able to make his escape, he jumped from the cart ere it had quit the village, and, as it is said, in defence of the barbarous act of his murder, struck at his guards, though how, unless with his feet, it is difficult to imagine, as his arms were still bound. In the scuffle he was mercilessly shot, sabred, hacked, and stabbed, as though he had been a mad dog, and not a pinioned and defenceless human being; and when the wretched man, maimed and bleeding from numerous wounds, sought shelter beneath the cart, he was dragged forth and foully murdered in the presence of a crowd of spectators. No more savage act marks the whole annals of Canada. And yet one of the barbarous villains who perpetrated it was subsequently acquitted, at Montreal, by a perjured jury of his countrymen."

Although this victory raised the hopes of the insurgents, they were speedily dashed again by a defeat of the rebels at St. Charles, where Wetherall came up with the insurgent force under Brown. Desirous to avoid the shedding of blood, Wetherall sent word that if they dispersed peaceably they should not be injured. Brown replied that, if Wetherall's troops laid down their arms, they should be permitted to pass unmolested. This proved to be a bit of braggadocio; for before the action had fairly begun, Brown fled, leaving his followers, about 1,000 in number, to shift for themselves. Wetherall speedily captured the entrenchment, the rebel loss being about sixty killed, with a number of prisoners. Gore returned to St. Denis with a stronger force, intending to attack Nelson; but the latter had fled. All the buildings were razed to the ground.

Martial law was proclaimed in the district of Montreal on the 5th of December, and a reward of £500 was offered for the apprehension of Weir's murderers. The prompt measures taken by Sir John Colborne suppressed the rebellion along the Richelieu before it could receive aid from the United States. Lieutenant-Colonel Hughes, with his military and volunteer troops, swept the counties of the disaffected, and among the prisoners taken was Wolfred Nelson. General Colborne made a movement against St. Eustache, and on the 16th of December captured the rebel position. The loss of the insurgents was upwards of 100 killed, about the same number wounded, and 118 prisoners. The leader, Girod, like Brown at St. Charles, deserted his followers, soon after the firing commenced, under the pretence of bringing up reinforcements; but he was pursued for some days, and when he found it impossible to escape, he shot himself in the head a few miles below Montreal. General Colborne next received the surrender of 250 insurgents at Montreal, all of whom he suffered to depart except the leaders.

On the 13th of January, 1838, Lord Gosford was recalled, and Colborne assumed the reins of the civil government until his successor should arrive. In February, a rising, under Robert Nelson—brother of Wolfred—and a Dr. Cote, was suppressed, and the whole force of 600 surrendered. Meanwhile, an Act was passed in the British Parliament in February, suspending the Constitution of Lower Canada, and making temporary provision for its government by the creation of a Special Council, whose decrees were to have the same force as the acts of a Legislature. At the same time, the Earl of Durham was appointed Governor-General, and her Majesty's High Commissioner "for the adjustment of certain important affairs affecting the provinces of Upper and Lower Canada." The Special Council met at Montreal on the 18th of April, and suspended the Habeas Corpus Act until the 14th of August following. Other protective measures were taken, which came into force at once.

The Earl of Durham arrived at Quebec on the 27th of May, assumed charge of the government, and two days afterwards issued a proclamation, briefly stating the policy he proposed to pursue. " The honest and conscientious advocates of reform and of the amelioration of defective institutions will receive from me," he said, " without distinction of party, races, or politics, that assistance and encouragement which their patriotism has a right to command ; but the disturbers of the public peace will find in me an uncompromising opponent. People of British America, I beg you to consider me as a friend and an arbitrator, ready at all times to listen to your wishes, complaints, and grievances, and fully determined to act with the strictest impartiality. If you, on your side, will abjure all party and sectarian animosities, and unite with me in the blessed work of peace and harmony, I feel assured that I can lay the foundation of such a system of government as will protect the rights and interests of all classes, allay all dissensions, and permanently establish, under divine Providence, the wealth, greatness, and prosperity, of which such inexhaustible elements are to be found in these fertile countries." He amply redeemed his promise. Never did any public man act more disinterestedly than Lord Durham. His celebrated report is a lasting monument of elaborate research, impartial scrutiny, and historical worth. Considerable reinforcements had already arrived from England and Halifax, as well as several vessels of war, and the prospect of successful revolt was now more slender than ever. Still, disaffection had not yet ceased to exist, and Papineau's partizans were already organizing another armed force with a view to the establishment of the Republic of Lower Canada. One of Lord Durham's first measures was to procure an accurate return of the prisoners in the several gaols of the province, with the depositions against each, and a list of the unexecuted warrants against parties who had fled the country. The old Executive Council was next dissolved, as well as the Special Council recently constituted under the Suspension Act. A new Executive Council was, however, soon appointed. A commission formed to enquire into the mode of disposing of Crown lands brought many abuses to light. Its report was favourable to the squatters, and recommended that they should be allowed the right of pre-emption. Up to the present, no persons had been tried for high treason, and large numbers still remained in the Montreal gaol to be disposed of. In the excited state of the public mind, it would be difficult to find an impartial jury, should they be brought to trial; and Lord Durham's mission being one of peace, he was unwilling to resort to court-martial. In this dilemma, he had recourse to an expedient, which, being at variance with all established precedent and law, created a large amount of criticism in both Canada and England. It was determined to release the minor offenders; and the principal ones were induced to place themselves at the disposal of the Governor-General, waiving all right to a trial. A new Special Council was accordingly summoned, in order to give its sanction to the line of policy Lord Durham now determined to pursue. On the 28th of June, the day on which this Council assembled, they issued an edict banishing Wolfred Nelson, Bouchette, Gauvin, Viger, and five others of the leading insurgents, then in prison at Montreal, to Bermuda, and threatening the penalty of death on Papineau and others, if they returned to Canada without permission. This was certainly a high-handed procedure; but, at the same time, it released the Governor-General from a serious dilemma, leaned to mercy's side, and, although it established an arbitrary and dangerous precedent, was therefore to a great extent excusable."

The English Government approved of these measures; but the Imperial Parliament annulled Lord Durham's ordinance, though it passed an act of indemnity to shield the Governor and his Special Council from any future proceedings which might arise out of their illegal course. In Canada, the Governor's action was endorsed as being necessary, owing to the condition of the country. The acquittal of the murderers of Joseph Chartrand, a volunteer private of St. John's, in spite of the clearest evidence, as well as the acquittal of one of Weir's murderers, also did much to exonerate the Governor.

After the censure passed upon him, Lord Durham resigned his position as Governor-General, leaving Sir John Colborne in charge of the government. The loss of Lord Durham was deeply regretted by the Canadians. Although his term of office had been short, he had done more for the country than any other governor, while his admirable report to a great extent paved the way for the subsequent union of the provinces.

Early in November, 1838, a second rebellion broke out in Lower Canada, headed by Dr. Robert Nelson, who was to be president of the proposed new republic. The rising was general throughout the whole district of Montreal. Martial law was again put in force, and the Habeas Corpus Act suspended. General Colborne took the field, and moved towards Napierville, where Nelson had collected a large body of insurgents, and issued a second declaration of independence, which caused a run on the Montreal banks. The loyalist militia of Odelltown organized themselves, with the view of interrupting the communication of Nelson with Rouse's point in his rear. They took up a strong position at La Colle Mill, where they were reinforced by the Hemmingford militia. A considerable body of insurgents under Cote and Gagnon endeavoured to dislodge them; but they were severely defeated, and the whole body driven into rapid and inglorious flight.

"Nelson's position at Napierville now became extremely critical. In his rear was the victorious frontier militia; while Sir John Colborne was steadily advancing against his front, with an overwhelming force of regular infantry and cavalry. He accordingly determined to fall back upon Odelltown with part of his forces, disperse the militia, 200 in number, posted there, and thus open his line of communication with the United States, so as to secure a safe retreat in case of necessity. In pursuance of this resolution, he moved against Odelltown, on the morning of the 9th, with 800 men armed with muskets and fowling-pieces, and 200 more carrying pikes and swords.

Fortunately, as this formidable force was about to enter the village, Lieutenant-Colonel Taylor, an officer sent out expressly from England to organize the militia, arrived on the ground, assumed command of the 200 loyalists, and posted them in the Methodist church, or in good position close by. Nelson began the battle at eleven o'clock by driving in Taylor's advanced picket, and then moved his force in solid column against the church. The gun captured at La Colle now did good service. Loaded with grape, its first discharge raked the advancing enemy with deadly effect, and opened a long lane through his ranks. Two other discharges were also given with success; but the insurgents pushed boldly on, and soon compelled the gunners to abandon it, and retire to the church, on the road immediately by which it was posted. Again and again did the enemy endeavour to capture this gun ; but the militia, although harassed and fatigued by long and arduous duty, fought stoutly, swept them back with close and well-aimed volleys, and even sallied out and made repeated charges with the bayonet. For two hours and a half did the action continue, and then, repulsed in every attempt to carry the church, the appearance of a body of a hundred militia, advancing to aid their comrades on their flank, completely disheartened the insurgents, who fled in every direction—part back to Napierville, another across the lines into the United States. Among the latter was Robert Nelson, who, soon procuring a horse, rode full speed to Plattsburg. Previous to the battle, some of the insurgents suspected he was about to desert them, and were with difficulty prevented from giving him up to Sir John Colborne. He gladly seized the first opportunity, therefore, to escape from his *Patriot* associates, and leave them to their fate. In this action, the loss of the rebels was nearly sixty killed, besides a large number wounded. The loyalists had one captain (M'Allister) and four men killed, and one lieutenant and nine men wounded. A considerable body of insurgents still remained at Napierville; but on the approach of General Colborne, they betook themselves to flight. The British cavalry, who made several prisoners, started rapidly in pursuit, and the chase was continued from daylight till the evening of the 10th."

Insurgent bodies at Beauharnois and Chambly were next defeated and dispersed, and in the short space of seven days the second Lower Canadian rebellion was suppressed. It was felt that the lenity displayed towards the prisoners in the first insurrection would now be entirely misplaced, and would afford no hope for the future safety of the country. As trial by jury would have proved abortive, a court-martial assembled for the trial of the captive insurgents. Twelve suffered the extreme penalty of the law, and a number of others were sentenced to transportation.

As to events in Upper Canada during this critical period, Major Sir Francis Bond Head had been appointed Governor. Sir Francis proved a rash and headstrong governor, who sought to retain power in his own hands by pitting Reformers against Tories in his councils. As an agitator, he beat Bidwell and Mackenzie on their own ground. By votes of the Assembly, he was requested to carry out responsible government, but refused. He dissolved Parliament, and the Reform party were beaten at the elections. Mackenzie, Bidwell, and other popular leaders were among the defeated ; and Mackenzie now apparently gave up all hopes of redress of existing evils by constitutional means, and secretly resolved to have recourse to illegal measures to carry out his views. He issued a newspaper called the *Constitution*, which did much to inflame the public mind, and pave the way for rebellion.

Although Sir Francis B. Head had secured a triumph at the elections, he began to experience considerable friction with the Colonial Office. Lord Glenelg, the Colonial Secretary, directed the Lieutenant-Governor to carry out responsible government in Upper Canada, but he refused, and the Home Government hesitated in recalling him. In the spring of 1837, a commercial crisis arose in the province, and Parliament was summoned to deal with it. Fortunately, sound maxims of political economy prevailed ; specie payment was continued, the banks safely weathered the storm, redeemed their bills when presented, and thus preserved the credit of the province untarnished.

But there was a storm approaching of another character. The vast majority of the Reform party were sincerely attached to the connection with the mother country, and they never dreamed that Mackenzie, Rolph, and other popular leaders had formed the design of establishing a republic by open rebellion, thus abandoning the constitutional and legal position they had hitherto occupied for an illegal and treasonable one. Yet there was already a secret correspondence with the insurgent leaders in Lower Canada, and a line of operations had been agreed upon ; while vigilance committees were being organized, and other treasonable measures set on foot. In spite of all this, Sir Francis B. Head himself still disbelieved in any idea of rebellion. He even sent troops away from the province, neglected to embody militia in their place, and committed the care of 4,000 stand of arms and accoutrements in Toronto to the city corporation.

Mackenzie and his sympathizers, however, were making active preparations for revolt ; and when at length the Governor called out the militia, Mackenzie in his newspaper called upon the people to rise. This being an overt act of treason, a warrant was issued for his arrest ; but he fled before he could be apprehended. Shortly afterwards, he was advancing to attack Toronto, at the head of a band of armed followers. Organized bands from various parts of the country had been directed to meet at Yonge Street, about four miles from Toronto, on the 7th of December. It was expected that the insurgent force would then be 4,000 strong, and the plan was to seize upon the arms in the City Hall, and to capture the Governor and his chief advisers, and hold them in safe custody. Indefinite rumours of these plans reached the Executive ; but they were discredited, and the Governor went on his course in blind security. In all probability, the city would have been captured, had not Dr. Rolph deranged Mackenzie's plans by altering the date of the attack from the 7th to the 4th. Van Egmond, an old French colonel, was appointed commander of the insurgent army, which also included Lount and other officers.

At last the flames of insurrection burst forth, and Lieutenant-Colonel Moodie lost his life in riding to Toronto to warn Sir Francis B. Head of the approach of the insurgents. Alderman John Powell had already done this, however, though he had been compelled to shoot down a prominent insurgent named Anderson, who was taking him prisoner, before he could make for the city. Anxiety now prevailed where security had hitherto been felt. The insurgent gathering swelled to 800 men, armed with rifles, fowling-pieces, and pikes. Every preparation was made by the authorities to strengthen the weak force in the city; but every effort would probably have been in vain, had the insurgents made the most of their advantages.

"Alarmed at the prospect of an immediate attack," remarks Macmullen, "and desirous to gain time, the Governor at midday sent the secret traitor Rolph and Robert Baldwin to the insurgents with a flag of truce, ostensibly to learn what they demanded. Mackenzie replied that they wanted independence; and added that, as they had no confidence in the Governor's word, he would have to put his message in writing, and within one hour. As two o'clock approached, the insurgents advanced towards the city, and were met at its immediate borders by a second flag of truce, bringing answer that their demand could not be complied with. But their farther advance was now stayed, by the secret advice of Rolph to wait till six o'clock, and enter the city under cover of night, when the disaffected there, to the number of 600, would be prepared to join them. At the appointed hour they again moved forward, and when within half a mile of the city were fired upon by a picket of loyalists, concealed behind a fence, and who immediately afterwards retreated. This unlooked-for attack produced the greatest confusion among the insurgents, who, after firing a few shots in return, were soon speeding away in disorderly flight, leaving one of their number killed, and two wounded, behind. Mackenzie endeavoured to rally the flying mob; but they absolutely refused to renew the attack, the majority throwing away their arms and returning to their homes. During the night, a few fresh bodies of insurgents came up; but on the following day, Mackenzie's force, all told, had dwindled down to about 500 men. Despairing of success, Rolph had fled to the United States during the preceding night, and was speedily followed by a number of others, who had effectually compromised themselves. Meanwhile, intelligence had spread far and wide that the rebels had advanced against Toronto. At two o'clock on Tuesday afternoon, Sir Allan M'Nab learned the news at Hamilton, and immediately mounting his horse he rode to the wharf, seized a steamboat lying there, put a guard on board, and despatched messengers in various directions to summon loyal men to the rescue. In three hours' time, that steamer was under weigh, freighted with stout hearts and stalwart arms, to be received at Toronto with cheers, that, reverberating to Government House, told the anxious Sir Francis B. Head that the 'men of Gore' had first arrived to aid him. Next day, the loyal militia crowded in to his assistance from all directions, and were armed and organized as well as circumstances would permit. Early on Thursday morning, Van Egmond arrived to take command of the insurgents, and detached a force of sixty men to cut off communication with Toronto to the eastward, burn the Don bridge, capture the mail from Montreal, and draw out the force of the enemy in that direction. They succeeded in capturing the mail and setting the bridge on fire; but the flames were shortly afterwards extinguished, and no intelligence of consequence was acquired by the insurgents. Meanwhile, it having been determined to attack their main body at Montgomery's Tavern, on Gallows' Hill, every preparation was fully made by eleven o'clock. Six hundred men, with two field-pieces, formed the main column of attack, under Sir Allan M'Nab, while another force of 320 men were detached to take the insurgent position in flank. It was situated at a small wood near the road, which afforded partial cover to some 400 badly armed men, who still clung to the desperate fortunes of their leaders. Their defence was of the weakest kind. The fire of the artillery speedily drove them from their first position, when a few volleys of musketry and a bayonet charge put them into rapid flight, hotly pursued by the enraged militia. The loss of the insurgents was thirty-six killed and fourteen wounded, while the loyalist force only sustained a loss of three slightly wounded. Little mercy was shown to the defeated, and two trembling prisoners were alone brought in, to be immediately discharged by the Governor, who subsequently directed Montgomery's Tavern, and the dwelling of Gibson, a member of the

Assembly, and who had a command under Mackenzie, to be burned down. During their stay at Gallows' Hill, the insurgents made prisoners of fifty-four loyalists, who were treated as well as circumstances permitted of, and were not subjected to any cruelty whatever. And thus terminated the attempt to capture Toronto."

By great good fortune, the insurgents had not been led by skilled and capable men, otherwise the result must have been different ; and if Toronto had fallen, the insurrection would have spread through the whole province.

A reward of £1,000 was offered for the capture of Mackenzie, but he escaped to Buffalo; and rewards of £500 each were offered for the capture of David Gibson, Samuel Lount, Silas Fletcher, and Jesse Loyd, the other principal rebel leaders. Rolph had already escaped, and Bidwell exiled himself, and became a citizen of the United States, settling in New York city, where he acquired fame as a lawyer. Kingston and Toronto were placed in positions of defence, Conservatives and moderate Reformers alike rallied round the Government, and thousands of militia came in to proffer their loyal services. Dr. Duncombe attempted a rising in the London district ; but it was speedily quelled, and Duncombe, like other rebel leaders, took to flight, leaving his deluded followers to shift for themselves.

Mackenzie got together a band of insurgents and adventurers at Buffalo—Canadians and Americans— and he and Rolph and the other members of the executive committee placed at the head of it a clever but unscrupulous person of the name of Van Rensselaer. Mackenzie made himself ridiculous by offering £500 for the apprehension of Sir F. B. Head. The insurgent force, to the extent of 1,000 strong, gathered on Navy Island, near Niagara. They were mostly of a worthless American type, and few responsible Canadians joined the rising. Open American aid was furnished to the so-called " Patriots," and the *Caroline* steamboat was employed to convey men and stores from the mainland to Navy Island. Governor Head gave permission for the *Caroline* to be captured, and she was gallantly boarded and taken by a detachment under Lieutenant Drew of the Royal Navy. An apology was subsequently made for the destruction of the vessel to the United States.

The Legislature met in December, and suspended the Habeas Corpus Act. In January, 1838, Van Rensselaer was driven from Navy Island to the American mainland. The " Patriots," under a Scotchman named Sutherland, next threatened Amherstburg. They were in considerable force, and the loyal militia of the district hastily assembled to repel them. But Sutherland retreated to one of the American islands instead of beginning the attack. The militia captured the rebel schooner *Anne*, and drove the insurgents from Point Pele Island.

Meanwhile, the Home Government had recalled Sir Francis B. Head, and appointed Sir George Arthur in his place. The new Governor arrived at Toronto on the 23rd of March. Imprisoned " Patriots " were now put on trial at Hamilton and Toronto, and the insurgents at large desisted at present from their

THE REBELLION OF 1837-38. 219

designs. But the Government distributed troops all along the frontier, while strong positions were soon held by 40,000 of the most efficient militia in the world. Lount and Matthews, two leaders of Mackenzie's attack upon Toronto, were executed for treason, but mercy was shown to the political prisoners generally.

A dastardly outrage was committed on the 29th of May, when a ruffianly gang, under one Johnson, boarded the *Sir Robert Peel*, one of the finest steamboats plying on the St. Lawrence, turned the passengers adrift, rifled the vessel, and then set on fire and destroyed it. The Governor of New York State took immediate measures to arrest the perpetrators, but the leader escaped; and he, with some others of his stamp, followed up his previous act by spoliations on land.

On the 12th of November, a body of 250 insurgents, led by Von Schultz, a Polish adventurer, landed at Prescott, on the Canadian side, and took up a strong position at Windmill Point, a little distance away. Von Schultz expected to be joined by many of the Canadians, but in this he was completely disappointed.

"By the morning of the 13th, a force of over 400 militia and 80 regulars had been drawn together, and, supported by the *Victoria* and *Coburg*, armed steamers, moved forward at seven o'clock under the command of Major Young, one of the military officers sent out from England to organize the militia, to dislodge the enemy from the breastwork he had formed, by connecting the stone walls around the mill with entrenchments of earth. The 'Patriots' fought desperately, but were gradually driven from point to point, and finally compelled to take shelter in the stone buildings within their position, where, as the attacking force had no artillery, and the guns of the steamers made no impression on the mill, they were permitted for the present to remain. Strong pickets, however, were posted so as to prevent their escape during the ensuing night. The loss of the Canadians during this action was severe. Two officers and six men were killed, and three officers and thirty-nine men were wounded. The ' Patriots ' suffered still more severely. Two of their officers and eleven men had been killed, a large number wounded, and thirty-two taken prisoners. During the battle, several boats filled with men had attempted to cross from the opposite side, but were prevented by the armed steamers. The American shore was crowded with spectators, who cheered vigorously whenever they supposed their countrymen had the advantage of the Canadians. Meanwhile, the schooners, which had sought shelter near the American shore, were taken possession of by a United States marshal, aided by some troops. The steamer *United States* was also seized, and the unhappy adventurers at Windmill Point left to their fate, although they repeatedly begged to be taken off. During the 14th, the enemy was permitted to retain his position undisturbed, the *Experiment* keeping a sharp watch to prevent his escape. On the following day, heavy artillery was forwarded from Kingston, as well as a body of troops, under Lieutenant Colonel Dundas ; but owing to some delays, these did not reach Prescott till the afternoon of the 16th. As night approached, the troops and militia moved forward to the assault, and being well supported by the fire of their guns, the 'Patriots' were soon driven from the dwelling-houses, and compelled to retreat to the mill. This effectually resisted the fire of the artillery ; but its destruction being apprehended by the 'Patriots,' who still numbered over a hundred, they surrendered at discretion. Several others were afterwards captured, who had hidden in the vicinity, so that 130 were taken altogether, of whom several were wounded ; their loss in killed was probably about fifty, there being no certainty on this point, many of the dead being burned in the buildings. On the side of the Canadians, only one soldier was killed, and a few wounded in the final assault."

The movement against Amherstburg, which also proved unsuccessful, was intercepted at Sandwich, a village two miles away. The insurgents were defeated. They had disgracefully stained their character by the brutal murder of Surgeon Hume, of the regular army, who happened to meet them when some of them were wounded, and offered his medical aid. Vengeance was quickly exacted for this by Colonel Prince, who unfortunately marred his victory by ordering four prisoners to be shot. The insurrection now died out, the last painful incident in the rebellion being the melancholy death of nineteen insurgents, who were frozen to death on the shore near Detroit.

The rising having been suppressed, courts-martial assembled at Kingston and London, for the trial of the prisoners taken in arms at Prescott and Windsor.

Von Schultz, and nine others, chiefly Americans, were executed at Kingston. Three were executed at London for an outrage committed at Windsor, several were also executed in Lower Canada, and a large number from both provinces were transported to the penal settlements at New Holland. The bulk of the prisoners taken at Prescott, being under age, were pardoned, and allowed to return to their homes.

The insurrection had its disastrous side in dislocating trade and commerce, and it also involved a large expenditure to the State. The moral blame for the rebellion very largely attaches to the name of William Lyon Mackenzie. This man of restless spirit and energies had led a chequered career, and he was so unstable that he was constantly in difficulties of some kind or other. His action was such that probably the taint of insanity was already at work in his mind, for he ultimately died of softening of the brain. Like Gourlay in Lower Canada, he completely failed in his aims and intentions; and well was it for the future of the two provinces that the projects of these two men were successfully overthrown.

CHAPTER X.

UNION OF UPPER AND LOWER CANADA.

THE insurrection having been quelled, in 1839 the two Canadian provinces completed the various military works in progress. Every important defensive position was re-established, and the entire Canadian frontier from Maine to Michigan was placed in a state of security. The militia was reorganized as a permanent corps, with a certain number of years' service. For Upper Canada alone, the militia army list showed 106 complete regiments; and with a total population of 450,000, the province could readily assemble 40,000 men in arms. The regular army in Canada consisted, in 1839, of seventeen regiments of the line, one regiment of Cavalry, and a proper proportion of the Royal Artillery, Sappers, Miners, and Royal Engineers. A naval force was also stationed on Lakes Ontario and Erie.

The finances of the Upper Province were unfortunately in a bad condition, and the Governor drew attention to the urgency of this in opening the session of 1839, as also to the necessity for settling the question of the Clergy Reserves. The publication of Lord Durham's report early in the year led to the feeling that the union of the sister provinces would be an excellent remedy for many of the evils under which both were suffering. The Assembly passed a resolution in favour of union, but it was thrown out in the Upper House. An Act was passed giving the Government the control of the Welland Canal; but an attempt to settle the Clergy Reserves difficulty proved abortive. Mackenzie, who was now at Rochester, was arrested, and indicted for promoting armed expeditions against Upper Canada to overturn its government. He was found guilty, and sentenced to eighteen months' imprisonment in the gaol of Monroe County, and to pay a fine of ten dollars.

Sir John Colborne, having been appointed Governor-General of the Canadas, continued the measures necessary for their complete pacification. Being indisposed, however, by reason of his long and arduous exertions, he was recalled at his own request, and Mr. Poulett Thomson arrived at Quebec in October as his successor. The new Governor, who was subsequently created Lord Sydenham, was a very capable statesman and able financier, and a close student of human nature. Though his appointment was not received with much favour in Canada in the outset, it was ultimately acknowledged that he was one of the best governors ever sent out from England.

The Home Government at length came to the conclusion that it would be the best policy to effect a union between the two provinces, and to concede responsible government to the majority which supported British rule. The Governor-General agreed with this, and he perceived the necessity for making the Executive Council harmonize with the House of

Assembly, by rendering its principal members dependent for their position on the majority in the latter, as in England. In this way the Canadian Ministry would be directly responsible to the people. But the difficulties in the way were great, as there was no one party entirely in favour of union. Nevertheless, the Governor went to work with the materials he had, and by the straightforward methods which he pursued he was enabled in the end to achieve success.

At a meeting of the Special Council held at Montreal on the 11th of November, the Governor brought the question of union before it, strongly recommending it in the interests of peace and the prosperity of the country. "Mutual sacrifices," said his Excellency, "were undoubtedly required, and mutual concessions would be demanded; but I entertain no doubt that the terms of the union would be finally adjusted by the Imperial Parliament, with fairness to both provinces, and with the utmost advantage to their inhabitants."

On the 13th, a series of six resolutions were agreed to by the majority of the Special Council, as the basis on which they were willing to unite the Lower with the Upper Province. The wishes of the French population were not consulted in this matter, for they had forfeited all right to consideration; but the policy which was soon carried proved as much to their benefit as to that of the loyal population.

The preliminary steps towards union having been completed in Lower Canada, the Governor-General then proceeded to the Upper Province, arriving at Toronto on the 21st of November. On the following day, he assumed temporary charge of the Administration, and was sworn in at the council chamber, when the Lieutenant-Governor, Sir George Arthur—who was opposed to responsible government—placed the Great Seal of the province in his hands. The Legislature of Upper Canada met on the 3rd of December, and the Governor-General addressed it in a judicious speech. He knew that there was considerable opposition to the union scheme in some quarters. The Family Compact saw that its monopoly of seats, offices, and positions must be destroyed if it were carried. Fortunately, the Governor-General published at the right moment a lucid despatch from Lord John Russell in support of his views. In the course of a few days, the scheme got through the Upper House, and no further difficulty was apprehended. The House of Assembly had already favourably considered the measure, and it now proceeded to pass resolutions in accordance with the recommendation in the Governor-General's message. Thus was a great question finally set at rest.

The sanction of the Imperial Parliament was now alone necessary to complete the work, and Lord Sydenham forwarded to England the draft of a Union Bill, principally prepared by Sir James Stuart. This bill provided for the union under the name of the Province of Canada.

"For the constitution of one Legislative Council and one House of Assembly, under the title of 'The Legislative Council and Assembly of Canada.'

"The Council not to be composed of fewer than twenty natural-born or naturalized subjects of the

Queen, the tenure of such office being for life, excepting the member chooses to resign, is absent from his duties without cause or permission for two successive sessions, shall become a citizen or subject of any foreign power, or become bankrupt, an insolvent debtor, public defaulter, or attainted of treason, or be convicted of felony, or of any infamous crime.

"The Speaker of the Legislative Council to be appointed by the Governor, who may remove him and appoint another. Ten members to constitute a quorum, including the Speaker.

"The Houses of Assembly to consist of members chosen from the same places as heretofore divided into counties and ridings in Upper Canada; but that the counties of Halton, Northumberland, and Lincoln shall each be divided into two ridings, and return one member for each riding. That the city of Toronto shall have two members; and the towns of Kingston, Brockville, Hamilton, Cornwall, Niagara, London, and Bytown one each. That in Lower Canada every county heretofore represented by one member shall continue to be so represented, excepting Montmorency, Orleans, L'Assomption, La Chesnaye, L'Acadia, La Prairie, Dorchester, and Beauce. These to be conjoined as follows : Montmorency and Orleans into the county of Montmorency; L'Assomption and La Chesnaye to be the county of Leinster; L'Acadia and La Prairie, that of Huntingdon; and Dorchester and Beauce, that of Dorchester; and each of these four new counties to return one member. The cities of Quebec and Montreal to return two members each, and the towns of Three Rivers and Sherbrooke one each. The qualifications of a member to be those of *bona-fide* possession of landed estate worth £500 sterling. The English language only is to be used in all written or printed proceedings of the Legislature.

"The passing of any bill to repeal the provision of the 14th George III., or the Acts of 31st of the same reign, relating to the government of the province of Quebec, and the dues and rights of the clergy of the Church of Rome; the allotment or appropriation of lands for the support of a Protestant clergy ; the endowments of the Church of England, or its internal discipline or establishment, or affecting the enjoyment or exercise of any form or mode of religious worship in any way whatever ; or which may affect her Majesty's prerogative touching the waste lands of the Crown, must be first submitted to the Imperial Parliament previous to the declaration of the sovereign's assent ; and if the Imperial Legislature shall petition the Queen to withhold her assent within thirty days after such Act shall have been received, it shall not be lawful to affix the royal assent thereto. The levying of Imperial and Colonial duties ; the appointment of a court of appeal ; the administration of the civil and criminal laws ; the fixation of the Court of Queen's Bench within the late province of Upper Canada ; and the regulation of trade were provided for—as well as the consolidation of all the revenues derivable from the colony into one fund, to be appropriated for the public service of Canada."

Out of this Consolidated Fund, £45,000 was to be payable to her Majesty, her heirs and successors, for the purpose of defraying the expenses of the administration of government and the laws. A further sum of £30,000 was to be paid out of the Consolidated Fund for defraying the various salaries of officials and others employed under Government. The total sum of £75,000 thus raised and paid for the Civil List, to be accepted and taken by her Majesty by way of civil list, instead of all territorial and other revenues then at the disposal of the Crown. The first charge upon the Consolidated Revenue Fund to be its collection, management, and receipt; the second, the public debt of the two provinces at the time of the union; the third, the payment of the clergy of the Church of England, Church of Scotland, and the ministers of other Christian denominations, agreeably to previous laws and usages; the fourth charge to be the civil list of £45,000; and the fifth, that of £30,000, payable during the lifetime of her Majesty, and for five years after her demise. The sixth charge to be that of the expenses and charges before levied and reserved by former Acts of the two provinces as long as they are payable. All bills for appropriating any part of the revenues of the united province to originate with the Governor, who shall have the right of initiating the same, as well as of recommending the appropriation of any new tax or impost, and that, having thus been recommended, the Legislative Assembly shall first discuss the same. The formation of new townships to originate with the Governor, as well as the appointment of township officers. Power was vested in the Queen to annex the Magdalen Islands to the Government of the Island of Prince Edward, in the Gulf of St. Lawrence; and with her lay the appointment of Governor of the province of Canada—to be understood as meaning Governor, Lieutenant-Governor, or person authorized by her Majesty, her heirs and successors—to execute the office of Governor of that province.

On receiving intelligence of the proceedings in the Legislature of Upper Canada, Lord John Russell laid the Union Bill before the House of Commons. With the exception of clauses for the creation of municipal councils, which were properly left for local legislation, the Bill passed through both Houses, and received the royal assent on the 23rd of July. Owing, however, to a suspensory clause, it did not take effect until the 10th of February, 1841, when it was declared in force by proclamation. Another important stage in the history of Canada was attained by the passing of this Act of Union.

CHAPTER XI.

GOVERNORS FROM SYDENHAM TO HEAD.

THE session of 1840 was rendered important by the passing of a Clergy Reserves Act. This Act empowered the Governor to sell the Reserves—part of the proceeds to be applied for payment of the salaries of the existing clergymen of the Church of England. One half of the remainder was to go to the Churches of England and Scotland, in proportion to their respective numbers; the other half to all other denominations of Christians recognized by the existing laws. The measure, however, did not finally settle this vexed question. Another triumph for which the Reform party had long struggled was likewise secured this session; namely, the engrafting of the principle of responsible government upon the Constitution of Canada.

The monument raised on Queenston Heights to the memory of the gallant Brock was shattered by an explosion of gunpowder on the 17th of April, 1840. It was the work of some ruffianly enemy of Canada, who was never discovered; but a great meeting was at once held, and a movement for another monument inaugurated.

In February, 1841, the Lieutenant-Governorship of Upper Canada ended, and Sir George Arthur retired. The elections for the province were held in April, and a small Reform majority was returned. An Executive Council for United Canada was also summoned, and various official appointments were made. The Legislature met at Kingston in June, and the session was opened by the Governor-General in person.

Lord Sydenham, however, had great difficulties to grapple with in administering the government. He had to contend against Tory prejudices on the one hand, and extravagant Reform expectations on the other. Mr. Robert Baldwin, Solicitor-General, and the principal leader of the constitutional Reformers, resigned, and threw in his lot with the opposition, which consisted of twenty French members and fifteen Upper Canadian Reformers. The formation of the Legislative Council likewise engendered much dissension. But the Governor-General nobly laboured on behalf of the best interests of Canada. He took over the Welland Canal for the Government, and through the Executive introduced into the Legislature bills for revising the customs laws, regulating the currency, promoting education, creating an efficient Board of Works, and erecting municipal corporations or district councils. He also did much towards healing the political feuds in the Legislature, and inducing all parties to unite on measures for the public good.

But the Governor-General's incessant toils told upon his naturally delicate constitution, and an accident which occurred to him by a fall from his horse on the 4th of September hastened his end. Canada's ablest governor, as well as one of her greatest benefactors, died on the 19th of September, 1841. " Short as his administration had been," remarks one historian, "his wise and vigorous policy had effected an immense improvement in the condition of these provinces. He found them suffering from recent intestine rebellion and foreign lawless aggression, their exchequer empty, their inhabitants mistrusting one another; and left them in the enjoyment of peace, mutual confidence in a measure re-established, restored credit, and the possession of a system of government which promised the most beneficial results, while the union with the mother country was placed on the broad and secure basis of mutual interest and natural affection. The name of Wolfe is a great one in Canadian annals, and that of Brock will never be forgotten by its people; the memory of Sydenham, the merchant pacificator of Canada, is equally worthy of reverence and honour. His reputation was a Canadian and not an English one; and when he desired to be buried at Kingston, he felt he was about to lay his ashes amid a people with whose history he must be for ever associated. No column as yet has arisen to honour him, but the union itself is a fitting monument to his memory; and the national peace and prosperity which it has produced should teach every true patriot to cherish that memory with gratitude and respect."

On the day before Lord Sydenham's death, Parliament had been prorogued by his deputy, General Clitherow. Three days later the *Kingston Herald* wrote: "It is finished! Parliament is prorogued, and the Governor-General is no more. *Sic transit gloria mundi!* Let us now be calm, and reflect on these occurrences as men and Christians. The first Parliament of United Canada has ended well—well beyond all expectation, and much good has been achieved. The main positions of the new Government have been sustained, and some of the most essential measures of reform effected. Conflicting opinions have not been carried out to an injurious extent in any way, and the members have all parted in good humour." The creator of the new Canada passed away just as he had affixed his signature to the Acts passed by the first Legislature of United Canada.

The Tories having come into office in England, they appointed as Sydenham's successor Sir Charles Bagot, a High Churchman and a Tory, imagining that he would carry out their views. But the new Governor-General, who arrived at Kingston in January, 1842, first made himself acquainted with the state of parties and the position of public affairs, and then determined to use that party which should be found most capable of supporting a Ministry. He accordingly made overtures to the French Canadians, and that section of the Reform party of Upper Canada, led by Mr. Baldwin, who then formed the opposition. The new Ministry included a man whose name afterwards figured prominently in the history of Canada, Mr. Francis Hincks, who was appointed Inspector-General of Public Accounts. Matters were progressing favourably, when, owing to failing health, Bagot requested his recall, and he died in England in the following year.

Sir Charles Metcalfe was now appointed Governor-General of Canada, and he arrived at Kingston on the 25th of March, 1843. He was a self-made man, and a man of much ability; but he soon showed a decided bias towards the Conservative party, led by Sir Allan M'Nab, and an open rupture ensued with the Reform party. When the Governor-General sought to form an irresponsible Cabinet for a time, his proceedings were severely denounced. In June, 1844, the seat of government was removed to Montreal. Parliament was dissolved, and the new elections gave a small Conservative majority. Shortly afterwards the Governor-General was raised to the peerage, and his policy was sustained by the Home Government. In 1845, however, Lord Metcalfe began to find that his policy was not appreciated by the country; and as he was suffering from cancer in the cheek, he requested his recall, and died shortly afterwards in England from this painful malady. Although his government was not successful, Lord Metcalfe was highly esteemed for his kindly disposition and private liberality.

Lieutenant-General Earl Cathcart, commanding the forces in Canada, temporarily assumed the government. He took no part in the political disputes of the rival parties. His administration was chiefly distinguished by an agitation with regard to the payment of losses caused by the destruction of property in Lower Canada during the rebellion. A commission was appointed, which reported on the claims made, some of which were deemed to be altogether inadmissible, and others as entirely too extravagant. But there was a total want of legal authority strictly to examine into and apportion the claims. Nevertheless, the Conservative Ministry under Mr. Draper drew up a bill as a basis for legislation, dealing with these losses.

At this juncture the Earl of Elgin—a man of culture

and refinement, like his father, the donor of the Elgin marbles—was appointed Governor-General of Canada, and he arrived at Montreal on the 30th of January, 1847. Party spirit was at a fever heat in the city, the Draper Administration was tottering towards its fall, and the Reform party was already agitating again upon the question of the Clergy Reserves. Yet all parties united in a work of philanthropy, and sent generous contributions to the famine-stricken population of Ireland. But a great immigration to Canada now set in, threatening fresh difficulties for Canada. Many of the poor suffering people came from Ireland, and up to the 7th of August, 1847, no fewer than 70,000 immigrants had landed at Quebec.

Parliament was dissolved in December, and at the general election held in January, 1848, the Reform party was victorious, and all its leaders were amongst the successful candidates. Papineau and Wolfred Nelson were in this Parliament; but the former had entirely lost his popularity, while the latter had repented of his revolutionary folly, and was now a loyal British subject.

A Lafontaine-Baldwin Ministry was constituted, in which Hincks again became Inspector-General. The country was quite tranquil when the new Parliament met in January, 1849. In his opening speech, the Governor-General announced the speedy completion of the St. Lawrence Canals, and the transfer of the Post-Office Department to the provincial authorities. A stormy debate took place on a measure introduced by Mr. Lafontaine for the payment of the losses sustained during the rebellion. The opposition complained that persons implicated in the rebellion were to receive payment for losses; and that it was unjust to charge this payment on the Consolidated Fund of the country, thus making Upper Canada liable for its proportion. On the other hand, the Ministerialists urged that it was not the intention to pay one shilling to parties concerned in the rebellion, but only to reimburse those whose property had been wantonly destroyed; that the present Government were merely carrying out the views of their Conservative predecessors; and that, as the payment of the Upper Canada losses had been drawn from licences forming part of the Consolidated Fund, it was no injustice to make that fund also liable for the same purpose in the sister province.

But explanations were of no avail. The cry of "No pay to rebels" was raised, and great popular excitement ensued, the old antagonism of races bursting forth again with extraordinary virulence. The more violent Tories even spoke of annexation to the United States. Those who were the most loyal in 1838, were now those who were most treasonable in speech and action. But the bill was pushed forward, notwithstanding the fierceness of the storm, and it was finally carried in the Lower House by forty-eight to thirty-two votes, and likewise passed the Legislative Council. The bill authorized the issue of debentures chargeable on the Consolidated Fund, to the amount of £100,000, for the final liquidation of the losses.

The passing of the bill was the signal for disturbance and rioting throughout the Upper Province. In Toronto, especially, there were scenes of great violence, and the Reform leaders were burnt in effigy. It was believed that Lord Elgin would either refuse his assent to the bill, or refer it to the consideration of the Home Government—which would have been a judicious step, in view of all that subsequently occurred. But on the 26th of April, in giving the royal assent to a Customs Bill, he likewise gave it to the Rebellion Losses Bill.

When the Governor-General left the House, he was received with hootings by an unruly mob, and missiles were thrown at his carriage. The Assembly went on with its sittings, however, although Sir Allan M'Nab predicted a riot at any moment, and urged the calling in of the military. Owing to the imprudent confidence of the Government, no measures had been taken against a possible riot when evening set in.

"Towards eight o'clock, the fire-bells were rung to create an excitement, and a large number of persons speedily assembled at the Champ de Mars, where several inflammatory speeches were made. Presently a cry was suddenly raised, 'To the Parliament House!' Thither the crowd immediately proceeded in a state of great excitement; and encountering neither police nor military to check their progress, their loud shouts and yells gave the first information to members, now discussing the Judicature Bill for Lower Canada, of the commencement of what was evidently a formidable riot. A few moments more, and a shower of stones dashed in at the windows, when the Strangers' Gallery was immediately deserted. Some of the members made their escape by this gallery, while others took refuge behind the Speaker's Chair. Meanwhile, stones continued to be thrown, till nearly all the windows were broken. Presently, this mode of attack was discontinued, and the mob began to force their way into the building. A few soon after made their appearance armed with sticks in the Hall of Assembly, at the opposite end of which the remaining members and clerks now disappeared as rapidly as possible. One of the rioters then seated himself in the Speaker's Chair, and waving his hand said, 'I dissolve this House.' The work of destruction was then rapidly proceeded with. Benches were pulled to pieces, and piled in the middle of the floor, with papers from the members' desks. Chandeliers and globe-lights were next broken, and the Speaker's mace was seized and carried off, despite the exertions of the serjeant-at-arms, who had the courage to remain. Messrs. Robinson and Gugy did their best to expel the rioters; and Sir Allan M'Nab employed himself in saving the Queen's picture, painted by Partridge, for which £500 had been paid. Presently, the cry was raised 'that the Parliament House was on fire!' and a lurid glare from the basement story bore painful testimony to its correctness. Several gentlemen now exerted themselves to save some of the valuable books in the library of the Assembly; but the flames spread so rapidly, that they were soon compelled to seek safety in flight. Some of them, however, remained so long in the burning building, that they were injured by the fire, and had to be rescued with ladders. The military, who had at length been sent for, were available in keeping back the dense crowd; but nothing could be done to arrest the conflagration, or save the valuable libraries and public records, the destruction of which inflicted a lasting disgrace and irreparable injury on the country. The Paris mobs, in the midst of revolution and anarchy, respected public buildings, the libraries, and works of art ; and it remained for the vandalism of Montreal rioters to inflict a public injury on themselves, of a character adopted by the Saracens and Huns, and other barbarians of the Middle Ages, to punish their enemies. Some fire-engines made a useless attempt to suppress the flames, which speedily illuminated the whole city, and threw out dense volumes of smoke, borne by the breeze towards the dark mountain, dimly visible in the background of the magnificent though painful spectacle. When the morning sun arose, the fire-charred and still smoking ruins of the Parliament House were all that remained of a vast amount of public property, equal in value, it was estimated, to the sum about to be expended under the Rebellion Losses Bill."

The mob conveyed the mace to Donegani's Hotel, and deposited it in the room occupied by Sir Allan M'Nab. Then they proceeded to wreck the *Pilot* office, where the Ministerial paper was printed. Next day (April 27th), the commander-in-chief, Sir Benjamin D'Urban, arrived in the city from his country seat, and made arrangements for the suppression of any future riots. Although several arrests were made, the mob insulted and beat several of the Reform members, and next attacked the Old Government House, where a Cabinet Council was being held ; but they were beaten back by a bayonet charge of the military.

"After nightfall, the mob received large accessions to their number, and presently a numerous body moved towards the St. Antoine suburb, where they completely wrecked the dwelling of the Premier, Mr. Lafontaine, and burned down his stables. The windows of Messrs. Baldwin's and Cameron's boarding-houses were next broken. Dr. Wolfred Nelson's house shared the same fate, as well as the houses of Messrs. Hincks, Holmes, and Charles Wilson. Objections being made next day to the military doing police duty, a body of French and Irish constables were sworn in ; and the rumour that these were being armed and drilled at the Bonsecours Market, threatened for a while to produce a fresh riot. The arrival of a deputation from Quebec (the inhabitants of which had a keen eye to the removal of the seat of government to their own city) to offer protection to the Governor-General renewed the excitement, and loud threats were made of violence to its members. But during the day they prudently remained in the French suburb, and entered the city in the evening without exciting observation. The loyal inhabitants of Montreal now held a public meeting, and circulated an address, signed by 200 respectable names, inviting the citizens to co-operate in the preservation of peace and order, which had a tranquillizing effect. But a new source of public uneasiness speedily arose. During the 28th, the Assembly had agreed upon an address to the Governor-General in connection with the recent riots, and it was arranged that he should receive it at the Government House instead of at Moncklands. Escorted by a troop of volunteer dragoons, and accompanied by several of his suite, Lord Elgin, accordingly, drove into the city on the 30th. He was greeted with showers of stones in the Haymarket, and in Great St. James and Notre Dame Streets with difficulty preserved his face from being injured. When he entered the Government House, he took a two-pound stone with him, which he had picked up in his carriage, as evidence of the unusual and sorrowful treatment her Majesty's representative had received. Captain Weatheral, a magistrate, read the Riot Act, and ordered the infantry on guard to charge. But the crowd had no ill-feeling towards the military, and cheered them as they ran out of their way. They waited patiently, expecting the reappearance of the Governor-General, in order to renew their assault upon him. But instead of turning round up Notre Dame Street, he doubled on the mob, and passed rapidly along in the direction of Sherbrooke Street. Cabs, calèches, and everything that would run were at once launched in pursuit, and, crossing his route, the Governor-General's carriage was bitterly assailed in the main street of the St. Lawrence suburbs. The good and rapid driving of his postilions enabled him to clear the desperate mob, but not until the head of his brother, Colonel Bruce, had been cut, injuries inflicted on the chief of police, Colonel Ermatinger, and on Captain Jones, commanding the escort, and every panel of the carriage driven in. It was the old war of races putting itself into a new shape, and British feeling was now venting its indignation in this riotous fashion for the imaginary triumph of the rebellious foe that had been so thoroughly crushed eleven years before. Nor did the excitement terminate with the assault on the Governor-General. A deputation from Toronto was made the occasion of a Ministerial dinner at Tetu's Hotel, when the cheering of toasts was met by groans from the mob outside. Presently, missiles were thrown, pistol shots fired, men wounded, and the arrival of a strong body of military alone prevented a serious loss of life. Next day, Lafontaine's house was again attacked ; but this time a volley of musketry compelled the mob to retreat—not, however, till one man had been killed. At the inquest, an attempt was made to fire the hotel where it was being held, and to do violence to Mr. Lafontaine during the confusion ; but he was saved by a party of the 71st Highlanders."

These disgraceful riots, combined with the insecurity of life and property in Montreal, determined the Legislature to remove the seat of government to Toronto for a period of two years, and to Quebec for four subsequent years.

The late serious events, as well as the personal insults to which he had been subjected, led Lord Elgin to tender his resignation to the Home Government. But the Queen and her Ministers at once expressed their entire approval of his conduct, and urgently desired him to remain at his post. Both Houses of Parliament, which had sustained the Rebellion Losses Bill, likewise endorsed the Governor-General's conduct, and pressed him to remain. When Sir Robert Peel's Government afterwards came in, it took the same view, as did the nation at large. Canada itself began gradually to settle down again, though bitter feeling still continued to exist in certain Tory circles, and the city of Montreal suffered considerably for its insensate action.

Dissensions arose among the Reformers in 1850, one section of the party desiring to overthrow the settlement effected on the Clergy Reserves question, and advocating the devotion of the Reserves to secular purposes. But the Government managed to hold their own through the session. The construction of railways was proceeded with, and postal improvements introduced. In 1851, a general election took place, and among those who lost their seats was Mr. Robert Baldwin, ex-Attorney-General, whilst among the new members returned was William Lyon Mackenzie. A terrible fire occurred in Quebec in July, 1852, which laid a great part of the city in ashes, and rendered 10,000 people homeless. The seat of government was removed to Quebec; and during the next three years, 1852-55, all the great questions which agitated the country were settled. A Reciprocity Treaty was concluded with the United States; the Clergy Reserves question was settled by an act of secularization, and the foundation of a permanent endowment; the Seignorial Tenure difficulty was adjusted; the Canada Ocean Steamship Company was incorporated; and a new Customs Tariff was passed.

In December, 1855, Lord Elgin resigned the post of Governor-General, which had long been irksome to him. His successor was Sir Edmund W. Head, a brilliant scholar, and a man of official experience as chief poor-law commissioner. Resigning this post, he was first appointed Governor of New Brunswick, and then Governor-General of British North America. Under Head's rule, the adoption of the principle of Free Trade largely increased the commercial prosperity of the country. In the ranks of the Reformers, Mr. George Brown now began to occupy a conspicuous position. He was an Edinburgh man, who emigrated with his father to Canada in 1838. Mr. Brown founded the *Toronto Globe* in 1844, and in 1851 he was elected to the Legislature, where his abilities and industry soon gave him a conspicuous position. In February, 1856, the Conservative Ministry was defeated. The Premier, Sir Allan M'Nab, resigned; and the Attorney-General, Mr. John A. Macdonald, became leader of the Conservatives. After a short spell of office on the part of Mr. Tache, Macdonald became Prime Minister. The new Government announced its abandonment of the "double majority" principle; that is, a majority in their favour from both Upper and Lower Canada separately, as well as collectively. Such a principle had never obtained in Great Britain, but it had been recognized for some time in Canada.

When the new Parliament met in February, 1858, at Toronto, amongst the members returned for the first time was the Fenian Thomas D'Arcy M'Ghee, who took the oath of allegiance without a murmur, and settled down into a peaceable and law-abiding citizen of Canada. Foiled in other attempts to overthrow the Government, the Reformers at length defeated it on the question of the proposed removal of the seat of government to Ottawa. The Ministry resigned, and Mr. George Brown formed a new administration.

He could get no support, however, and was soon compelled to resign. Mr. Cartier, leader of the Lower Canadian majority, then became Premier, and in his Ministry were Mr. Macdonald and Mr. Alexander Galt. Intense party spirit prevailed at this time; but, nevertheless, many valuable measures were passed. Two special events marked the course of the year 1858. One was the successful laying of the Atlantic Cable—though it proved to be only a temporary achievement, constant communication being delayed till some years later—and the other was the death of Robert Baldwin, the Nestor of Canadian reform, who was the victim of ingratitude and contumely. After his death, his great services to the country were more fittingly remembered than they had been during his life.

In the session of 1859, the question of the seat of government was finally set at rest, and it was determined to proceed at once with the public buildings at Ottawa. The Victoria Railway Bridge at Montreal was approaching completion, and a pressing invitation was given to her Majesty and any member of the Royal Family to visit Canada for the purpose of the opening. An agitation was now set on foot, chiefly by Mr. George Brown, calling for a more equal government and representation of the two provinces, and the first whisperings began to be heard of the principle of confederation.

When the Legislature met at Quebec in February, 1860, the Governor-General announced the Queen's regret that she could not visit the Dominion; but she acknowledged the affectionate loyalty of her Canadian subjects, and expressed a hope that the Prince of

Wales would be able to open the new Victoria Bridge in her name. As the result of a Reform Convention at Toronto, Mr. Brown brought forward resolutions condemning the existing constitutional relations of Upper and Lower Canada, declaring that the union could no longer be continued in its present form, and affirming that the true remedy for the evils complained of was the formation of two or more local governments, and the creation of some joint authority to dispose of the affairs common to all. These resolutions were defeated by a large majority, as was also a motion of want of confidence in Ministers.

The visit of the Prince of Wales to Canada in 1860 was one of the most important and auspicious events in the history of the Dominion. " From one end of the country to the other it evoked a feeling of the most loyal enthusiasm, and people of all classes and of all shades of politics now united most cordially to do honour to the Imperial representative of their good Queen. From every direction along the proposed route of progress arose the din of preparation, and city and town and village corporations voted money to decorate their localities and make fitting arrangements otherwise. At Quebec, a portion of the Parliament buildings had been handsomely fitted up for the reception of the Prince and his suite ; and here, on the 21st of August, he was received in state by both Houses of the Legislature, headed by their Speakers, Narcisse Belleau of the Council, and Henry Smith of the Assembly, both of whom received the honour of knighthood. The festivities having terminated at Quebec, progress westward was resumed to Montreal, where a grand ovation awaited his Royal Highness. As the steamer *Kingston*, which carried him and his suite, entered the harbour, the batteries of St. Helen's Island thundered out a royal salute, the sailors of the vessels of war manned the yards and made the welkin ring with cheers, which were taken up by the vast multitude who lined the substantial wharves, while the city bells reverberated far and wide their sonorous tones of welcome. A little farther on, the current of the noble river still chafing angrily from its descent of the Lachine Rapids, was spanned by the Victoria Bridge, the idea of which first assumed tangible shape in the mind of a talented Canadian engineer, Thomas C. Keefer, to be elaborated and perfected by the genius of a Stephenson. Stretching 10,000 feet from shore to shore, with pier openings 200 feet in width, and rising in the centre 100 feet above high-water mark, to permit lake steamers to pass beneath, this colossal structure stood, the eighth wonder of the world. And this was the bridge now formally opened for traffic by the Prince of Wales, in the name of his august mother, after whom it was most fitly called. Next day, Montreal literally ran riot with joy. A grand ball collected all that was bright and beautiful in the city to greet the heir-apparent of their sovereign, and night was turned into day by the blazes of illuminations and fireworks, that lit up the dark mountain-side in the background, or flashed over the broad current of the St. Lawrence as it sped murmuringly oceanward. From Montreal, the Prince of Wales proceeded to Ottawa, where, on the 1st of September, in the presence of the Duke of

Newcastle, the Governor-General, many of the notabilities of Canada, and a most brilliant suite, he laid the foundation stone of the new Parliament buildings, and subsequently shot the timber slides of the Chaudière on the usual lumberman's crib. Proceeding up the Ottawa to Arnprior, he crossed the country by carriage and railway to Brockville, where he arrived at night, and a most brilliant reception awaited him. This loyal little town greeted him with a grand firemen's torchlight procession, with triumphal arches, fireworks, an illumination, and bonfires among the islands in the river. Embarking on board the *Kingston*, the royal party proceeded next day westwards through the beautiful lake of the Thousand Islands. But no landing was made either at Kingston or Belleville, in consequence of the Orange societies of those neighbourhoods insisting on receiving his Royal Highness with party flags, processions, and music. Further unpleasantness, in connection with the Orange body, awaited him at Toronto, where a triumphal arch on his proposed route was decorated with its flags and emblems, but beneath which he declined to pass. This raised a storm of Orange indignation against his advisers, and the Duke of Newcastle and the Governor-General were burned in effigy on Colborne Street. His progress through the Western Peninsula evoked no additional demonstrations of this nature, and the most joyous welcome everywhere awaited him. His Royal Highness finally passed, at Windsor, out of Canada into the United States, to be exceedingly well received in all the great northern cities visited by him, and particularly at Boston, but to have his passage southward stopped at Richmond, the gateway of the slave states, by insulting demonstrations on the part of its mob."

The case of the fugitive slave Anderson caused great excitement in Canada during the closing days of 1860. Anderson, in making his escape from bondage in Missouri seven years before, had killed a man who sought to arrest him. He succeeded in reaching Canada, where, after a long residence, he was now recognized by a Missouri slave-dealer. He was charged with murder, and his extradition demanded under the provisions of the Ashburton Treaty. After magisterial proceedings, the case was argued before the Court of Error and Appeal at Toronto, on a writ of Habeas Corpus, when Chief Justice Robinson delivered judgment—Judge McLean alone dissenting—to the effect that Anderson must be given up. Intense public feeling was excited, the alleged murder being regarded as an act of self-defence, and therefore no murder. Steps were being taken to bring the matter before the English Court of Queen's Bench, when Anderson was set free by the Court of Common Pleas at Toronto, on the ground of informality in his warrant of committal. The Anderson case led to a revision of the Canadian Act, enforcing the Ashburton Treaty ; and primary jurisdiction, as regarded foreign fugitives from justice, was taken from the control of ordinary magistrates, and left with judges of county courts and police justices.

A census of the population, declared early in 1861, showed the total population of Canada was 2,506,755.

But the most remarkable fact in the census was the great advance revealed in the Upper Province as compared with the Lower. In 1841 the population of Upper Canada was 465,375 ; in 1851 it was 952,061 ; while in 1861 it had reached 1,396,091. On the other hand, the population of Lower Canada in 1841 was 690,782 ; in 1851, 890,261 ; and in 1861 it stood at 1,110,444. This excess of population in the Upper Province gave the supporters of representation by population fresh courage, and in the session of 1861 they renewed their efforts in the Legislature in favour of a constitutional change, but were again defeated. The session was practically fruitless in useful measures, and at the end of May Parliament was dissolved. In Upper Canada the ensuing elections resulted in a victory for the Reform party, though its leader, Mr. Brown, was defeated in Toronto by a combination of Orangemen and Roman Catholics. At the same time, the Premier, Mr. Cartier, defeated the Rouge leader, Dorion, in Montreal East.

The American Civil War now broke out ; but Canada, like Great Britain, maintained a strict neutrality. Events went on peacefully in Canada, the only incident of importance for some time being the death of William Lyon Mackenzie, the once prominent citizen, who died in great pecuniary embarrassment, and with all his political hopes shattered in the dust.

Sir Edmund Head retired from the office of Governor-General in October, 1861, and Lord Monck was sent out as his successor.

CHAPTER XII.

CONFEDERATION OF THE PROVINCES.

THE grand idea of confederation was destined to be carried out while Lord Monck was Governor-General of Canada. The new Viceroy was a native of County Tipperary, Ireland, where he was born in 1819. He was educated at Trinity College, Dublin, and was called to the Irish bar in 1841. In 1849, he succeeded to the title and estates, and three years later was returned to the House of Commons for Portsmouth. Making a good impression in the House, he was appointed a Lord of the Treasury in the Palmerston Government, and held that office for two years. It now remained to see how he would comport himself in a much wider sphere.

During the early months of Lord Monck's rule, two events cast a deep shadow over the Canadian people. One was the death of the Prince Consort, which drew forth expressions of the deepest sympathy with the Queen in her great loss; and the other was the affair of the British mail steamer *Trent*, which had been boarded by Captain Wilkes, of the United States Navy, who forcibly seized Messrs. Slidell and Mason, the Confederate Commissioners. For a time, this incident threatened to cause a war between England and the United States, with consequent disturbance to the peace of Canada ; but happily the matter yielded to a peaceable adjustment.

In March, 1862, Lord Monck opened Parliament at Quebec in considerable state. After a lengthy debate on the address, business was proceeded with. On the 7th of April, an address of condolence to the Queen, on the death of the Prince Consort, was agreed to in the Upper Chamber, of which Sir Allan M'Nab was now the Speaker, and sent down to the Assembly for its concurrence, which was at once signified. As the session progressed, it became evident that the Government were losing ground, owing to the prevalence of certain abuses, the deficiency in the revenue, unpopular fiscal changes proposed by Mr. Galt, and other causes. On the 30th of May, they were defeated on a Militia Bill by sixty-one to fifty-four, and resigned office.

A new Cabinet was formed under the leadership of Mr. John Sandfield Macdonald and Mr. L. V. Sicotte. The policy of the new Administration was announced to be—the restoration of the double-majority principle in all matters locally affecting either section of the province ; the readjustment of the representation of Upper and Lower Canada respectively ; an amended Militia Law ; a revision of the tariff, so as to produce increased revenue, and afford protection to manufacturing industries ; an Insolvent Debtors' Act ; a system of retrenchment in the public expenditure ; the maintenance of her Majesty's decision on the seat of government question ; and an investigation into certain alleged abuses in connection with the construction of the Parliamentary buildings at Ottawa. This programme was received with much favour by almost all classes of the community; though Mr. Brown, in the *Toronto Globe*, fiercely assailed the Upper Canada section of the Administration for not making representation by population, without any regard to a dividing line between Upper and Lower Canada, a Cabinet question, and for having yielded to French domination.

In August, Sir Allan M'Nab died at his residence near Hamilton, having survived his Reform contemporary William Hamilton Merritt but a brief space. One by one the links with the past generation in Canada were being severed. The Governor-General first visited Upper Canada in September, in order to open the Provincial Exhibition at Toronto. Wherever he went, he created a favourable impression by his frank bearing and genial manners. Canada now enjoyed a spell of great agricultural and commercial prosperity, and this gratifying condition of things was accompanied also by a diminution of crime.

Parliament assembled at Quebec on the 13th of February, 1863, when the Legislative Council elected Alexander Campbell as their Speaker, in the place of the late Sir Allan M'Nab. The hostility of the Reformers towards the Government was soon made apparent. An amendment was moved to the address, asserting the principle of representation by population; but this was defeated by sixty-four to forty-two. A second motion for increasing the representation of Upper Canada without disturbing the existing number of members was negatived by eighty-one to thirty-three. Still, the Government was felt to be in a position of insecurity. A measure called Scott's

Separate School Bill, which conceded certain privileges to Roman Catholics, awoke afresh the hostility of western Reformers, while the statement of the Finance Minister proved that Ministers had not been able to redeem their promises. Mr. John A. Macdonald took advantage of these circumstances, and on the 1st of May moved a direct vote of want of confidence in the Government. This was carried by sixty-four votes to fifty-nine. Whereupon the Premier resolved to appeal to the country, at the same time making a reconstruction of his Cabinet, in order to appease the electors of the Reform party and the Lower Canadian Rouges.

When Parliament again assembled in August, the Government were strong enough to carry their candidate for the Speakership of the Assembly, Lewis Wallbridge, by sixty-six to fifty-eight votes. They also managed to struggle through the remainder of the session, notwithstanding their financial and other difficulties. But early in 1864 the Government further lost ground by a declaration made by Mr. M'Dougall, Commissioner of Crown Lands, to the effect that he had abandoned representation by population, because he had found it to be impracticable. This highly incensed Mr. Brown and the Reformers; and when, subsequently, the new Solicitor-General, Mr. Albert N. Richards, was rejected by his constituents on his appeal for re-election, the actual majority of Ministers in the Assembly was reduced to one.

Seeing that they could not hope to continue the successful conduct of public affairs, Ministers resigned in March, and a new Government was formed under

Sir E. P. Tache, a Lower Canadian Conservative, which included Messrs. Cartier, Galt, M'Gee, Langevin, and J. A. Macdonald. But its difficulties began almost as soon as it was constituted. A factious spirit had sprung up in the Assembly, and parties appeared to be only desirous of defeating each other. Ministers having advised the issuing of an order in council reducing the canal tolls, the opposition moved a vote of want of confidence in them, which was only defeated by sixty-four to sixty-two. In June, an actual defeat was sustained on the question of a Government loan of $100,000 made to Montreal in 1859, the votes being—for Ministers, fifty-eight; against, sixty.

Constitutional government in Canada now seemed to have arrived at a dead-lock. Dissolutions of Parliament and changes of Cabinet had been repeatedly tried, and yet the public business could not be carried on. The public were dismayed but helpless over the condition of affairs, while the friends of constitutional government were in a state of bewilderment and despair. At last, many of the best statesmen on both sides came to the conclusion that the only solution of the difficulty was that suggested by Mr. Brown many years before—the scheme of a joint authority. It had been ridiculed and defeated again and again, John A. Macdonald being especially strong in his opposition to it. But Mr. Brown had an ample revenge when his political foes were brought to acknowledge that his plan was the only one to afford relief.

"The negotiations which now ensued between the rival political leaders speedily resulted in a satisfactory understanding, based upon a project of confederation of all the British North American provinces on the federal principle, and leaving to each province the settlement by local legislation of its own municipal and peculiar affairs. In order to ensure the satisfactory arrangement of all the details of the project, Mr. Brown was to have three seats in the Cabinet placed at his disposal. He accordingly became President of the Council; William M'Dougall, Provincial Secretary; and Oliver Mowatt, Postmaster-General. Thus a strong coalition government was formed to carry out the newly accepted policy of confederation; and although extreme parties here and there grumbled at these arrangements, the great body of the people of all shades of opinion, thankful that the dangerous crisis had been safely passed, gladly accepted the situation, and calmly and confidently awaited the progress of events. Never before had a coalition been more opportune. It rendered the Government of the country again respectable, elevated it above the accidents of faction, and enabled it to wield the administrative power with that firmness and decision so requisite during the trying and critical period which speedily ensued. It would, indeed, seem as if a special Providence was controlling matters for its own wise purposes, and evoking results from the ambitions and passions of partizan leaders, directly tending to elevate this country to a position of greater eminence, and to increased usefulness among the nations. The curtain fell on the Parliamentary drama on the 30th of June. But faction even yet was not wholly extinct, and soon found a prominent exponent in Matthew Crooks Cameron, who now contested

North Ontario with Secretary M'Dougall, and beat him by a hundred votes. The latter was not, however, left without a seat in the Legislature. He was subsequently returned by the thoughtful Scotch settlers of North Lanark, who gave him a large majority over a Mr. Rosamond, whose father, an Irish Conservative of the straitest school, showed his appreciation of the coalition by voting for the Secretary, and against his own son."

Difficulties arising out of the American Civil War speedily demonstrated the necessity for a strong government in Canada. Perceiving no prospect of European intervention, the Confederates attempted in September, 1864, to effect a diversion in their favour from the Canadian frontier. By menacing the defenceless borders of the Northern States, they hoped to cause a war between them and Great Britain. In pursuance of this policy, Confederate bands seized two American steamboats, the *Philo Parsons* and *Island Queen*, on Lake Erie, with the immediate design of releasing a number of Southern prisoners confined on Johnson's Island, and of destroying the lake shipping. Although these objects were not carried out, great excitement ensued; and this was intensified in October, when a body of twenty-three Southern refugees made a raid on the little Vermont town of St. Albans, close to the Canadian frontier, shooting an American citizen there, robbing its banks of $233,000 in current funds, and then hastily retreating across the border. The Canadian authorities promptly arrested fourteen of these marauders, who were committed to the gaol at Montreal.

Other unfortunate incidents succeeded. In the meantime, the bitter feelings provoked by the Lake Erie outrage and the St. Albans raid, as well as by the expression of sympathy for the South on the part of many of the Canadian journals, when the vast majority of the people abominated slavery, reacted very unfavourably on Canada, and materially tended, with other adverse causes, to the speedy abrogation of the Reciprocity Treaty. The inexplicable discharge of the St. Albans raiders by Judge Coursol, of Montreal, in December, and the illegal surrender to them of $90,000 of the stolen money by the police—which the Government were subsequently obliged to repay—still further complicated matters, and increased the tension of Canadian relations with the United States.

At this juncture, proposals for a confederation of the North American provinces began to assume definite shape, and to be viewed with favour by many British and Canadian statesmen. The union question had already been agitated in the maritime provinces, and an enlarged project of confederation was laid before the Governor-General, the several Lieutenant-Governors, and thirty-three representatives of all shades of politics, in a council at Quebec, early in October. The negotiators " proceeded to business methodically and cautiously, the representatives of each province having a close eye to its local benefits, and seeking to place its peculiar advantages in the best possible light. Canadians pointed to their vast territorial area, their national wealth, and their important population as their contributions to the proposed State ; while the maritime provinces plumed themselves on their noble harbours, their great merchant fleets, and their foreign commerce. In addition, Newfoundlanders set forth the value of their fisheries and their mines; New Brunswickers pointed to the vigorous and growing trade they would bring into the partnership; Nova Scotians alluded complacently to their vast coal-fields; while Prince Edward Islanders coquettishly asserted their claims to consideration as representing the Isle of Wight of British North America. Gradually difficulties were smoothed down, local pretensions regulated, a harmonious basis of action settled upon, and resolutions adopted, on which subsequently the Imperial Act of Confederation was based."

When Parliament met at Quebec in January, 1865, the Governor-General announced that her Majesty's Secretary of State for the Colonies was prepared to introduce a measure into the Imperial Parliament to give effect to the Acts of Union which might be passed by the different local Legislatures. During the debates on the address, the divisions showed that a great majority of the Legislature supported the principle of confederation; and the question was finally disposed of by a vote of ninety-one to thirty-three. Parliament was then prorogued, in order that Ministers might put themselves into communication with the Home Government on this all-absorbing question.

Shortly afterwards, dramatic incidents occurred in the United States. President Lincoln, the friend of the slave, was assassinated; but the preservation of the Union was already assured. The Confederate Generals Lee and Johnston surrendered, the war was over, and the dream of a Southern Empire had vanished. Slavery was abolished, nor was the price too heavy to pay for the removal of this dark stain for ever from the statute books of a free people.

On the 23rd of June, a second and most disastrous fire occurred at Quebec, which rendered 3,000 persons homeless, and destroyed property to the extent of $1,000,000. The narrow streets and wooden buildings of Old Quebec made the city peculiarly liable to these conflagrations, which have been far less frequent since the building of more commodious stone structures in wider thoroughfares.

The Legislature of United Canada assembled for the last time in Quebec on the 8th of August, to receive the report of the deputation to England with respect to confederation, and for the completion of public business left unfinished at the close of the previous session. The Premier, Sir E. P. Tache, had died a few days before, and he was succeeded by Sir Narcisse Belleau, a member of the Upper House. The various measures quickly passed through the House, including an Act imposing a stamp duty on notes and bills. Towards the close of the year, the seat of government was at length removed to Ottawa.

Early in 1866, Mr. Brown resigned his seat in the Cabinet, on a question arising out of the Reciprocity Treaty. All the members of the Government except himself were in favour of making a good many concessions to the United States, and of accepting legislative reciprocity if they could not secure treaty reciprocity. Mr. Brown declared that he could not accept legislative reciprocity, which might be terminated at any moment by a vote of Congress, nor could he accept what he deemed to be unnecessary concessions. As it soon afterwards appeared that neither the American Government nor Congress would agree to a renewal of the treaty in any shape which would make it acceptable to Canada, many of Mr. Brown's friends regretted that he did not remain in the Government until confederation had been carried through.

The effects of reciprocity were thus described by a Canadian authority: "As the period drew near for the termination of the Reciprocity Treaty, Canada presented a most unusual spectacle. American dealers in farm stock and produce spread themselves in every direction throughout the country, already largely denuded of saleable articles, and purchased everything buyable. The various international ferries were choked up continually with vast droves of cattle, sheep, and horses, as though a hostile army had harried all Canada; while the conveying capacity of the railways, in every direction, was taxed to its utmost limits to meet the needs of produce-buyers at this juncture. Under the provisions of the Reciprocity Treaty, the international commerce between the United States and this country had swelled to the enormous sum of £70,000,000 per annum. Its termination produced a great disturbance of trade, and the New England States, now so accustomed to the cheap markets of Canada lying almost at their doors, were largely the sufferers, and had to look elsewhere for supplies for their manufacturing population. The brewers of New York and Pennsylvania experienced the greatest inconvenience in having their supplies of Canadian barley cut off, while woollen and worsted manufacturers found it utterly impossible to replace the long staple they had hitherto drawn so abundantly from this country; and railway companies and produce merchants bewailed the loss of a profitable and growing tributary commerce. Never before were the calculations of American politicians so thoroughly at fault. They had vainly supposed that Canada could not possibly survive the loss of reciprocity, that its abrogation must hasten annexation to the United States, and they hoped in this way to rid themselves of an independent and lightly taxed country lying conterminous with their northern frontier for many hundreds of miles, and never once imagined they were about to seriously injure themselves. And yet it so turned out that the termination of the Reciprocity Treaty was much more detrimental to the United States than to Canada. Here its loss was much less sensibly felt than could have been supposed possible even by the most sanguine, and it scarcely raised an adverse ripple on the current of our prosperity. Its operations had already swept away all surplus farm stock, trenched largely even upon necessary animals, enriched the country, and placed it in an admirable position to start forward on its own account. Instead of being tributaries and customers of the United States, the Canadians would henceforth be competitors; and the loss of reciprocity, while it greatly tended to stimulate confederation, led the commercial men of this country to push their trade far outside its accustomed limits, and rendered the prospect of annexation infinitely more remote than it ever was before."

As the abrogation of the Reciprocity Treaty led to no desire for annexation on the part of the Canadians, the American supporters of annexation cast about for other means to further their ends; and open countenance began to be given to the Fenian associations in many of the principal towns in the Northern States. Military supplies of all descriptions were procured, and early in March the plan of Sweeny, the Fenian leader, was published. A series of combined movements were arranged for the 17th of March, St. Patrick's Day; and to these threats of invasion the Canadian Government immediately responded by calling out 10,000 volunteers. In less than twenty-four hours, no fewer than 14,000 men offered themselves for the defence of the country. No Fenian advance took place on the day named; and although there was a ludicrous demonstration of a few badly armed men, in April the agitation soon apparently died down.

But as time wore on it became evident that the Fenian organization in the United States was more formidable than at first appeared to be the case. It was divided into two sections, one of which, led by Stephens and O'Mahony, contemplated a move against Ireland; the other, the larger section, led by Roberts and Sweeny, proposed to conquer Canada in the first place, and to make it the base of subsequent operations against Great Britain. The American Republican leaders did more than temporize with the Fenians, in order to gain the Irish vote, and at the same time harass Canada and Great Britain; and the Fenian leaders were permitted to make hostile preparations without restraint. Ambitious politicians and others contributed largely to the invasion fund, and a number of disciplined men, discharged from the American army, gladly embraced the opportunity to join the enterprise. Sweeny himself was formerly an officer in the American regular service, and he had associated with him a number of well-trained military men who had held commands in the late Civil War.

In May, the Fenian leaders laid their plans for a simultaneous descent upon Canada. Three lines of operations were determined on : one from Chicago and other western cities, on the Lake Huron coast ; another from Buffalo and Rochester, across the Niagara frontier ; and the third and most formidable from the cities of the Atlantic seaboard, to organize in the vicinity of Ogdensburg. This last force was to menace Ottawa, to capture Prescott, and operate along the exposed frontier in the direction of the eastern townships. By the end of May, the city of Buffalo, at the foot of Lake Erie, swarmed with Fenian bands. On the 1st of June, a body of about 1,200 strong, under the command of General O'Neil, crossed the Niagara River at Blackrock, and landed unopposed on Canadian soil. They took possession of the ruins of Fort Erie and of the depot of the Buffalo and Lake Huron Railway. But the Fenians were utterly disappointed as to a Canadian rising in their favour.

Having made a purposely delusive reconnaissance down the Niagara, O'Neil quickly retraced his steps, and moved in the direction of the Welland Canal, until he came to an elevated woodland termed Limeridge, where he constructed a temporary breast-work. Meantime, the Canadian military authorities had not been idle. Volunteer corps were called out, and General Napier, commanding the Western District, was instructed to adopt any measures he deemed necessary. A Toronto volunteer force, under the command of Colonel Booker, a volunteer officer of no experience, was despatched to Port Colborne, at the Lake Erie entrance of the Welland Canal, to cover that important work. Another column of 1,800 troops, including 750 regulars and a battery of artillery, under Colonel Peacock, took up a position at Chippewa, two miles above Niagara Falls. Booker and Peacock were to unite and attack O'Neil, and in moving forward to do this Booker unexpectedly encountered O'Neil's outposts at Limeridge. He drove back the advance line of O'Neil on his main body, and had this success been skilfully utilized a real victory might have been gained. But at the critical moment, owing to confused orders and want of ammunition, a panic ensued, and Booker's force was speedily in full retreat. It was now O'Neil's turn to take advantage of his good fortune; but he failed to do so, and ordered a retreat on Fort Erie. He there defeated a small body of volunteers under Colonel Dennis, and made forty prisoners.

" Worn out with marching and fighting, the Fenians began to understand that campaigning in Canada was not the holiday affair they had anticipated; and after night had set in, many of them stole down to the river, and crossed to the American shore in small boats. Meanwhile, their friends in Buffalo were making the most strenuous exertions to reinforce them; and towards midnight a tug, towing two canal-boats laden with 400 well-armed men and abundant supplies, left the harbour for Fort Erie, while the lower part of the city swarmed with armed sympathizers, and the American authorities were powerless to interfere. But O'Neil and his officers had already given up every hope of success, and all they now desired was to escape in safety from the attack which daylight must bring with it from Peacock's column, lying on its arms a few miles distant. A small boat carried the order from O'Neil to the officer commanding the reinforcements to return to Buffalo, and to send the tug and canal-boats to take off his force from Fort Erie. This order reached the reinforcing party when about midway in the river, was obeyed, and shortly after one o'clock on the morning of Sunday the 3rd, the bulk of the Fenian force, to the number of fully 900, without even drawing in their pickets, stole on board the boats sent for them, and were speedily on their way to the American shore. Before they could land, however, they were intercepted by the United States armed propeller *Harrison*, compelled to surrender, and were soon anchored under the guns of the war steamer *Michigan*. The rest of the Fenians endeavoured to cross as best they could, some even, in their extremity, pulling the planks from the wharves, and pushing out into the current upon them. Many also escaped in small boats sent over by their friends ; while the remainder, who were probably about 200 in number, hid themselves in the vicinity, or skulked off into the bush. The prisoners they had captured were all abandoned at Fort Erie, as well as most of their dead and wounded ;

and when Colonel Peacock came up on Sunday morning, he found he had nothing to do beyond arresting the straggling Fenians still lingering in the neighbourhood, who were sent to Toronto gaol. And thus ingloriously terminated the Fenian invasion of the Niagara frontier. The New York leaders sought to conceal their chagrin at its ill success by describing it as a mere feint designed to cover a more important attack to be made elsewhere."

Turning now to the important movement on Ogdensburg and Prescott, it was completely circumvented by the rapid massing of over 2,000 volunteers and regulars at the point threatened, and by the placing of a British gunboat in the river. The Fenians then moved downwards, as though to attack Cornwall; but a garrison there of 3,000 troops and volunteers convinced them of the futility of their designs.

As by the 5th of June no fewer than 5,000 Fenians had congregated on the borders of the eastern townships, the President of the United States could no longer ignore the representations of the British Minister at Washington, nor shut his eyes to the fact that war was being made on a friendly country from the United States. He accordingly "issued a proclamation calling on the Fenians to disperse, and commit no overt acts; while General Meade, an honest and capable officer, was ordered to arrest their leaders and seize their supplies. In pursuance of this order, he speedily captured a large amount of arms and ammunition, which arrived by railway at Ogdensburg, and prevented the passage north of further reinforcements. On the 8th, however, a body of Fenians, 2,000 strong, under the command of General Spear, crossed the frontier near St. Albans, and marched three miles into the interior. There they formed a sort of camp, whence they spread out over the country, plundering every description of property which could possibly be of any use to them. But the advance of troops against them caused them to retreat across the border, where Spear and other leaders were arrested by General Meade, and the masses of mischievous men rapidly dispersed, the American Government granting them free conveyance home on the different railway lines. Thus terminated the Fenian invasion of the Canadian frontier. The actual injury to property it produced was not of much account; but the indirect loss sustained by this country—40,000 volunteers being at one period under arms—was very considerable. No new Fenian attempts were made against Canada. During the summer, gunboats guarded the lake and river approaches; and troops and volunteers, stationed at every assailable point, demonstrated the folly of further efforts at invasion. Canada bewailed the death of her college youths and young men of Toronto. But their blood was not shed in vain. It speedily bore fruit ; and, in connection with the gallant manner in which a great volunteer force had sprung to arms, raised this country in the opinion of the world, and greatly stimulated the project of confederation."

On the 8th of June, the Legislature assembled in the new Parliament buildings at Ottawa. In his opening speech, the Governor-General said he had convened a Council of Trade, which included representatives from the different provinces of British North America. The termination of the Reciprocity Treaty with the United States rendered it necessary to seek new avenues of trade, and it was intended to develop and extend commercial relations with the West Indies and Brazil. He also referred to the Fenian rising, which called for protective measures.

A new Tariff Bill, rendered necessary by the cessation of the Reciprocity Treaty, was brought forward by Mr. Galt. It reduced the duty on the great bulk of imported goods 5 per cent., leaving the maximum rate 15 per cent., admitted articles which entered largely into the manufactures of the country free, and provided for the deficiency thus produced by increasing the import on whisky thirty cents a gallon. This tariff was not only a considerable relief to importers of foreign goods, but it largely stimulated the manufactures of the country. It passed with few modifications. The writ of Habeas Corpus was suspended for a year, the assessment law of Upper Canada was amended, and its municipal law was subjected to very important alterations, which raised the franchise in towns, and effected other changes that were well received by all classes.

On the 3rd of July, Ministers brought forward resolutions in the Legislature defining the Constitutions of Upper and Lower Canada respectively, under the proposed Confederation Scheme, and these resolutions were subsequently embodied in the Imperial Bill. The American Congress, still angling after annexation, passed a measure granting facilities for the admission of British North America into the American Union as four separate States, and providing for the assumption of their public debt by the General Government. The bill completely failed, and its overtures were treated by the Canadian people with indifference and contempt.

Before the summer ended, another disastrous fire occurred at Quebec, which resulted in the whole of the St. Roch suburb, and likewise much of that of St. Sauveur, being burnt down ; 2,119 houses were destroyed, and upwards of 20,000 persons were left homeless. This disaster, which scattered a large portion of the population, combined with a serious decline in the commerce of Quebec, quite paralyzed the city for a long time to come.

In the autumn, the Fenian trials took place at Toronto, when the grand jury ignored many of the bills against the prisoners. In a large number of cases, however, true bills were found, and the prisoners were convicted and sentenced to death ; but the sentences were afterwards commuted by the Queen to a period of imprisonment in the provincial penitentiary.

The great confederation project now moved towards its final consummation. In December, delegates from the provinces of Canada, Nova Scotia, and New Brunswick assembled in London to arrange the final terms of the Act of Union to be submitted to the Imperial Parliament. The Earl of Carnarvon, the Colonial Secretary, introduced the measure on the 7th of February, 1867, in the House of Lords. It quickly passed through its various stages, and was sent down to the Commons. There likewise it passed with few amendments, and on the 28th of March it received the royal assent and became law. A bill was next day brought forward in the Commons, to guarantee a loan of £3,000,000 sterling for the Intercolonial Railway, and this duly went through its various stages and became law. Her Majesty then issued her royal proclamation, appointing the 1st of July as the day on which the Dominion of Canada should begin its new existence, at the same time nominating its seventy-two senators.

The British North America Act of 1867, better known as the Confederation Act, " gives jurisdiction to the Provincial Governments over administration of justice (except in criminal matters), municipal, and all purely local affairs. In the territories, not yet constituted into provinces, there is a small elective body or house who select a financial committee to assist the Lieutenant-Governor. These territories are also represented in the two Houses of the Dominion Parliament. The Central or General Government of the Dominion is administered by a Governor-General, with the assistance of a Ministry responsible to a Parliament, composed of a Senate appointed by the Crown, and a House of Commons elected under an electoral franchise, practically the very threshold of universal suffrage. This Government has jurisdiction over trade and commerce, post office, militia and defence, navigation and shipping, fisheries, railways and public works of a Dominion character, and all other matters of a general or national import. Education is under the control of the Provincial Governments, but the rights and privileges of a religious minority with respect to separate or denominational schools are protected by the Constitution. The common law of England prevails in all the provinces except in French Canada, where the civil law still exists. The criminal law of England obtains throughout the Dominion. The Central Government appoints all the judges, who are irremovable except for cause. Although the Constitution places in the Central Government the residue of all powers not expressly given to the provincial authorities, conflicts of jurisdiction are constantly arising between the general and local governments. Such questions, however, are being gradually settled by the decisions of the courts—the chief security of a written Constitution—although at times the rivalry of parties and the antagonisms of distinct nationalities and creeds tend to give special importance to certain educational and other matters which arise in the operation of the Constitution. All these are perils inseparable from a federal constitution governing two distinct races. The appointment of the Governor-General by the Crown, the power of disallowing bills which may interfere with Imperial obligations, and the right which Canadians still enjoy of appealing to the judicial committee of the Queen's Privy Council from the subordinate courts of the provinces, including the Supreme Court of Canada ; the obligation which rests upon England to assist the colony in time of danger by all the power of her army and fleet, together with the fact that all treaties with foreign powers must be necessarily negotiated through the Imperial authorities, will be considered as the most patent evidences of Canada being still a dependency of the Empire."

The great scheme of confederation answered admirably in welding the populations of the various provinces into one harmonious whole, and in ensuring the prosperity and progress of the Dominion.

British Columbia, which includes Vancouver Island, entered the Canadian Confederation in July, 1871. The province is represented in the Dominion Senate by three members, and in the House of Commons by six. The Provincial Government is represented by a Lieutenant-Governor, appointed and paid by the Dominion, and a Legislative Assembly of twenty-seven members, elected by the inhabitants. Education is compulsory, and free between the ages of seven and twelve. This province, with its magnificent if rugged scenery, was isolated from the rest of the Dominion until the completion of the Canadian Pacific Railway in 1885. Its commerce is now increasing rapidly, and lines of steamers pass between Vancouver and Hong Kong.

Prince Edward Island entered the Confederation in 1873. It is situated in the Gulf of St. Lawrence, and is separated from New Brunswick and Nova Scotia by Northumberland Strait. Free education has prevailed in the province since 1853. The government of the island is administered by a Lieutenant-Governor, appointed by the Governor in Council, and paid out of federal funds. The Legislative Council consists of thirteen members, and the Assembly of thirty members. In the Dominion Senate the province is represented by four members, and in the House of Commons by six.

CHAPTER XIII.

THE RED RIVER REBELLION.

CANADA was greatly agitated by two important occurrences in 1869-70. The first was another Fenian raid from the United States, which happily proved a fiasco, and the other was the formidable rising known as the Red River Rebellion.

The restless Fenian adventurers who congregated in some of the great cities of the American Union subsisted by contributions from Irish immigrants who were hostile to the rule of Great Britain. In May, 1870, these people began to collect in arms under the so-styled general, O'Neil, at two points on the frontier, between Canada and New York and Vermont States respectively. The United States, although charged by Canada and her friends with supineness in allowing these armed bands to assemble, acted with singular promptitude when the alarm respecting their movements was given.

On the 23rd of May, the intended rising was reported at Washington. On the 24th, the President issued a proclamation, stating that he had received information of the preparation of illegal expeditions against the people of Canada by inhabitants of the United States, and that all participation in or furtherance of such proceedings would forfeit the protection of the United States Government, and render the promoters amenable to justice. However, the first body of Fenians, under O'Neil in person, crossed from Vermont in considerable strength. On the 25th, General Meade was despatched from Philadelphia to the frontier, but the necessary work had been accomplished before he arrived. The Fenians had been repulsed at Williamstown by a detachment of the 69th Regiment and some Canadian volunteers, under General Lindsay. One man was killed. The Fenians were just ninety minutes on Canadian soil. As soon as O'Neil recrossed the frontier, he found the United States marshal, Forster, in waiting, who arrested him after some show of resistance, and carried him off in a carriage. On the 27th, another band, under a Fenian leader named Gleeson, crossed the border from Malone; but these too were easily repulsed, also with the loss of one man only, and in their flight Gleeson and others were captured by the American authorities. The prisoners were placed in confinement to await their trial for a breach of the neutrality laws. For his action in this matter, President Grant received an expression of satisfaction from the British Government through Mr. Thornton, the British Minister. The Fenian leaders were tried in the course of the summer, and received sentences of imprisonment, but with recommendations to mercy, which were subsequently acted upon; while at the same time a stringent proclamation against future raids was issued by the President.

The Red River Rebellion demands explanation in

greater detail, because of the circumstances which gave rise to it. "The Hudson's Bay Company, under their charters from Charles II. and other authorities, had enjoyed powers of proprietorship and exclusive trade in the vast region north of the American boundary-line, 49° north, to the Frozen Ocean. Early in this century, the great projector, Lord Selkirk, had established in the extreme south of this region, and close to the American line, a colony of mixed French Canadians, chiefly half-bred, and English and Scotch descendants of servants of the Company, in a strip of fertile land on the banks of the Red River flowing from what is now the American State of Minnesota into Lake Winnipeg. These people, though established under a very rigorous winter climate, increased to the number of some 8,000 or 10,000, living on the rich agricultural produce of their short summer, and on trade with the surrounding Indians. They inhabited, perhaps, the most secluded spot ever reached by European colonists, in the exact centre of the North American Continent equidistant from the Atlantic and Pacific east and west, and from the mouth of Mackenzie's River and that of the Mississippi north and south. The Company sent them supplies by way of a long land journey from Hudson's Bay, itself inaccessible from ice except for three months in the year. The nearest American railway station is distant from them about 600 miles; the western end of Lake Superior, in Canada, about 400; all between them and these points is wilderness of prairie and of forest. This insulated community had been ruled after a fashion by the Company under a 'Governor of

Assiniboia' and a Recorder. But they had always been troublesome subjects. In 1869, the Company had succeeded in effecting an arrangement for parting with all their general territorial rights in Rupert's Land (that is, their dominion east of the Rocky Mountains) to Canada for £300,000. This cession, of course, included the Red River."

The Canadian Ministry, of which Sir John Macdonald was Premier, at once took measures to assume possession of the country, where they proposed to establish a provisional government. These measures are thus described by the Hon. J. G. Bourinot, in his recent volume on Canada : " Mr. William M'Dougall, a prominent Canadian Liberal, one of the founders of confederation, always an earnest advocate of the acquisition of the North-West, was appointed to act as Lieutenant-Governor as soon as the formal transfer was made. This transfer, however, was not completed until a few months later than it was at first expected, and the Government of Canada appears to have acted with some precipitancy in sending surveyors into the country, and in allowing Mr. M'Dougall to proceed at once to the scene of his proposed government. It would have been wise had the Canadian authorities taken measures to ascertain the wishes of the small but independent population with respect to the future government of their own country. The British as well as French settlers resented the hasty action of the Canadian authorities. The half-breeds, little acquainted with questions of government, saw in the appearance of surveying parties an insidious attempt to dispossess them eventually of their lands, to which many of them had not a sound title. The British settlers, the best educated and most intelligent portion of the population, believed that a popular form of government should have been immediately established in the old limits of Assiniboia as soon as it became a part of Canada. Some of the Hudson's Bay Company's employés were not in their hearts pleased at the transfer, and the probable change in their position in a country where they had been so long masters. Although these men stood aloof from the insurrection, yet their influence was not exercised at the commencement of the troubles in favour of peace and order, or in exposing the plans of the insurgents, of which some of them must have had an idea. The appearance of Mr. M'Dougall on the frontier of the settlement was the signal for an outbreak which has been dignified by the name of rebellion. The insurgents seized Fort Garry, and established a provisional government, with Mr. John Bruce, a Scotch settler, as nominal president, and Mr. Louis Riel, the actual leader, as secretary of state. The latter was a French half-breed, who had been superficially educated in French Canada. His temperament was that of a race not inclined to steady occupation, loving the life of the river and plain, ready to put law at defiance when their rights and privileges were in danger. This restless man and his half-breed associates soon found themselves at the head and front of the whole rebellious movement, as the British settlers, while disapproving of the action of the Canadian Government, were not prepared to support the seditious designs of the French Canadian Métis. Riel became president, and made prisoners of Dr. Schultz, in later times a lieutenant-governor of the new province, and of a number of other British settlers who were now anxious to restore order and come to terms with the Canadian Government, who began to show every disposition to arrange the difficulty. In the meantime, Mr. M'Dougall issued a proclamation which was a mere *brutum fulmen*, and then went back to Ottawa, where he detailed his grievances, and soon afterwards disappeared from public life. The Canadian authorities by this time recognized their mistake, and entered into negotiations with Red River delegates, representing both the loyal and rebellious elements, and the result was more favourable for the immediate settlement of the difficulties. At this critical juncture, the Canadian Government had the advantage of the sage counsels of Sir Donald Smith, then a prominent official of the Hudson's Bay Company, who at a later time became a prominent figure in Canadian public life. Chiefly through the instrumentality of Archbishop Taché, whose services to the land and race he loved can never be forgotten by its people, an amnesty was promised to those who had taken part in the insurrection; and the troubles would have come to an end, had not Riel, in a moment of recklessness characteristic of his real nature, tried one Thomas Scott by the veriest mockery of a court-martial, on account of some severe words he had uttered against the rebels' government, and had him mercilessly shot outside the fort. As Scott was a native of Ontario, and an Orangeman, his murder aroused a widespread feeling of indignation throughout his native province.

The amnesty which was promised to Archbishop Taché, it is now quite clear, never contemplated the pardon of a crime like this, which was committed subsequently."

The Canadian Government now decided to act with resolution, and the British troops in Canada furnished a contingent for immediate action. One battalion of infantry, two of Canadian militia, and a small party of artillery and engineers were selected for the purpose, under the command of Colonel Garnet Wolseley, now Lord Wolseley, the Commander-in-Chief of the British Army. "The expedition which followed—in the summer of 1870—though not exciting the same public interest, very much resembled in its general character that against Theodore, King of Abyssinia, in 1868, and illustrated in like manner the power of endurance, resource, and discipline of trained men employed in a very trying service. Between the head of Lake Superior and the Red River, about 500 miles were to be passed of country without a road (one had been projected by Canada, but a small portion of it only was even marked out), a region composed of thick forest, swamp, bush-covered rocks, and small lakes of intricate navigation. The route is described by a member of the expedition as 'forty-eight miles by road through the forest to Shenandowan Lake, and thence about 310 miles by rivers and lakes, with about seventeen portages to the Lake of the Woods. Some of these portages were more than a mile in length; and when it is remembered that all the boats, stores, etc., required for the expedition had to be carried by the soldiers over these breaks in the navigation, an idea can be formed of the physical labour which such an operation would entail. From the Lake of the Woods to Fort Garry was about 100 miles in a direct line by hand; but there was only a road made for about sixty miles of that distance, the unmade portion being laid out over most difficult swamps'; and ultimately it was necessary to avoid the difficulties of this last portion by a circuitous movement down the Winnipeg River. The expedition reached Fort Garry, the headquarters of the Hudson's Bay Company, and now of Riel and his rebel followers, on the 23rd of August. They were welcomed enthusiastically by the loyal party, and met with no opposition from the disaffected. Riel had disappeared: the latest accounts represent him as having taken refuge, with a considerable amount of plunder which he had collected, in the neighbouring American territory. The British force did not experience the loss of a single man, thanks in great measure to the foresight and sagacity with which the whole enterprise was conducted. 'It had to advance,' says an eye-witness, 'from its point of disembarkation on Lake Superior, for more than 600 miles, through a wilderness of water, rocks, and forests, where no supplies were to be had, and where every pound weight of provisions and stores had to be transported for miles on the backs of soldiers. . . . The total expense was under £100,000, of which one-quarter only was to be paid by England. There was no reckless waste in either material or money . . . . It may be safely asserted that no such distance has ever been traversed by an efficient brigade, numbering about 1,400 souls, in any of our numerous little wars, at such a trifling cost.'"

Order having been re-established, the province of Manitoba was constituted, and added to the Dominion of Canada. Manitoba was given a complete system of local government, with guarantees respecting education, as in the old provinces. The first Lieutenant-Governor was Mr. Adams Archibald, a Nova Scotian lawyer, and a statesman of distinction. Representation was given to the province in the two Houses of Parliament. The vast territory outside of the new prairie province was subsequently divided into six districts for purposes of government—Alberta, Assiniboia, Athabasca, Keewatin, and Saskatchewan. In the great northern unsettled districts, four new provisional districts were marked out in 1896, under the names of Franklin, Mackenzie, Yukon, and Ungava.

During the last twenty years, Manitoba has made remarkable progress from the agricultural point of view, but its political history has been comparatively uneventful.

CHAPTER XIV.

THE DOMINION SINCE CONFEDERATION.

BEFORE tracing the further progress of Canada, it will be fitting here to make some references to the men who, both before and since confederation, bore so large a share in the making of the Dominion.

First, in point of time, was the Hon. George Brown, an able but sometimes injudicious statesman. Earnest and eloquent, and possessing wide financial and political knowledge, he was responsible during his career for the raising of many difficulties which almost made government for a time impossible. Prior to the union of 1867, both in speech and through his newspaper, the *Toronto Globe*, he attacked French Canada and its institutions with great bitterness, and thereby aggravated the racial antagonisms. Yet it must not be forgotten that it was largely through his advocacy of confederation, when the plan was most fiercely assailed, that this great boon was eventually secured. Mr. Brown died from a wound he received at the hands of a reckless printer who had been in his employ, and grateful Canadians erected a fine monument to his memory in Queen's Park, Toronto.

Sir George Etienne Cartier was the leader of the Liberal-Conservative party, and it was through his influence that the French Canadian race came to be a real factor to be reckoned with in Dominion affairs. He was distinguished for his sound sense and excellent judgment in times of national difficulty and danger. He died in 1873, and was awarded a State funeral; while a statue was raised to him on one side of the Parliament buildings at Ottawa.

Mr. Alexander Mackenzie was a statesman who raised himself from the humble position of a stonemason to the highest place in the councils of the country. A Liberal in politics, he had a thorough knowledge of Canadian questions, and was Premier from 1873 to 1878.

But the statesman who held the most prominent position in the public eye for fully a generation was Sir John A. Macdonald, the leader of the Conservative party after the death of Sir Allan M'Nab. With exception of Mr. Mackenzie's four years of office above-mentioned, Sir J. A. Macdonald was Premier of the Dominion from 1867 till his death in 1891. He has been described as the most successful statesman that Canada has yet produced, both on account of his long tenure of office, and of the importance of the measures which he was able to carry during his remarkable career. Both in physical features and statesmanship he has frequently been compared to the Earl of Beaconsfield. "A lawyer by profession," says the Hon. J. G. Bourinot, speaking of Sir John Macdonald, "but a politician by choice, not remarkable for originality of conception, but possessing an unusual capacity for estimating the exact conditions of public sentiment, and for moulding his policy so as to satisfy that opinion, having a perfect understanding of the weaknesses and ambitions of human nature, believing that party success was often as desirable as the triumph of any great principle, ready to forget his friends and purchase his opponents when political danger was imminent, possessing a fascinating manner which he found very useful at times when he had to pacify his friends and disarm his opponents, fully comprehending the use of compromise in a country of diverse nationalities, having a firm conviction that in the principles of the British Constitution there was the best guarantee for sound political progress, having a patriotic confidence in the ability of Canada to hold her own on this continent, and become, to use his own words, ' a nation within a nation,'—that is to say, within the British Empire,—Sir John Macdonald offers to the political student an example of a remarkable combination of strength and weakness, of qualities which make up a great statesman and a mere party politician, according to the governing circumstances. Happily, for the best interests of Canada, in the case of confederation the statesman prevailed. But his ambition at this crisis would have been futile, had not Mr. Brown consented to unite with him and Cartier. This triple alliance made a confederation possible on terms acceptable to both English and French Canadians. These three men were the representatives of the antagonistic elements which had to be reconciled and cemented." On Sir John's death in 1891, a State funeral was awarded to the deceased, and statues were afterwards erected to his memory in the cities of Montreal, Ottawa, Toronto, Hamilton, and Kingston.

That at Ottawa is on the opposite side of the Parliament buildings to the statue of Cartier. On the occasion of the Queen's great Jubilee, Lady Macdonald was created a peeress in her own right.

To these names worthy of remembrance should be added Sir Charles Tupper and Sir Leonard Tilley, the Premiers of Nova Scotia and New Brunswick, who co-operated with the statesmen of the upper provinces in the successful formation of the Confederation. Among other names of men prominent as Liberal leaders in Nova Scotia were those of Sir Adams Archibald, Mr. Jonathan McCully, and Mr. Joseph Howe.

Reverting now to the history of Canada since confederation, and subsequent to the Red River Rebellion, the most important event for several years was the signing of the Washington Treaty of 1871. This convention settled the Alabama and other questions of difference between the United States, Great Britain, and Canada. The direct interest of the Dominion in the subjects under consideration was recognized by England in the selection she made of Sir John Macdonald as one of the commissioners. It has been observed that the most satisfactory result of this conference was the appointment of a commission which, after full deliberation, gave Canada and Newfoundland a compensation of $5,500,000 for certain concessions which were made to the United States with regard to the valuable fishing grounds of British North America. Further, during the diplomatic discussions between England and the United States as to the seizure of Canadian vessels while engaged in catching seals in the open waters of Behring Sea, the British Government was greatly influenced by the views and arguments of the Canadian Ministry.

The scheme for the construction of the Great Canadian Pacific Railway led to the fall of Sir John Macdonald's Government in 1873; but a few years later the contract for its construction was signed, and Parliament having ratified the scheme, the work was vigorously proceeded with. Now there is a complete system of railway communication from the Atlantic to the Pacific Ocean.

In the year 1879, the new Conservative Ministry carried a higher customs tariff, called the national policy, as a measure of protection against the United States fiscal policy, and also in order to foster native industries.

In 1885, another rebellion was instigated and set on foot by the Indian half-breed Louis Riel. This restless spirit, who was really a man of intelligence and energy, began his insurrectionary work in March in the North-West territories of the Dominion, and for some time the rising threatened very serious consequences. The scene of the outbreak was on the North Saskatchewan River, Manitoba. The police sent to restore order met the rioters at Fort Carleton, but were repulsed with the loss of fifteen men. Three Indian chiefs joined the revolt, by which the numbers of the insurgents were raised to 1,500. The insurrection spread rapidly over a large portion of Winnipeg territory.

Fort Pitt, on the North-West frontier, was attacked in April by a body of Indians. For two weeks it was completely surrounded, and at length it was entered by night and seized. The garrison and settlers, however, had embarked on board a boat under the leadership of Inspector Francis Dickens, of the mounted police, a son of Charles Dickens the novelist. The Indians pursued them along the bank, firing at every opportunity; but ultimately Mr. Dickens brought the whole of his party, with the exception of one man, in safety to Battleford.

Fears were entertained of a general rising of the Indians, of whom it was estimated there were in all about 90,000 in the Canadian dominions. If that deplorable event had occurred, the mission stations and the small and scattered European and Canadian settlements in the North-West would in all probability have been exterminated. The postponement of the opening-up of the North-West by means of the New Pacific Railroad was one of the less serious results anticipated if the Riel revolt had proved successful. But the energy of the Government, aided by the gallantry and patriotism of the Canadian militia and volunteers, led by General Middleton, " quelled the disturbance before it had extended very far. For nearly two months, however (March to May), the state of affairs was exceedingly critical, and there was much excitement throughout Canada. The capture of Batoche by the troops under General Middleton, and the subsequent surrender of Riel (May 15th), put an end to the rebellion. With his capture, another difficulty began. He was not without a large number of sympathizers, apart from his own immediate followers. The halfbreed leader was a native of the North-West. He was born near Fort Garry, now called Winnipeg, in 1844, and was marked by some features of an Indian, with

19

the fair complexion and blue eyes of a European race. He was well-educated, having been trained at Montreal for the Roman Catholic priesthood. He had much of the craft of the Indian, combined with the tact of the Frenchman. He was popular with the whole of the French population of Lower Canada, while his ascendency over the Indians and half-breeds of the North-West had been shown in two rebellions."

After Lord Wolseley had driven Riel over the border in the rising of 1869-70, the rebel leader had remained some years in exile. He was then elected to the Dominion Parliament, but never took his seat. "His presence now in the Saskatchewan district was due to an invitation sent to him in the summer of 1885 by the half-breeds to come back and assist them in obtaining a redress of their grievances. In accepting the invitation, he announced his intention of spending some months among them, in the hope that redress might be got by petitioning the Government. The movement, however, developed into an armed insurrection, and Riel himself received much sympathy from the French population, which constitutes a fourth part of the people of Canada. Riel afterwards stated that his papers, captured at Batoche, would show that he was not the leader of the rebellion, but that it had been encouraged by people of good standing around Prince Albert. This statement was significant in connection with the fact that, in a speech at Prince Albert in the preceding summer, Riel urged that the three districts of Assiniboia, Alberta, and Saskatchewan should apply for admission to the Confederation with governments of their own. The white settlers in the Alberta district subsequently sent in a petition with a similar prayer. They not only used Riel's language, but asserted that the half-breeds in the North-West were entitled to the same privileges as their brethren in Manitoba. This was what Riel asked. He probably had no intention either in 1869 or 1885 of taking up arms. But he was an enthusiast, with a strong sense of the wrongs of his race, and much power of attaching them to his person. In 1869, he made great professions of peaceful intentions; and it is worthy of note that, as soon as the rebellion was suppressed, the Canadian Government gave the half-breeds of Manitoba the measures Riel had demanded for them. In July, 1885, Riel was put upon his trial for high treason. His counsel made an eloquent appeal, alleging justification, urging extenuating circumstances, and finally advancing the plea of insanity. Afterwards, Riel himself (by permission of the presiding judge) addressed the jury at length, setting forth his grievances and those of the half-breeds, and alleging that petition after petition had been sent to the Federal Government, but without effect. These, it is believed, had reference to a more generous policy in the allotment of land claims. The jury returned a verdict of 'guilty,' with a recommendation to mercy. Riel was sentenced to be hanged. Notice of appeal was immediately given, and the full court of Manitoba, sitting at Winnipeg, subsequently disallowed the appeal and confirmed the sentence. It held that the jury arrived at the only decision possible on the evidence, and decided that the court, originally trying the case, had undoubted jurisdiction, which, it had been alleged, it had not. The plea of insanity the full court declared to be not sustained, as the evidence showed that Riel, while acting strangely sometimes, was a clever and designing man. A reprieve was granted, to allow of a further appeal to the Lords of the Privy Council. The appeal was heard in the House of Lords at Westminster, at the meeting of the Law Courts in October, and was again dismissed. Every effort was made by his Canadian sympathizers to have the sentence of death commuted to one of imprisonment, but without effect. Louis Riel was hanged on Monday, the 16th of November. On the following day, a demonstration of French Canadians numbering some 10,000 persons was made in Montreal, but no harm resulted. There were somewhat similar demonstrations in Quebec and elsewhere. The agitation, however, soon subsided."

But in the course of two years another matter arose, which caused great excitement and agitation in Manitoba. The Canadian Pacific Railway Act contained certain provisions known as monopoly clauses, and a cry now arose for their abolition. A local Act was passed for the construction of the Red River Valley Railway to a boundary-line which connected it with the United States railways. The Act was disallowed by the Governor in Council ; but the railway was commenced, notwithstanding. An injunction was obtained in the provincial law courts, and this compelled a cessation of the work. In the same year (1887) an agreement was arrived at between the British and United States Governments to discuss the fishery disputes in conference at Washington. The British plenipotentiaries appointed were the Right Hon. Joseph Chamberlain, Sir Lionel Sackville West, and Sir Charles Tupper. The meetings of the conference began early in December.

The treaty for the settlement of the fishery disputes was signed by the British and United States representatives on the 15th of February, 1888, and it was afterwards ratified by the Legislatures of the two countries. The treaty recognized the right of Canada to fisheries within the three-mile limit, which was to follow the coast-line, except, first, in the case of bays of ten miles wide and under, when the line was to be drawn from headland to headland; and, secondly, in the case of certain bays specially exempted from the operation of the treaty. Fishing vessels of the United States were to be allowed to land, sell, and tranship cargoes only in cases of distress; but they might enter the ports for wood, water, shelter, and repairs, and, on obtaining a licence (given without charge), to purchase casual supplies and stores, excepting bait. Concessions were also to be made as to reporting at customs ports, and as to pilot, harbour, light, and other dues. If the United States agreed at any time to admit Canadian fish and certain fish products free of duty, their vessels might in addition, so long as privilege remained in force, land, sell, and tranship their cargoes, and also purchase bait and all other supplies. The treaty was to be ratified within two years, and in the meantime, to avoid friction, a *modus vivendi* was arranged, providing that United States fishing vessels might have all the privileges mentioned above, on payment of a tonnage licence fee of 1·50 dollars per ton.

The question of commercial union between the United States and Canada came on for discussion in the Dominion House of Commons early in April, 1888. The motion for unrestricted reciprocity was rejected by 124 to 67 votes. The Government amendment carried was to the effect that Canada was desirous, in the future as in the past, of cultivating and extending trade relations with the United States, in so far as it might not conflict with the national policy of Canada. At a later date, the Government arranged with the Canadian Pacific Railway Company for the cancellation of its monopoly clauses, on terms satisfactory to Manitoba. An abortive conference was held at Ottawa, in June, between Canada and Newfoundland, to discuss the question of the entry of the latter into the Confederation.

Lord Monck, who was Governor-General at the time of the passing of the Confederation Scheme, resigned in 1868, and was succeeded by Lord Lisgar, who held the office for four years. Lord Dufferin became Governor-General in 1872, and his brilliant administration was signalized by the remarkable development of the province of Manitoba. His lordship resigned in 1878, and was followed by the Marquis of Lorne, who held the office for five years, during which he and the Princess Louise were popular with the people. The Marquis of Lansdowne held the appointment from 1883 to 1888, when he was succeeded by Lord Stanley of Preston, who resigned on succeeding to the Earldom of Derby in 1893. His successor was the Earl of Aberdeen, who has just resigned this high office.

The province of Quebec was greatly agitated by a series of official scandals in 1891-92. Towards the close of the former year, Mr. A. P. Bradley, Secretary of the Railway Department, was dismissed for having drawn a year's pay for his son as a clerk in his department while the latter was actually attending college. Soon afterwards the Royal Commission issued its report on the Chaleur Bay Railway Scandal, and Mr. Mercier's Cabinet was at once dismissed, Mr. Mercier protesting strongly against the proceeding as arbitrary and unconstitutional. A new Cabinet was formed, with Mr. de Boucherville as Premier and President of the Council. A further charge was now preferred against the late Mercier Administration. It was discovered that letters of credit for $60,000 had been issued for stationery, while only $10,000 worth had been supplied. In January, 1892, a Royal Commission was appointed to enquire into the alleged corrupt practices during Mr. Mercier's Premiership. A civil action was likewise entered against Mr. Pacaud to recover $100,000 of the Chaleur Bay Railway subsidy, but this was dismissed. It was soon stated that another batch of letters of credit had been discovered by the Quebec Government, pledging the credit of the province for a year in advance to the extent of $300,000.

The majority and minority reports of the Chaleur Bay Commission were made public in February. The President, Judge Jette, a Liberal, exonerated Mr. Mercier and all his Ministers, and only condemned Mr. Mercier's political agent, Pacaud, and the contractor, Armstrong. The other judges, Baber and Davidson, both Conservatives, unreservedly condemned Mr. Mercier and Mr. Langelier, ex-Secretary. The elections in Quebec resulted in the signal defeat of Mr. Mercier, fifty-three Government members being returned and only seventeen Liberals, including Mr. Mercier, who now resigned his seat, and issued an address to his friends, announcing his retirement into private life. He next voluntarily executed an assignment of his estate for the benefit of his creditors; but on the 9th of June, he and Pacaud were committed for trial, on the charge of conspiracy to defraud. The charge against Messrs. Pacaud and Langelier was dismissed; but two fresh charges of fraud were brought against Mr. Mercier, in connection with the Hereford and the Montreal and Ottawa Railways. Judge Chauveau committed Mr. Mercier for trial on all three of the charges brought against him. No bills, however, were returned on the indictment against him of malfeasance as to the Hereford Railway subsidies, and against Mr. Pacaud of bribery. Eventually, in November, both Mr. Mercier and Mr. Pacaud were acquitted of the various charges of malfeasance brought against them.

Another scandal which caused much comment arose out of a charge brought against the Postmaster-General for the Dominion, Sir A. P. Caron, of having employed money from railway subsidies for electioneering purposes. A Royal Commission was appointed by the Dominion House of Commons to investigate the matter. But in September, the prosecuting counsel, Mr. Edgar, refused to proceed before the Royal Commission with his charges against Sir A. P. Caron, on the ground that the charges had been changed by the Government so as to no longer include his original allegations of fraud and conspiracy.

With regard to Imperial matters, the 250th anniversary of the foundation of Montreal was celebrated in May, 1892, with great ceremony. In August the province of Ontario kept the 100th anniversary of its existence, the proceedings taking place principally near Niagara, where the Legislature of the province met after its creation. In the Dominion Parliament, the Hon. G. Foster, Finance Minister, stated that the outcome of the conference with the United States was to make it clear that unrestricted reciprocity must inevitably lead to the annexation of Canada. At a later date, all idea of reciprocity between Canada and the States was quashed by a message sent by President Harrison and the Senate, urging Congress to retaliate against Canada for what he called the persistent denial of the rights of American citizens, guaranteed by the Treaty of Washington, in connection with the navigation of Canadian canals. A bill was afterwards passed to prevent Canadian vessels from passing through the Sault Sainte Marie Canal.

In the Canadian House of Commons, the following resolution was adopted by ninety-eight to sixty-four votes : "That when the Parliament of Great Britain admits Canadian products to the British markets on more favourable terms than it grants to foreign products, Canada will be prepared to extend corresponding advantages of reduction of duties to British manufactured goods." It was afterwards resolved to open negotiations with the Imperial Government to secure a fuller representation of Canadian interests at Washington and in other countries, where it should be found desirable and consistent with proper relations between Great Britain and Canada. A Redistribution of Seats Bill was carried through the Dominion Legislature during the session, which took away a seat each from Prince Edward Island and Nova Scotia, and two seats from New Brunswick, and gave two new seats to Manitoba.

In the session of 1893, when introducing the Dominion Budget, the Finance Minister said that free trade was impossible in Canada; but the Government were in favour of giving preference to all places within the bounds of the British Empire, and of a fair measure of reciprocity with the United States. A Ministerial crisis arose through the action of Mr. Wallace, the Comptroller of Customs, who publicly promised that the Canadian Orangemen would assist Ulster to resist Home Rule. The Ministry, though not in sympathy with their colleague, had a narrow escape from a hostile vote.

A great Liberal Convention, attended by nearly 2,000 delegates from all parts of the Dominion, was held at Ottawa in June, the Hon. Wilfrid Laurier presiding. Tariff reform on the basis of revenue only, and reciprocity, were indicated as the leading planks in the Liberal platform, as against the Conservative principle of protection. The convention also declared in favour of an elective Senate.

Much interest was manifested this year by a new commercial development; namely, the opening up of a new steamship route to Australia and New Zealand *via* Vancouver and Honolulu. The Canadian Pacific Railway were to act as the agents of the new line in Europe, Canada, and the United States. The advertised time of the through train from Montreal to Vancouver was reduced by twenty-four hours, the journey now occupying only five days.

Fiscal and commercial measures were again the chief points of discussion in 1894. Sir John Thompson, in the course of a speech delivered at Picton, Nova Scotia, said that the Government were in favour of reducing the tariff to as low a basis as was compatible with the revenue requirements. He had no hope of obtaining a reciprocity treaty from the United States Democrats; but for every step taken by them in abolishing or reducing duties on Canadian products, the Canadian Government would take corresponding steps to make trade between the two countries freer; always, however, having regard to Canada's revenue requirements, commercial independence, and the bonds of attachment uniting her to the mother country.

In the Dominion Parliament, a new Tariff Bill was introduced by the Government on March 26th, with the object of imposing only *ad valorem* duties on imported goods in place of the existing system of mixed specific and *ad valorem* duties. Reductions were proposed on many goods imported from Great Britain. The new tariff scheme passed, and the reductions in the import duties had a favourable effect on commerce, as had also the passage of the Wilson tariff in the United States. An Intercolonial Conference was held at Ottawa in June, when the Governor-General, Lord Aberdeen, received the delegates. A loyal address to the Queen was first adopted, and then the conference devoted itself to the practical work of devising means for providing commercial intercourse between all parts of the empire.

Sir John Thompson, the Dominion Premier, visited England in December, 1894, for the purpose of discussing, amongst other things, the question of Canadian copyright. He died suddenly, however, on the 12th of that month, at Windsor Castle, whither he had been summoned to have an audience of the Queen, and to be sworn of the Privy Council. On the receipt of this melancholy news in Canada, the Hon. Mackenzie Bowell succeeded in forming a new Ministry, which met with general approval. An Imperial man-of-war conveyed the remains of Sir John Thompson to the city of Halifax, where an official funeral was given to them, the ceremony being attended by all the chief officers of the Dominion, and by an immense number of people gathered from all parts of Canada. The appointment of this highly esteemed statesman on the Paris Court of Arbitration had been regarded by the Canadians as a direct acknowledgment of the importance of the Dominion in Imperial councils.

The Dominion Parliament had many important matters before it in the session of 1895. In February, the Minister of Trade stated that the tenders for laying the proposed Pacific cable had been received, and that the lowest amount was £1,517,000. The route suggested was from Vancouver to Fanning Island, Fiji, and Norfolk Island to New Zealand and Australia.

A subject which caused great dissension at this time was one known as the Manitoba Schools Question. In March, the Governor in Council declared that the rights and privileges enjoyed by the Roman Catholic minority in Manitoba in relation to education prior to the 1st of May, 1890, were prejudicially affected by Acts passed by the Provincial Legislature in that year, and that a provincial law should be passed re-enacting the provisions of the law in force prior to May, 1890, so as to remove the grievances of which the Catholics complained. The Acts of 1890 had abolished the existing separate Protestant and Catholic sections of the School Board, and brought all the school districts, both Protestant and Catholic, under one system of free and non-sectarian schools, supported by the proceeds of a public school rate. Schools not conducted in accordance with this system were expressly excluded from all share in the grants. The Roman Catholics appealed, with the result above stated. But the decision of the Government immediately raised both a Catholic v. Protestant and a Province v. Dominion question. Sir Charles H. Tupper, the Minister of Justice, maintained that the proper constitutional course was a dissolution, and therefore resigned office. He was afterwards, however, prevailed upon to return. The Manitoba Provincial Government declined to comply with the remedial order of the Dominion Government, and pointed out the difficulty, which amounted almost to an impossibility, of maintaining separate schools in so large and scattered a country. The Dominion Government then announced that it would not take any further immediate steps; but if no amicable settlement could be arrived at before, it would bring forward legislation to remedy the grievance of the minority by the ensuing January at the latest. This caused the resignation of Mr. A. R. Angers, the Minister of Agriculture, who wished for remedial legislation at once; but the House, by 114 votes to 70, endorsed the action of the Government.

The financial difficulties of Newfoundland revived

the idea of the union of that colony with the Dominion, and a conference was held between Dominion and Newfoundland delegates, which it was stated resulted in the basis of a union. But the negotiations subsequently fell through, as the Whiteway Government of Newfoundland found themselves unable to bear the financial burdens which would still be left to them under the Canadian terms.

The Royal Commission on Prohibition, after sitting for two years, reported against the abolition of the liquor traffic, and recommended instead its curtailment, with the prevention of adulteration, and a system of high licences. The Dominion House of Commons rejected a resolution in favour of Women's Suffrage by 105 to 47 votes.

In October, 1895, the Dominion Government issued a proclamation setting apart various unorganized portions of the Dominion into provisional districts. The territory east of Hudson Bay, having the province of Quebec on the south and the Atlantic on the east, was designated as Ungava. The territory embraced in the islands of the Arctic Sea was named Franklin, the Mackenzie River region Mackenzie, and the Pacific Coast territory lying north of British Columbia and west of Mackenzie, Yukon. The extent of Ungava and Franklin is undefined, Mackenzie covers 538,600 square miles, and Yukon covers 225,000 square miles, in addition to 143,000 square miles added to Athabasca and 470,000 to Keewatin.

In the course of a special interview, "General" Booth laid his plans for the establishment of an agricultural Salvation Army colony in the North-West

Territory before the Governor-General, the Cabinet, and the permanent officials; and he warmly urged his request for a grant of public land and money. The matter was reserved for further consideration.

The great difficulty in the session of 1896 was again the Manitoba Catholic Schools Question. Ministerial changes occurred in January; Sir Mackenzie Bowell still retained the Premiership, however, but being joined by Sir Charles Tupper, senior, and others. The Manitoba Schools Remedial Bill was introduced into the Dominion Parliament, giving the Catholics the right to establish denominational schools under strict guarantees as to their efficiency. The measure was fiercely contested, one sitting alone lasting for 129 hours. The Premier announced his resignation, the bill was not carried, and Parliament was prorogued. Sir Charles Tupper became Premier, and Sir Donald Smith was appointed High Commissioner in England.

The elections, which were held in June, resulted in a crushing defeat for the Conservatives. They only succeeded in returning 86 members, as against 118 Liberals and 8 Independents. The great change took place in Quebec, which, in spite of all the pressure applied by the Roman Catholic hierarchy, and the strict episcopal injunctions to vote for the Conservative party, went almost solidly Liberal. The education question had much to do with the result, which was a triumph for civil freedom over clerical influence; but tariff reform was also an important factor in the contest. Sir C. Tupper and his colleagues resigned, and Mr. (now Sir) Wilfrid Laurier took office with a strong Liberal Cabinet, including no less than five provincial ex-Premiers. In September, a compromise as to the Manitoba Schools Question was proposed between the Dominion Government and the Manitoba Ministry. It was suggested that provision should be made for voluntary religious instruction in the schools by the clergy of the different Churches after school hours, and that a fair proportion of Catholic teachers should be appointed in those schools which were attended by many Catholic children.

A remarkable outburst of loyalty occurred in the Dominion House of Commons on the 23rd of September. A reference to the Queen led to the whole House joining in singing, " God save the Queen," and giving three cheers for her Majesty, whose reign had then exceeded in length that of any other British sovereign.

It is interesting to note the position of political parties in Canada. The two leading divisions are known by the old and familiar titles of Conservative and Liberal. From the date of confederation, in 1867, the Liberals were only in power once, until their signal victory in 1896. In this latter struggle, the Conservatives were led by Sir Charles Tupper, and the party advocated protection and preferential trade, if possible, with Great Britain and the Colonies, new steam and cable services, the strengthening of the defences of the Dominion, and the redress of the grievances of the Catholics with regard to the Manitoba Schools. The Liberals, led by Mr. Wilfrid Laurier, advocated fiscal reforms in the direction of free trade, modified only by revenue requirements, the extension of the franchise, the enlargement of the trade of Canada, and a policy of non-interference with provincial politics, especially with regard to Manitoba. A third party, the McCarthyites, seceded from the Conservative party, on account of the administrative scandals a few years ago, and advocated purity of administration. A fourth party, the Patrons of Industry, formed practically the Labour party. The eight Independent members returned at the elections of 1896 were, on the whole, supporters of the Liberals.

So intense was the feeling which still remained over the Manitoba Schools Question, that the Roman Catholic bishops of Quebec interdicted the Liberal paper the *Lecteur*; but a new organ, the *Soleil*, was immediately issued to take its place, with the Premier as one of its directors. The *Lecteur* was denounced solely because of the support it gave to the Manitoba Schools settlement in opposition to the Roman Catholic hierarchy. This settlement, which had been arranged shortly after Mr. Laurier's accession to power, was approved by the Legislature of Manitoba on the 18th of March, 1897. Only five out of the forty members present voted against the measure which was introduced to carry out its provisions. The attitude of the Roman Catholic clergy, however, especially in Quebec, remained uncompromisingly hostile. Every means of influence, even a threat that those who voted against the wishes of the Church should be refused burial in consecrated ground, was brought to bear, but in vain. The electorate generally stoutly claimed their political independence, and in spite of the clergy returned candidates who approved the settlement. When the provincial general election took place throughout Quebec in May, fifty-three

Liberals were returned, and only twenty Conservatives and one Independent. The provincial election in Nova Scotia also resulted in a great triumph for the Liberals, only three Conservatives being returned against thirty-five Liberals.

In consequence of the galling effects of an Alien Labour Law, put into force against Canadians by the United States, the Dominion House of Commons now took similar and retaliatory measures.

The Finance Minister for the Dominion, Mr. W. S. Fielding, brought in his Budget on the 22nd of April, estimating the revenue for the year at $37,300,000, and the expenditure at $37,900,000, the deficit being attributable to the fiscal policy of the previous Government. But the great feature of Mr. Fielding's Budget speech was his epoch-making announcement on the question of the tariff. He stated that the Government had resolved to maintain the existing tariff, but freed from some of its enormities and injustices, and to a large extent from specific duties, for those countries which were not prepared to deal favourably and on reciprocal terms with the Dominion. They would, however, set up a preferential tariff which would apply at once to Great Britain, and to any other country that should afterwards grant reciprocal terms to Canadian products. With regard to the general tariff, specific duties were abolished in numerous instances—for example, iron, clothing, woollens, and glass; while they were largely reduced in others, such as textile fabrics; but the duties on luxuries were increased.

The following were the important resolutions dealing with the preferential tariff. On all the products of the countries entitled to the benefits of this reciprocal tariff, the duties mentioned in schedule (a) of the general tariff shall be reduced as follows : Until the 30th of June, 1898, inclusive, the reduction shall in every case be one-eighth of the duty mentioned in the general tariff, and the duty to be levied, collected, and paid shall be seven-eighths of the duty mentioned in the schedule. On and after the 1st of July, 1898, the reduction shall in every case be one-fourth of the duty mentioned in the schedule, and the duty to be levied, collected, and paid shall be three-fourths of the duty mentioned in the schedule : provided, however, that these reductions shall not apply to any of the following articles ; namely, ales, beers, wines, and liquors, sugar, molasses, and syrups of all kinds, the production of the sugar-cane or the beetroot, tobacco, cigars, and cigarettes. The foregoing would apply to Great Britain immediately; and as regards other countries, the application would be governed by this resolution when the customs tariff of any country admits the products of Canada on terms which on the whole are as favourable to Canada as the terms of the reciprocal tariff herein referred to are to the countries to which it may apply. Articles which are the growth, product, or manufacture of such country, when imported direct therefrom, may then be imported direct into Canada, or taken out of the warehouse for consumption therein, at reduced rates of duty, provided in the reciprocal tariff any question that may arise as to the countries entitled to the benefits of reciprocal tariff shall be decided by the Comptroller of Customs.

During the debates on the tariff, Mr. Fielding stated

that, though the Government still held that the German and Belgian treaties with Great Britain did not apply to Canada, yet they had inserted a clause in the Tariff Bill empowering the Governor in Council "to extend the benefits of such reciprocal tariff to any country which may be entitled thereto by virtue of any treaty with her Majesty." At a later date, the Imperial Government, in the interests of the tariff policy of the Dominion, denounced the existing commercial treaties with Belgium and Germany, finding that they interfered with the desire of the colony to give preferential treatment to Great Britain. This decision was hailed throughout Canada with satisfaction and approval. The Dominion Cabinet next found themselves compelled to extend the operation of the preferential clause of the tariff, which had already been applied to Great Britain, New South Wales, France, Belgium, and Germany, to the other countries entitled to it under the most-favoured-nation treaties —namely, Spain, Russia, Denmark, Sweden, and Norway; but these countries were to cease to be so entitled during 1898. The passing of the new tariff soon began to exercise a beneficial effect upon the commerce of the Dominion. The Government sent a representative to Europe to enquire into the best methods for developing the exports of Canadian agricultural produce. Railway extension was vigorously proceeded with, and the Dominion benefited considerably by the increased demand for timber in Great Britain, a very large proportion of the increase consisting of increased shipments from British North America.

Intense excitement prevailed in Canada in July, owing to the wonderful discoveries of gold reported from the Klondike district in the North-West Territories, and the Yukon Territory generally. As the new gold-fields were in remote and inclement regions, the Government issued emphatic warnings as to the dangers from cold and starvation to which miners going thither exposed themselves. A royalty was imposed on the out-put of placer diggings, and every alternative claim in placer grounds was reserved as Government property. The Klondike discoveries and mining developments generally made for increased trade, while the arrangements for establishing a new weekly fast steamship service between the Dominion and Great Britain were expected to tend in the same direction.

In the course of 1897, the status of a province was conferred upon the North-West Territories, and a Ministry was accordingly formed with Mr. F. W. Haultain as Premier.

On the occasion of the Queen's great Jubilee in 1897, there were loyal demonstrations throughout Canada. The Governor-General attended a review at Ottawa, and was present at other loyal gatherings in honour of her Majesty. Popular enthusiasm was everywhere displayed. The Colonial Premiers were invited to visit England for the Jubilee celebrations, and among them was the Dominion Premier, Mr. Wilfrid Laurier. He and the other Premiers were received at Windsor by the Queen, who conferred upon them the honour of knighthood. The Colonial Premiers subsequently visited Mr. Gladstone at Hawarden.

CHAPTER XV.

THE CANADA OF TO-DAY.

HAVING brought down the history of Canada to the present year, something now remains to be said concerning the extent and the physical characteristics of the Dominion, its resources, commerce, government, constitution, and people.

The Dominion of Canada embraces all the upper portion of the North American Continent except Labrador, which belongs to Newfoundland, and Alaska, which belongs to the United States. It is bounded on the north by the Arctic Ocean, on the west by the Pacific and Alaska, on the east by Newfoundland and the Atlantic, and on the south by the United States. Its total area is 3,456,383 square miles. Magnificent harbours and sheltered bays abound on both the Atlantic and Pacific shores. Hudson Bay, which is connected with the Atlantic by Hudson Straits, is really an inland sea with an area of 350,000 square miles, and the Gulf of St. Lawrence is 80,000 square miles in extent. A recent writer points out that the most striking physical features of Canada are the Rocky Mountains, the Laurentian Range, and the chain of immense fresh-water lakes. The Laurentian Range is about 3,500 miles in length, and extends along the north side of the St. Lawrence and the Ottawa River, stretching thence away to Lake Superior and the north. The range varies in height from 1,000 to 3,000 feet. The eastern and north-western portions of Canada are well timbered; but to the westward of the Red River there is an immense fertile plain, suitable for agriculture and grazing, extending almost to the Rocky Mountains. The highest peaks of the Rocky Mountains are Mount Brown, 16,000 feet, Mount Murchison, 15,789 feet, and Mount Hooker, 15,700 feet; and the average height of the whole chain is from 7,000 to 8,000 feet. With regard to the lakes and rivers of Canada, the system of the St. Lawrence alone—with its great lakes Superior, Huron, Michigan, Erie, and Ontario—drains an area of no less than 330,000 square miles. Between Lakes Erie and Ontario are the famous Falls of Niagara. The area of the lakes themselves is about 90,000 square miles; and Lake Superior and Lake Ontario, with their outlet, form the greatest fresh-water way in the world. Among other important lakes may be mentioned the Great Slave Lake, 12,000 square miles, the Great Bear Lake, 10,000 square miles, and Lake Winnipeg, 9,000 square miles.

With regard to the climate of Canada, the cold in winter and the heat in summer are greater than in Great Britain; but the climate is a healthy one, because the air is always dry, bracing, and exhilarating. British Columbia is thought to possess the finest climate in North America. All the grain and fruit crops grown in England flourish in Canada; and in the southern part of the Dominion, many species raised in England under glass—such as grapes, peaches, melons, and tomatoes—ripen in the open air.

The area of the various districts and provinces of Canada is as follows : Ontario, 144,600 square miles —not including some disputed territory; Quebec, 193,355; Nova Scotia, 21,731 ; New Brunswick, 27,322 ; Prince Edward Island, 2,133 ; Manitoba, 60,500 ; British Columbia, 390,344 ; Provisional districts— Assiniboia, 89,700 ; Saskatchewan, 106,700 ; Alberta, 106,500 ; Athabasca, 105,500 ; remaining territory, about 2,200,000. Canada is almost as large as the whole of Europe, and about 600,000 square miles larger than the United States without Alaska.

The province of Ontario, which contains the capital of the Dominion, is the best, the wealthiest, and the most thickly populated of all the Canadian provinces. It is a splendid agricultural region, and one well adapted for stock raising. A traveller through Canada thus describes the province of Quebec, the old home of the French : " The great River St. Lawrence runs through this province from the head of ocean navigation to the gulf of the same name, thus giving the country a most commanding commercial position. The scenery on the banks is always pleasing, and sometimes even magnificently grand, especially among the thousand islands. The climate is very healthy, the winter being cold and the summer of about the same average warmth as that of France. The dryness of the winter air renders the frequent extreme cold of that season not nearly so unpleasant as it would otherwise be, while the snowfall is even welcomed by the farmer as forming a warm covering for the ground, and enabling him to draw his firewood and other 'produce' to market with ease on sleds. On the other hand, while the climate is in winter not more severe than that of some of the Western Prairie States in America, the summers are freer from ague, which is the scourge of most parts of the American Continent below a certain latitude. Quebec and Montreal, both old French towns, and still maintaining a good deal of that Old World appearance which is so rare in America, are the chief cities of the province. The first, which has a population of between 60,000 and 70,000, is the capital of the province; while the latter, with a population of 216,000, is the commercial metropolis, and, indeed, the chief port in British North America. To travellers from Europe, Quebec will always have the greatest interest. It has historic associations which few of the other Canadian towns possess, and the man must be deficient in sentiment who can visit the Heights of Abraham, or walk under the shadow of its battlements, without memories that take him far back to the days when the Briton and the Frenchman fought here for the mastery of the New World. Quebec is essentially a French city of two hundred years ago."

Taking a sketch now from the Manitoba region, we read : " The prairie land passes into woodland in various localities to the north of the Saskatchewan, to reappear in higher latitudes. On Peace River, there are extensive prairies with extremely rich soil. In other localities there is an agreeable mixture of woodland and prairie, and this character of country appears to prevail as far as Hay River, 400 miles north of the River Saskatchewan. Although the prairie region is of vast extent, it is not at all fertile. A very large area adjoining the boundary of the United States, midway between Manitoba and the Rocky Mountain Zone, is arid and unfavourable for agriculture. In other quarters, a great breadth of rich pasture and cultivable land exists. The province of Manitoba is in reality a mere speck of the vast North-Western Territories, or Rupert's Land, out of which it is formed. It contains, nevertheless, about 9,000,000 acres, mostly prairie, consisting of rich alluvial soil, so clear that a 'buggy' can be driven for 1,000 miles over fertile lands capable of growing wheat and other vegetable products, in perhaps as great perfection as any other portion of the temperate North American Continent. Along the banks of the streams wood abounds, and the natural prairie is covered with rich nutritious grasses. The summers are hot, and the winters colder even than in other portions of Canada ; but both seasons are very healthy. Snow disappears and ploughing commences in April, while the crops are harvested in August. The regular frosts seldom set in later than November, while Red River is rarely open for navigation earlier than the end of April. There are thus in Manitoba, as in the rest of the colder portions of Canada, two seasons—the summer, which is the period of activity, and the winter, a time when the settler rests from his labours. Professor Daniel Wilson remarks, that early in April the alders and willows of the Saskatchewan country are in bloom, and the prairie anemone then covers the northern exposures to the very verge of the retreating snow. May is hotter than in the provinces along the banks of the St. Lawrence ; but the nights are cold, and even during the period of the greatest heats the cold night breeze brings heavy dews, and begets a pleasant change after the sultry hours of daylight. To use the language of the Rev. Professor Bryce, a resident of the province, 'The juncture of the seasons is not very noticeable. Spring glides superbly into summer, summer into fine autumn weather, which, during the equinox, breaks up in a series of heavy gales of wind, accompanied by rain and snow. These are followed by that divine aftermath, the Indian summer, which attains its true glory only in the North-West.'"

With regard to Canadian life in its general aspects, the traveller from whom we have already quoted says: "The people of that country differ in many respects from those of the United States and of England. They have an accent of their own—partaking of the general Transatlantic drawl—and in their character they have also some features which at once stamp them as a race not yet out of the gristle period, but hardening into the bone of manhood. The men are equally energetic in business with those of the United States, but are capable of greater physical exertion. They bear the reputation, perhaps undeserved, of being exceedingly careful of their money, though, possibly, a little more scrupulous in obtaining it than some of their neighbours over the border. Sweeping censure, like sweeping praise, is, however, always dangerous, and in some cases utterly erroneous. Accordingly, it may be as well not to generalize upon premises which will undoubtedly be declared erroneous, no matter what conclusions they may lead to. It cannot, at least, be denied that the Canadian women are as healthy in appearance as the men are robust. The true 'American' woman may be pretty, but she soon fades, and she is ageing at thirty. The Canadian girl is, on the contrary, like the English woman, in her prime at that period, and, being addicted to out-of-door exercise, maintains her freshness longer. She walks on snow-shoes, 'trabogens' and 'rinks' out of doors, while inside her daily domestic duties take so much of her time that she indulges in little of the lassitude and languor which unfortunately too often afflict her American sister. The moral character of the people is high. In the town, there are rogues, as there always are in large communities. In the country, the people are orderly and peaceable. Farmyards are rarely enclosed. Timber lies all winter on the banks of the stream, ready to be floated down when the ice disappears, and yet it is perfectly safe from depredation. In the farmhouse bolts and locks are unnecessary, while the farm implements lie in the field, and the stock often wander all summer through the woods till the autumn, when each owner claims his own. Education is free and compulsory, the teachers being paid by a school tax levied on every citizen, while every ratepayer over twenty-one is entitled to a vote. Lastly, it may be added that the 'manifest destiny' of Canada to go over to the United States is not believed in, except by a very small section of the country."

The population of Canada amounted, in 1897, to about 5,200,000. The French number 1,415,090, or 29 per cent.; and the Indians number about 100,000. The federal capital, Ottawa, has a population of 44,154; and the populations of the other chief cities are as follows: Montreal, 216,650; Toronto, 181,220; Quebec,

63,090; Halifax, 38,556; St. John, 39,179; and Winnipeg, 25,642. Some years ago there were by descent—1,298,929 French Canadians; 957,403 Irish, 881,301 English, 699,863 Scotch, and 9,947 Welsh— total, British population, 2,548,514; Germans, 254,319; Indians, 108,547; Dutch, 30,412; the rest of the population being cosmopolitan, and including Africans Swiss, Chinese, Scandinavians, Italians, Russians, Spanish and Portuguese, and Icelanders. The language generally spoken is English; but in some parts of the province of Quebec, French is the only language understood. In the Dominion, Quebec, and Manitoba Parliaments, members may address the House in either language. In the city of Quebec, French is the official language, as it is that of nearly all the inhabitants.

The fortunes of the Indians, who are now greatly diminished in numbers, are still followed with deep interest. Nearly all the survivors are to be found in the eastern provinces, in Manitoba and the North-West, and in British Columbia; but there are now very few Indians of pure blood in the older provinces. Although they are proving amenable to civilization, and are chiefly engaged in industrial and agricultural occupations, many still follow hunting and fishing as a means of livelihood. Those who possess the necessary property qualifications have enjoyed the franchise since 1886. The education of the young is being encouraged by the establishment of schools. The Indians are supervised by the superintendent-general of Indian affairs, which office is held by the Minister of the Interior, a member of the Dominion Cabinet; and the Government expenditure for the Indian service is upwards of $1,250,000. The public revenue of the Dominion for 1896-97 was £7,323,720 ; the expenditure, £7,389,830 ; the exports, £26,822,796; the imports, £22,276,000 ; and the net public debt, £52,073,000.

Canada enjoyed a system of free and unsectarian education long before the establishment of Board Schools in England. Good education is widely diffused throughout the Dominion, and the highest prizes the country offers are open to all, rich and poor alike. The principal universities are those of Toronto, McGill at Montreal, Laval at Quebec, Queen's at Kingston, Victoria at Coburg, and Dalhousie at Halifax. There are numerous scientific and historical societies, and both literature and science are now advancing by rapid strides.

There is no State Church in Canada, though the Roman Catholic Church in the province of Quebec enjoys still the privileges of collecting tithes, etc., which it possessed previous to British rule. The strength of the chief religious bodies is thus estimated : Roman Catholics, 1,992,017 ; Methodists, 847,765 ; Presbyterians, 755,326 ; Church of England, 644,059 ; and Baptists, 303,839. As regards social matters in the Dominion, local option prevails with regard to the liquor traffic; marriage with a deceased wife's sister has been legalized since 1882 ; religious liberty prevails, and there are fewer class distinctions than in the mother country ; in addition to free education, there is a free and liberal franchise; members of Parliament are paid for their services ; the Parliaments are quinquennial ; and there is no system for legalizing pauperism, though the aged, the sick, and the orphan are looked after.

The public lands are under the control of the various local governments, except in the case of Manitoba and the North-West Territories, where the lands are retained by the Dominion Government, the object being by sale, etc., to refund the money expended in acquiring the territory, and in constructing the Canadian Pacific Railway. The forest products constitute one of the most important sources of wealth, though live stock, agricultural produce, and manufactures play no unimportant part. The mineral deposits are practically inexhaustible, especially coal, iron, copper, and gold. The fisheries on both the Atlantic and Pacific coasts are very valuable. There are sixty-five main lines of railway working in the Dominion, with a total mileage of 16,091. The Canadian Pacific and the Grand Trunk of Canada Railways are the two principal systems.

Touching the constitution and method of government, the Federal Parliament is modelled after that of the United Kingdom, though the Upper House consists of 81 senators nominated for life by the Governor in Council—24 from Ontario, 24 from Quebec, 10 from Nova Scotia, 10 from New Brunswick, 4 from Manitoba, 3 from British Columbia, 4 from Prince Edward Island, and 2 from the Territories. The House of Commons consists of 213 members, elected on a popular suffrage—92 from Ontario, 65 from Quebec, 20 from Nova Scotia, 14 from New Brunswick, 6 from British Columbia, 5 from Prince Edward Island, 7 from Manitoba, and 4 from the North-West Territories. The limits of federal and provincial jurisdiction are regulated by the British North America Act of 1867, which formulated the Constitution of the Dominion.

Canada has led a chequered existence in the past; but now a spirit of union and loyalty prevails throughout the entire Dominion, which augurs well for the future happiness and prosperity of the country.

THE END.

Printed by Hazell, Watson, & Viney, Ld., London and Aylesbury.

www.ingramcontent.com/pod-product-compliance
Lightning Source LLC
Chambersburg PA
CBHW022020240426
43667CB00042B/1009